I don't know how long I contemplated my stomach.
But, during that time, the lunatic made a conscious
decision to become sane.

Nothing, I told myself, could be worse than this. It
wasn't possible to get lower than I was now. There was
no comfort beyond the breaking-point, no hidey-hole;
only a screaming void. From here on, I had to head the
other way. I had to go back to the other side. I had to
drag up every social skill I knew to convince the
authorities of my sanity.

'Senor,' said the civil servant. 'I do not think this abbey
exists. The other gringo is crazy.' He waved at folders
and documents scattered on his desk. 'If the abbey
exists, then where is it in my papers? Where? It does not
exist except in his head.'

"This is a tale of endurance, bravery and perseverance
which is often astounding. And it goes to prove that
truth can often be stranger than fiction."
Newcastle-upon-Tyne Journal

"Written with obvious honesty and sincerity...the reader
is kept on tenterhooks until the closing pages..."
Huddersfield Examiner

"A haunting story."
South Devon Journal

The Weaver and the Abbey

Abbey

*The Quest for a Secret
Monastery in the Andes*

Michael Brown

CORGI BOOKS

THE WEAVER AND THE ABBEY

A CORGI BOOK 0 552 12172 X

Originally published in Great Britain by Arthur Barker Limited

PRINTING HISTORY

Arthur Barker edition published 1982
Corgi edition published 1983

This book is set in 9½/10 Paladium
by Colset Pte Ltd., Singapore

Corgi Books are published by
Transworld Publishers Ltd.,
Century House, 61–63 Uxbridge Road,
Ealing, London W5 5SA

Made and printed in Great Britain by the
Guernsey Press Co. Ltd., Guernsey, Channel Islands.

*Let this be one bridge
between the physical, spiritual
and psychical worlds.*

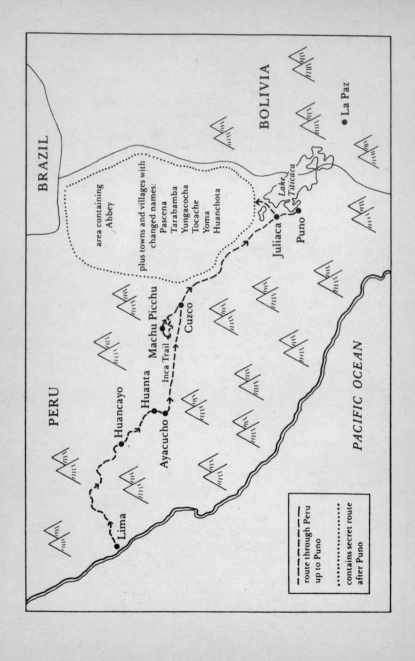

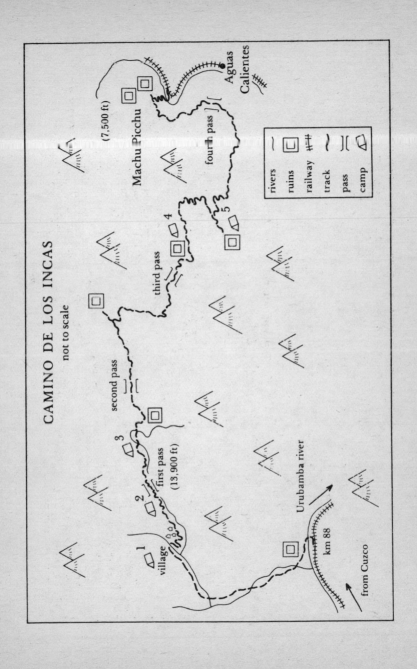

CAMINO DE LOS INCAS

not to scale

village

first pass
(13,900 ft)

second pass

third pass

fourth pass

Machu Picchu
(7,500 ft)

Aguas
Calientes

Urubamba river

km 88

from Cuzco

rivers
ruins
railway
track
pass
camp

Foreword

I've got very little evidence for what I'm going to write. When it all happened, Julie and I had no idea we would want to tell anyone. But we are certain of our memories; with Julie's help, I want to pour them out into black and white in a way that's believable. And, because we've kept it all to ourselves since we came home, this writing will be a kind of purging for us.

We know, now, that many people carry unspeakable torments inside them, as I did. Some carry theirs unspoken and unresolved until they die. Others drift, as I drifted, desperate for a clear direction through the currents that push them about. And if this book is to be for any particular person, then let it be for anyone who knows what it's like to be enclosed in a black tunnel that no one else can see.

There is a small number of widely scattered individuals who will feel no disbelief when they read part of this book . . . the people who have been dead for a short time, and then revived. I think, for them, it will be like recognizing a friend.

A few readers may feel like setting out across Peru, to find the abbey for themselves. Because of what happened to us, Julie and I can only wish them well. However, we plead with them to take every possible care: the journey is difficult and dangerous.

I'm going to change the names of some people and some places. I hope anyone who wants to find the abbey will understand why we can give them no more specific directions than we had when we started. However, we found indirect and subtle clues, which I'll include without waving flags.

Some of these events are going to be unpleasant to work through again. Other parts will be a delight to remember on paper. Perhaps I'll make people smile a little. I would like that. For the most part, I'm going to have more fun chasing words than a cocker spaniel at a party for ducks.

So will Julie, I think. It's all as fresh in her mind as it is in mine.

Part One

1

'Bend the knee, Brown. Beeeend the knee!'

There was no escaping Sensei Lee's voice. It hunted me down from the far end of the dojo, through the sounds of two dozen leaping, shouting karate students, and through forty feet of air turbulence.

Yells at me were usually triggered by my knee action, which was almost non-existent. I bent the offending joint and pushed off from the back foot, leaping into the offensive while I had Sensei's attention.

My opponent was an enthusiastic purple belt. It took him a fraction of a second to notice that my knee bend had turned my upper body into an imitation of the leaning Tower of Pisa. Enthusiasm and opportunity are fast dancing partners. He shuffled his rear leg back half a step, flicked aside my punch, then drove the flat of his front foot into the place I usually used for breathing. Each of my parts hit the floor simultaneously.

My opponent hovered apologetically while I inspected the floor boards. I had spent a considerable portion of my karate life inspecting the floor. I was beginning to cover the same boards twice.

I found no bloodstains. But I did find a foot which belonged to Sensei. I looked up.

'Brown! When you bend the knee, you must keep the back straight! And your head must stay back! If you go out on the street and wave your head in the air like that, someone will knock it off!' He turned to address the whole class. 'Yame! Everyone against the far wall. Kneeling down.'

Tall, continuous mirrors lined two opposite walls. The repeated reflections turned the dojo into a fantastic ballroom, peopled by hundreds of frenzied, black-suited dancers. But, on Sensei's command, the dance stilled. The dancers moved into a long, segmented, black line, waiting for twenty images of Sensei to start the last stages of the training session.

'Goodrowe and Halligan.'

The two leapt to their feet, bowed to Sensei, to each other, and launched into the contest. Medium contact karate: blows hard enough to hurt, but not to injure. Minimal head contact.

As Sensei monitored their excursion round the room, I wondered how much time he'd give me to recover from my last bout. Not long, I decided. Sensei thought of pain and suffering as little more than an opportunity for learning.

'Yame. Bow. Bow. Sit down. Brown and Kinder.'

In the last few weeks, without knowing why, I had become determined not to reveal my cowardly side in front of Sensei. So I was on my feet before Geoff Kinder, who rose with such power and co-ordination that speed would only have detracted from the movement.

'Bow.' We bowed to Sensei. 'Bow.' We inclined to each other and squared off.

Geoff Kinder was the club's star pupil, headed for the higher realms of karate fighting. He gave me bad dreams. He also gave me day-dreams in which I would conceive new tactics, then beat him with brilliant displays of speed and courage. But on the real training floor, the tactics almost never worked. And small successes were painfully discouraged with what I came to call 'Kinder's reminders'. I was more afraid of him than anyone I could remember, but two minutes with him was more valuable than a complete training session without him.

With a pleasant grin, Geoff floated a lazy, muscular arm down to my head, stopping just short of a hit. It wasn't meant to land; just to show me how useless my defences were against him.

We had only been fighting five seconds. So I couldn't shift into reverse without losing every shred of dignity. I tried a move I'd been practising: a feint to the chest with the left, followed by a right to the side of the head. To my horror, it landed. And because I hadn't expected it to work, the blow was out of control and struck too hard.

I successfully suppressed the nervous spasms in my throat, but my feet skittered back three steps in panic. I had just earned myself a banquet of Kinder's reminders. His eyes narrowed. The appetizer grazed my ear, not quite deflected by my block. The entrée went hard to my chest, and I was wide open for the main course: the kick. The Kinder Sidewinder. His right leg side-kicks were devastating.

But Sensei was watching. Again without knowing why, I altered my actions to suit. What I did was thoughtless, desperate, and completely graceless. It was something approximating a judo throw; not expressly forbidden on the bare boards, but it wasn't karate and it wasn't cricket. Geoff didn't fly through the air, but he was forced to sit down hard.

He came up fast and snarling, and he didn't waste time coming up vertically. His first blow was the side-kick, and it was the last blow I blocked. From then on, he took only a quarter of a minute to side-kick my left ribs in the same spot four times. The last kick ran me backwards into the mirrors. The glass was mounted firmly on the wall, so I stayed lucky.

'*Yame*. Bow. Bow. Sit down. Johnstone and Cowley.'

My contribution to the bowing was almost nil. I lurched back into the kneeling line, nursing my ribs and wondering why nothing had been said about the judo throw.

As the others got through their fights, I watched Sensei. He was intent on the sparring, with dark eyes shafting from a tan face. His movements were strong and precise, each extending from the centre of his body. Yet he moved quietly, sometimes adopting a better viewing position without seeming to have walked there. He had no superfluous movements that could be called mannerisms.

I had never seen him fight. He would go through demonstration moves with and without partners, but wouldn't join in the free sparring. What this reluctance to fight indicated, I had not yet worked out. He never smiled during training. Nor did he seem abstracted, thinking of other things. But he had the air of a man who has more to him than what he is seen doing. I had only noticed this underlying atmosphere in the last few weeks. I had no name for it. It puzzled me. It both attracted and repelled me.

Why had Sensei come to New Zealand? Why Christchurch? This was a backwater for someone with his karate reputation. A newspaper had quoted him as saying that he had searched the world a long time before deciding on Christchurch. It had the right vibrations, he'd told the reporter. For what? Perhaps for that indefinable thing in him that seemed larger than the training rooms.

Whatever the reason, I was convinced that Sensei had something I wanted. Perhaps needed. What, I didn't know. It certainly wasn't karate. Vague though it was, the feeling had nothing to do with karate. But the effort of trying to identify the feeling made me queasy. And that was disturbing. It made me afraid of him.

'Line up,' Sensei ordered. It was the end of the training session. Two dozen black suits pattered to the north end of the dojo and formed a graded line. Highest grades on Sensei's right, lowest on the left.

'Standing formal. Down.'

We knelt, sitting on our heels, looking at him through strands of sweaty hair. Pains ran around my body, finding unexpected places to sing. I always enjoyed those pains; even this morning, after a more than usually difficult session.

'Practise,' Sensei said. 'Practise, practise, practise. You *must* practise the basics. You can learn all the fancy moves you want, and you won't last a minute on the street without the basics. Practise on the kick-bag. Go through your techniques slowly in front of a mirror. Criticize yourself. Concentrate.

'Brown, see me after class. Backs straight. Head up. Bow. Up. Right wrist over left. Right leg to the side. Close. Bow. Sign the book. Practise.'

2

'Michael. Sit down.' Sensei nodded at the chair on the other side of his desk.

I sat, surprised. I had never before stayed long enough to merit using the seat. Possibly I was going to get a lecture about the judo throw. I shifted position and pulled money from my pocket.

'I owe you for last month,' I said.

'Ah, yes.' He scribbled out a receipt. Sixteen dollars. 'Thank you.' He leaned back in his chair, resting eight fingers on the front of the desk. 'Well, Michael. What's been happening?'

My eyebrows felt a touch of foreboding. For a moment I disliked him, but I couldn't think why. 'Not much,' I said carefully. 'Not my day for training, today.'

'Yes,' he said. 'You stopped tapping the reservoir.'

An electric shock ran from the bottom of my spine to the back of my head, behind the ears. It wasn't possible! How had he known about that? I took my eyes on a tour of the office to gain time. Trophies on the desk; books on a shelf; fighting weapons on the walls; and a pile of beginners' whites in the corner. Sensei's belt was slung over a peg on the wall. A fly crawled on the edge of the lowest end of the belt, upside-down. Black on black.

I brought myself together shaply; with the thought that his remark could well have been casual and innocent. 'What reservoir?' I said flatly.

'Universal energy.' His tone was matter-of-fact.

My hair prickled. 'You know,' I said, faintly.

'Yes.'

'And the connections? All the connections between . . .'

'Yes. Yes.' Sensei smiled as he nodded. But I felt bad. Nauseous. No one else was supposed to know about that; and he had stripped me of it in seconds. It was private. And not only was it private, it was the protective wall between me and my secret. Perhaps he knew my secret as well! No! Surely to God he couldn't know that!

His face was serious again. Patient. 'Look at all the energy you're using up now,' he observed.

My right arm was shaking. I looked at it. I tried to freeze it. That didn't work, so I removed it from his desk and held on to it with my left hand. Idiot! Twenty-nine years old and shaking like a schoolboy in front of the headmaster! I wanted to leave. But I couldn't, not without finding out how much he knew.

'These . . . this thing we're talking about – what is it?' I asked. 'What *are* we talking about?'

He didn't answer immediately, but went to the door and closed it. And he came back looking like a man who knows he's in the right place at the right time. 'For now, it's better that you keep this conversation to yourself.'

I nodded. The stake was at my back and the blindfold to my face. If he knew . . . If he knew . . .

He replaced his fingers on the edge of the desk. 'What you're really asking is "What is the Truth?", and "What is your place in it?" ' He paused, lifting his eyebrows to invite confirmation. I nodded, wanting, for the moment, to hear anything he had to say. 'Those two questions are really one question. And the answer to it is something you have to discover for yourself.'

My first reaction was one of relief: he didn't know my secret after all. The second was of puzzlement. His reference to 'the Truth' was the sort of thing I'd expect from a hermit in a Tibetan cave, or from a guru in India. But I didn't expect it from a karate instructor in conservative, more-English-than-England Christchurch, New Zealand.

On the other hand, he obviously understood a great deal about me.

The secret expanded inside me and whispered at my throat, urging release on a babbling string of words. After all, this time, I might have found someone who would understand, who could have the means of putting my hidden torment to sleep.

No. No. Impossible.

I became angry at my inability to control the shaking. 'Why *can't* you give me the answers?' I demanded. 'You obviously have the answers I need.'

'No.' He showed not the slightest ruffle at my rudeness. 'The answers will not strike a chord in you simply because you listen to them. It will take effort as well as knowledge. You will only grasp what you reach out for. I can guide you, but the effort must come from you.'

I couldn't shake the meaning of his words loose from my need to find the solution to my particular problem. The secret screamed to get out. And I tried to let it have its way.

'I have . . . I have something . . .' But a sob thrust upwards from the bottom of my stomach. I clamped down on it, and on my words. I couldn't tell him. I must not tell anyone. If I told anyone, I would be locked up again. And that could not, must not, ever happen.

'If you're not going to tell me, why did you start this?' I snapped. 'Why did you bring all this up in the first place?'

17

He waited silently and calmly, watching while I regained self-control. He seemed both detached and involved.

After a while, I said, 'I don't know how to start looking.'

He nodded, and still said nothing.

'Are you the only one I can get the answers from?' Testing him.

'No. The answers are all around you. The fundamental truths are not lost, but they have to be found.'

For some time after that, I listened more carefully. I questioned him more rationally. For the first time, I sensed the possibility of a positive solution to my secret; one that wouldn't get me locked up again. The more we talked, the more a peculiar sensation touched the inside of my temples. It was as if something immense and important were passing by, waiting for me to climb on.

But it was frustratingly intangible. Sensei would not give names to anything. He insisted that it was too soon, that I first had to go away and try to find my own explanations.

After half an hour, I felt both drunk and drained. 'Who are you?' I demanded.

'I'm a teacher and a student.'

'You're part of an organization?'

'Yes.'

'Which?'

He hesitated. 'Call it a brotherhood,' he said.

I stood up abruptly. 'I have to go. I have to think this over. I haven't told you . . . I don't . . .'

He reached behind him and pulled a worn paperback from the shelf. 'Take this with you. Please bring it back; it's precious to me.'

I glanced at the title. *Secret of the Andes* by Brother Philip.

Secret.

'Thank you,' I said, backing out. I crashed into the closed door, but he didn't smile. I avoided his eyes as I opened the door and escaped.

Secret. Secret. Secret. The word chopped and slashed at me as I started down the stairs. Half-way down, the sob broke through. By the time I reached the wintery street, I could hardly see the book and the towel around my karate suit.

A little boy and his father passed me a few seconds later, pushing quickly, hand in hand, through the chilled, smog-laden, night air. The boy regarded me solemnly, turning his face over the arm held by his father. He turned it so far that his chin rested momentarily on his shoulder, and the even slap of his shoes on the frozen pavement changed to a rhythmic, dit-dit-dit dah, dit-dit-dit dah, the morse code for V. V for victory.

His face turned away. The regular slapping sound resumed. He spoke in puzzlement to his father, as they forged ahead into the night. 'Daddy, why for is that man crying?'

18

3

I had to be alone. Completely alone.

From outside the dojo, I drove to my flat, stopping only to collect my back-pack, tent, and sleeping-bag. And three candles. With the book Sensei had given me sitting on the passenger seat, I kept driving: out of the city, past the estuary, through Sumner to the top of the hill to Taylor's Mistake. From there, and now in early winter darkness, I walked another quarter of a mile to the highest point of the Scarborough cliffs. And, with a few yards to go, I dropped the pack and continued out to the edge. To my rock. The place I always came when I wanted to be alone.

The rock juts out from the edge, hanging a thousand feet directly above the water. It points out to the east over the Pacific Ocean, which stretches from the extreme left of vision to the extreme right. The rock is a natural viewing platform and it contains a ledge big enough to seat one man.

Six feet down the cliff face to my left, a white shape shuffled awkwardly on a ledge. It mewed thinly, uneasy at my presence. A gannet, probably nesting. There was a three-quarter moon tonight, still low over the sea, stretching cold silver across the water. The light, trapped at the bottom of the cliff, whitewashed the swells surging among the rocks. The stars nodded shyly to the remnant of the day breeze wafting towards them up the cliff face. A dark pair of wings rose from below, riding the air. Effortless. A nightfisher. Once level with my rock it peeled quickly away, gliding out to sea, an irridescent spot in the velvet light.

The longer I sat there, the stronger grew the urge to stand up and take just one step forward. One simple step would return me to the universe which had cut me off, isolated me with a vision to torment me. To stand up and take that step would require the co-operation of a series of muscles, starting with the stomach muscles. I began the mental effort. But the muscles refused to respond. When I forced the issue they hardened and locked. I decided that I could achieve the same result by simply toppling forward. I tried to relax my back muscles, to let go. But they locked rigid also. So I stayed seated, looking about me into the unreachable, mocking unknown.

Eventually I remembered my original purpose in coming to the cliffs, and returned to the pack, clumsy, cramped by muscles reluctant to return to normal. I pitched the tent, shut myself inside, and lit the three candles, melting the ends of each on to separate stones. The wall of the tent shifted hesitantly back and forth in response to the moving air outside, and, for a few minutes, I watched the flames of the candles tilt minutely in sympathy.

Then, in the orange light of the canvas, I read the book Sensei had given me. Perhaps here would be the solution to my secret. 'Please,' I murmured to the book, 'please let there be an answer.'

The Abbey of the Brotherhood of the Seven Rays has been built in a remote valley in the mountains of Peru. This hidden valley is a place of magnificent natural beauty. Its vertical walls are silvered with a hundred waterfalls, and its floors laid with streams, bush, grassed slopes and flowers.

The valley hangs so deeply between the mountains that the climate on its floor is semi-tropical. The flowers bloom throughout the year, and an enormous variety of food is grown in the rich soil.

The valley is kept secret from civilization by high mountain ranges, and by passes covered in snow. But there is one entrance for those who would find it: a llama trail winding down from the heights of the last pass. Any traveller who succeeds in finding the trail is welcome at the abbey. There is no other restriction on entry.

The abbey is one of the mystery schools; a learning centre for those of the outside world who look for the secrets of life. Many of those secrets are contained in a library holding thirty thousand years of the history of the brotherhood, and the true history of man.

Students are expected to follow the few rules established by the brotherhood. The rules are designed to create a simplicity of lifestyle conducive to learning. Jewellery is discouraged, with the exception of wristwatches. Students can, if they wish, wear a plain white robe, made from materials of the valley.

Students are expected to support themselves financially. However, this should be no hardship. For most non-Peruvians, the cost of living in Peru is reasonable, and in the valley, even more so.

Only those students who are fit and well should attempt the journey. The way through the mountains is long and arduous, much of it on foot. Those who cannot make the journey should not be discouraged. There are other outer retreats, other mystery schools, and other ways to serve the truth once it is learned.

Just before sunrise, I took my seat on the rock, and watched the light concentrating its energies for the thrust out of the sea. At the critical moment, nothing happened; some refractive trick of the

20

atmosphere delayed the arrival. Then, in less than a second, nearly a quarter of the golden disc rushed out of the sea and into the new day.

I was a journalism student. I had an assignment for that Saturday morning. But in the last months, as my desperation had grown, the training had meant less and less to me. I cancelled my appointments and went back to the dojo, just after morning class.

'Michael.' Sensei gestured to the chair, glancing through the office door to the mirrors where two blue-belts were flowing through a complex series of set moves. I closed the door on their stylized shouts and sat. I consciously adopted a relaxed pose, determined, this time, not to lose my self-control. I realized that I had not greeted him at all. But since he had offered me a dangerous journey to solve my problems, there didn't seem to be the same need for such niceties.

'The abbey,' I started carefully. 'Does it exist? Or is it another Shangri-la?'

'It exists. The abbey is real.' Finality. Assurance.

'Have you been there?'

'No.' I lifted a hand, but he answered the question before I spoke it. 'I am indirectly in touch with those who run it.'

'What religion is it?'

'That's for you to find out.'

'I suppose you're also not going to tell me where it is.'

He nodded, smiling. 'No.'

'But all I have is that it's in Peru, to the north of Lake Titicaca.' I had looked it up. There were a hundred thousand square miles of mountain and jungle north of Lake Titicaca. 'That's hardly a pin-point location . . .' But I tailed off, somehow knowing that it was better for him not to tell me: that I wouldn't, later, thank him for giving me a map or a bus ticket.

He waited. Then, 'You must understand that no one needs to go and find an abbey in Peru. Nothing is taught there that is not around you wherever you go. The answers you look for are with you now, just waiting for you to recognize them.'

Again there was that feeling of something moving by.

Briefly, I day-dreamed. I pictured myself standing at a lonely crossroads, waiting for a carriage. Beside me was a rich leather, velvet-lined suitcase containing my secret, and the suitcase was padlocked to my leg by a red-hot, gold chain. I heard the sound of the carriage approaching, and looked around eagerly, knowing that on the carriage was a key which fitted the padlock. I heard the thud of the wheels on the dirt road, I heard the squeak of the harness and the breath of horses, as the carriage passed slowly by. But I saw nothing. The carriage was invisible. I didn't know how to step on board.

I blinked. My eyes had been closed. Sensei had his elbows on the desk, chin on clasped hands, looking, it seemed, through me.

'I must find the key,' I murmured. I was in danger of beginning to tremble. Time to go.

'Yes. And no one can find it for you. I can guide you, but you must do the looking.'

'You don't understand. If you knew why I have to find it . . .' My voice was beginning to squeak. 'If you knew what was chained to me, you wouldn't want anything to do with me. No one would. You'd condemn me.' Giving him no chance to respond, I stood. 'I have to go.' I opened the door on a now empty dojo, and, on impulse, turned back to face him. 'You say the answers are already with me. Will the abbey help me to recognize them?'

'Yes.'

'And my key?'

'Yes. But realize that you have already begun the process of making your key visible.'

4

Now, rather than look for solitude, I looked for the other extreme. I didn't have to make such a decision now, I thought. Desperate though I was, a decision to drop everything and travel into the Andes Mountains couldn't be made in a moment. And I was exhausted with the self-searching and the mental churning. So that night I went to a party for student journalists; expecting only to immerse myself in company and forget.

The evening was unusually cold. More than twenty had arrived before me, yet the party atmosphere was only now pushing out from the fireplace. The logs hissed and spat, crackling sharp bursts of orange-white light across a dozen faces. One side-lamp glowed softly in the small end of the L-shaped room. Its light ventured out just beyond a mahogany coffee table, then faded apologetically into green and gold carpet. Newcomers from the outside cold were at first disconcerted by the subdued lighting, but the heat from the fire quickly found them, and the expanding warmth of the party just as quickly absorbed them.

When I saw her first, she was manœuvring wine and port from group to group; handing crystal goblets into frays of cultivated wit and informed comment that, later, would be re-run through numerous student typewriters. Quiet, relaxed; she responded easily and cheerfully when spoken to, but took no part in intricate dialogue. Fair hair curled on her shoulders and swung shining in the firelight when she moved. Graceful movements, unstudied. Slim waist and beautifully proportioned figure. And there was something fascinating about her that was none of those things, something that tightened my attention and defined my concentration.

We first crossed glances over the piano, across the heads of thirty-two chess-men set for a game. And in that briefest of instants, I knew that she was equally aware of me. From that moment the party receded for both of us. The chatter, the chink of glass on glass, the movement; all formed a haze which shrank away from the space around her and around me, and between us. We were two figures locked in a transparent dumb-bell, around which swirled a party.

Now she was not quite as relaxed, not as assured; though I could have sworn that no one but me would have detected the difference. Nor was I the assured male I would have hoped to be. When we brushed glances, we would immediately throw our eyes elsewhere, and move away, each leaving behind a tiny shroud of self-consciousness.

A tongue beside me clucked in mock disapproval. 'Down boy, down. Hands off my waitress.' It was the hostess, a sub-editor with the Christchurch weekly newspaper that printed some of my student efforts.

'Grubby mind you have,' I complained. 'Who is she?'

'Shows how often you turn up with your articles, doesn't it? . . . She works for us, reporting. Just started a few months ago. Overseas before that, Asia, Europe . . .'

'But, her name . . .'

'Oh that.' Impish eyebrows rose in elaborate surprise that I should want to know. 'Julie Scott.' A heavy wink as she departed. 'Lovely girl eh?'

'Go away.'

I was standing with two students; both of them destined to shine in political journalism, and both of them in heated disagreement about some local issue. Julie's tray appeared between us and they broke off.

'Any port in this storm?' she asked. 'Or shall I fetch a teacup?'

'Begone hussy.' But since port was all she had left on the tray they departed to look after themselves. We were alone.

I took a glass. I hated port. 'Port's fine,' I said. 'I'm Michael Brown.'

She spoke her name as our eyes finally met, and held. And a lot happened in that time. We recognized each other. Not physically, but as if some sleeping part in each of us, knowing beforehand of this encounter, had woken and whispered, 'Here I am.' An impulse took hold of us, to lean towards each other, to touch in some way. But we came to with a start, looked away in confusion, said something polite, and parted once more.

For the next few minutes I was hardly conscious of people talking to me. I could only think of what I had just seen: there was pain behind her eyes, pain overcome. Sorrow overcome, hardship overcome. She had found answers. She was where I wanted to be, to have found the key and solved the mystery.

That was when I made the decision.

With just a little manœuvring, we met again near the chess-board, and pushed the pieces of moulded plastic around as we began to know each other.

After an hour or so, the hostess cruised by and growled, 'You're monopolizing each other.'

And shortly after that, Julie said, 'I'm going to travel again soon. To South America.'

I swallowed, picked a rook off the chess-board, and turned it over and over in my fingers. I could justifiably have complained that our hearts and souls had not been in the game. 'I'm going to Peru,' I said slowly. 'I'm going into the Andes to look for an abbey.'

Julie closed her eyes, then reopened them slowly, nodding at the chess-board. She looked up. 'That,' she said, 'is going to take some explaining, isn't it?'

My flat was filthy, cold, and almost completely bare: holes in the walls . . . flatmates to avoid in dark alleys . . . nothing at all in what should have been the lounge. The only place of warmth and comfort was the bedroom.

We sat on my rug on the floor with our backs to the bed, holding coffee mugs with both hands, and talking softly through the steam as the room warmed. She told me something of her background, mostly of the travelling. And even though she lightened her words about experiences in London and Thailand, I knew all the more certainly that she had not only overcome her problems but had also turned them to strength.

Suddenly, I felt helpless. Inadequate. How could I explain why I had to find the abbey? She, of all people, might understand; but how could I take the risk? If she walked out of the room in disgust it would finish me.

So, instead, I told her about the abbey itself and the valley it had been built in, its beauty, the flowers, the simplicity of life, the semi-tropical climate amid some of the world's highest mountains. And while I spoke, I could feel my traitor body beginning to undo me yet again: the smallest of tremors worried the elbows supporting me.

Throughout, she listened carefully, gravely.

'You see why I have to go?' I said lightly. 'That place is too good to be true. I have to satisfy myself that it's there. I just want to know for sure.'

Julie shook her head. 'No. You haven't told me why you have to go.'

I picked my guitar out of its cranny between the bookcase and the bed and plucked aimlessly at the strings. I studied the vibrations closely. But I ceased touching the strings and turned to her at the same instant that she reached over to lift my hand away from the guitar. Then, instead of speaking, we rose, in slow motion, to the bed, holding each other closer and closer as we went; intertwining, lowering ourselves inch by inch until we lay together.

The movements were very, very slow. No thought to the outside world, no thought to the room, no thought even to the bed. No thought to yesterday, or tomorrow. The moment of release wasn't connected to time at all, and it brought with it a new space which opened inside us, growing from a point within a point, flooding us with warmth.

We lay tightly clasped afterwards, holding on to as much of the warmth as would stay with us. And I thought how ironic it was that after all that had happened in the last thirty hours, I was about to let the secret out to someone other than Sensei.

I laughed, and Julie said, 'Tell me.'

So I did.

5

It began not with me, but with my grandfather. He was committed to a mental institution when he was twenty. He died there two years ago at the age of seventy. His family all but abandoned him. Until three years ago, I didn't know of his existence. When I was a boy, I was told simply that he had died in 1926. That was the year he was committed. My grandfather thought he was Jesus Christ, reincarnated. And, along with all the powers that gave him, he was on talking terms with the sun.

When I was a young boy, long before I had heard anything of my grandfather, I began to have wonderful, powerful dreams. I floated high above the sun, looking down on the orbital plane of the planets of the solar system. The sun was my friend. I rested in orbit around the earth. I walked a foot above the ground. Or two feet. Or twenty. I stood on a hill surrounded by a crowd of people.

In my teenage years the dreams clarified. They became specific, detailed, unmistakable in their meaning. The people around me on the hill were listening to something I was saying. I walked on water. I touched sick people and made them well, that was the most frequent dream. I looked down at faces I knew from a height of about ten feet. My arms were outstretched. Although I felt no physical pain, there was torment everywhere. The backs of my wrists felt the texture of wood. And by the time I understood the first significance of those invasions of my sleep, I knew enough not to speak about them. To anyone.

In my late teenage years I began what I thought must produce the answer. I would perfect myself. Through perfection the dreams would fall into perspective, would fall into the shape of the answer. At first I simply tried to eliminate visual defects in whatever I made or did. In later years, I chased perfection in thought, speech, action, and in situation. I was anxious for praise, but even more anxious to measure up to the flawless performance I felt was demanded by the dreams. Then I tried to eliminate the anxiety, because that, too, was a defect.

'Be careful,' my father warned me. 'You're the sort of person who could be emotionally overwhelmed by religion.' I still didn't know, of course, about his father. So I didn't know why he attached such importance to that warning. He, on the other hand, didn't know about my dreams. So he wouldn't know for many years why his warnings fell on such ready ears. And yet, in spite of his warnings and my fears, I sometimes stood in empty churches, brushed with the shame of being there, and not understanding why I had come.

I trained in physics because I thought that that science would perfectly and rationally describe the universe. I spent much time on calculating the orbital movements of the planets, and on calculating the production of vast amounts of energy from small lumps of matter. But I discovered that physicists' theories suffered from the same defect as all other kinds of models. They were approximations.

I tried school-teaching, convinced that I could create in every child a thirst for understanding and wisdom. But my subject was physics, and physics had blemished.

I married, at the age of twenty-one. I told my perfect wife that we would have a perfect marriage. Four years later, Stuart was born. He would be a faultless son. He would have an immaculate upbringing.

I experimented with psychic phenomena of every possible type. But nothing happened that couldn't be explained away by classical science. Without faith, I tried faith healing, furtively, on myself; trying to cure physical complaints as inconsequential as sandfly bites. Still I found nothing to connect me with the dreams.

I began a hunt for skills, and attempted mastery of every one. I reasoned that while the one great medium still eluded me, I had to allow for the possibility that the answer might lie in the perfection of all.

Eventually, I was surrounded by imperfection. Everything I touched, tarnished. Flaws and fissures clamoured around me; tearing at my job, my skills, my family, my marriage. And myself. There was no answer anywhere. One day, it all took me apart. In my twenty-seventh year, a few weeks before Andrea was born, I went berserk.

I entered the tunnel.

6

I had been watching an early afternoon television special. I was ironing a shirt at the same time; trying to watch the screen and move the iron without pulling its plug out of the all. A bumble-bee, caught inside, threw itself repeatedly at the window, making dull pinging noises. The sound put a worm of annoyance into my stomach. It twitched with every collision of the bee against the window.

I don't remember the name of the film. All I remember is one still scene – a few seconds long. A rescue party had just broken through into a ground cave in which a pregnant mother and her son had been buried alive. As the dust settled, the rescuers' lights began to pick out what was in the cave.

The mother stood weakly. She leaned at an odd angle against the rock wall. Her little son clung to her leg – about Stuart's age he was – his head came to just above his mother's knees. Complete, horrible insanity writhed on the mother's face. Her stomach was not so swollen now; she had given birth. The baby lay silent and still on the floor a few feet away.

A baby girl, I decided. And an instant later I was certain that our child, my child about to be born, would be a girl. Then the worm in my stomach was joined by a hundred cousins, and they began eating their way up to my chest. I went to bed. I would get rid of the worms by lying down and resting.

Five seconds after closing my eyes, I sat rigidly upright on the bed and screamed. A vast black tunnel thundered over me; blinding and deafening. Then I flew through the tunnel, faster and faster until the dark walls blurred and all I could see was a faint light a long, long way ahead.

The light went in and out of view. There was something trying to get between me and the light. Some evil, formless thing. A feeling, a purpose, rose inside me. I flooded urgently up my spine and through my flying body: so powerful, that my scalp, my hands and my feet all burned with rhythmic fiery waves. *I must overcome whatever is in my path and reach the end of the tunnel.*

Then the tunnel disappeared. Flick. I whimpered on the bed. My wife was in the room, calling out something. I couldn't remember her name. But there was no time to think about that; an eerie moaning sound floated into the house from higher up in the hills.

Within one minute, I was forcing our car down the hill, leaving rubber marks on every curve. Banshees moaned on my shoulder, fading back into the hills as I skirted the city towards the main road west.

Mount Rolleston, I thought. Up till that point I hadn't known why I was headed west. I stopped for petrol: it was going to be about a hundred and fifty kilometres to Mount Rolleston. The purple petrol climbed up the petrol tank.

By now, I knew I'd gone utterly insane. I was a lunatic. Off my trolley. Gleepy. There could be no other explanation. I rolled the word 'insane' on my tongue to test the flavour. Strange that I should be aware of being insane; unreasonable that everything around me looked so icy-clear. I felt a little cheated.

'You alright, mate?' The attendant looked anxious.

I didn't answer him. The driver's door closed itself as I accelerated away. I don't remember paying him, so he was probably the first to call the police. At the time I wondered why I hadn't yet heard traffic sirens.

I played chicken with the first on-coming car. He ran off the road. After that I ran every car off the road, improving my technique as I went along. Open road. All mine. Everything going my way to Mount Rolleston and the sun.

Some of the drivers wanted to cheat round me on the wrong side. So I snaked continuously to discourage them. Some ploughed into the shingle before their drivers even thought about the brakes. But I never looked back to see what happened to them.

When there were no cars to frighten, I swerved lazily from side to side, enjoying the hypnotic swaying. I sounded the horn continuously, taking command of the air as well as the road. This was my day.

Somewhere past Darfield, with one swerve, I ran off two cars at once. Well done, Michael. The second one was a traffic patrol car. Wonderful. His U-turn was so aggressive he almost did the full circle. Then he came howling through the trees after me, with full orchestral and visual effects. Oh glorious day.

He wasn't happy when I didn't pull over. He came up close behind, adding his horn to the persuasion. I gave my brakes a sharp stab. Then he took more care, pulling back a few metres. As an afterthought I gave him the fingers. Delightful – I'd never done that to anyone. I'd never sworn at anyone either.

'Fuck off,' I said, experimentally. 'Fuck off!' I screamed out the window in high joy. But he wouldn't have heard me.

For a long time he stuck behind me, content to do his own noisy swerving to warn cars coming from ahead. Even so, I managed to send off a motorbike coming out of a blind corner.

So, the traffic cop became determined. Perhaps he had more instructions. He came up abreast and swung to scare me. I kept driving straight. He had a red face and I waved to it. He tried moving forward then, to cut me off, but dropped back smartly when I tried to put my car where his was.

On the next long straight, he came alongside and started to ram sideways. Once. Twice. He shouldn't have done it, because his car wasn't built like mine. On the third ram, I swung to meet him.

The whole left front of the patrol car folded up like a used handkerchief. I watched in my rear vision mirror as his vehicle shuddered and bounced to a stop. I could see the driver's lips moving.

'Fucking bastard,' the lips said. His cap was askew.

Oh joy, joy – my car was still running perfectly. Now nothing would stop me getting to Mount Rolleston. Everything was going well. My smile felt like one of those moustaches that climb up towards the cheekbone and drop downwards at the end. If I didn't change my expression soon, the smile might have to be removed surgically in a hospital.

Heh, heh . . . 'remove the smile in a hospital,' that was a good one. If I could think up jokes about insanity, maybe I wasn't crazy.

There were no cars at all through Porters Pass, but that didn't bother me. The day was mine; everything was mine; exhilaration was mine – especially driving past the sheer drops at that speed. For the next sixty kilometres, time made no more impression on me than the disturbance a needle makes when it is fired point first into a pond.

Just a few kilometres short of Mount Rolleston, one kilometre from the village of Arthur's Pass, two men standing off the road waved their arms frantically in the air as I shot past.

On the approach to the village, there's a long one-way bridge. As I cleared the last corner and came within sight of the river, a Land-Rover rolled to a stop on the far end of the bridge. Two men in khaki uniforms flung the doors open and put greased distance between themselves and the bridge. Park rangers. How unreasonable: I didn't want to die yet. And how inconsiderate to leave their Land-Rover right there: I had to get to Mount Rolleston.

I braked hard and stopped just clear of the Rover. Now I would need every second. Five or six bounds put me behind the Rover's wheel. In his hurry, the driver had left the door open and the keys in the ignition.

But I couldn't find reverse and, after three attempts, hands were snatching at me through the window. I couldn't jerk them off; I'd already jolted the Rover forward on to my car. And I couldn't hold shut both the door and the window, as well as fiddle round finding reverse.

I tumbled into the covered rear section, but three more uniforms reached the tailboard before I found my feet. I had to reach Rolleston. There was only one way left. I had to fly.

The Land-Rover's radio hissed and crackled behind the driver's seat. I picked up the microphone and spoke into it urgently.

'Charlie Victor Bravo to taxi. One person. Arthur's Pass area. Two hours.'

No answer. They must be asleep up there.

'Ground control, this is Charlie Victor Bravo . . . do you read me?'

No answer. Some days there was this wild impulse to bowl out on to the runway and take off without asking anybody. Today . . . this was my day . . . I'd take off now, and to hell with them.

But then I noticed all the watching faces. They were perfectly still, staring into the cockpit with their mouths open.

'Must be from the airforce,' said one.

'Yeah,' said another, 'Look at his moustache.'

'Loop-the-loop,' said the first one.

They didn't seem to know what to do. But I couldn't take off with them standing in the way, and if they took it into their heads to climb aboard, they'd damage the rudder. So I laid about those heads with the shovel I'd fallen on when I rolled into the back. I knew it was a shovel.

One of the men wasn't in uniform. He had a motorbike helmet on and he was angry about something. Then one of the uniformed arms grabbed the business end of my shovel and yanked it. I toppled forward, and they had me by an arm and leg faster than Rikki Tikki Tavi snatching a cobra.

The trouble with being manhandled that way was that one of my legs wanted to stay on the inside of the tailboard, and the Rangers were hauling downwards on the outside leg. That became excruciatingly difficult for me in the region where my legs join together. I saw the logic of their argument, shrieked with pain, and carried the debate out into the road.

Most of the really painful blows came from the motorbike rider. He was persistent – seemed to have something personal against me. He still had his helmet on, too, which I thought was an unfair advantage.

I stopped wasting energy only when I was horizontal, with my wrists and elbows tied behind me, a rope around my chest and upper arms, a rope and a belt on my ankles and knees, a strap bringing my ankles up towards my wrists, and a rope connecting my wrists to the Land-Rover's towbar.

They were very angry. There was a lot of milling about and shouting. I thought a great deal about why I was attached to the towbar. I thought about them having to shift my car before they could do it. If I could just make them understand, all this fuss wouldn't be necessary.

Spittle dribbled out the right side of my mouth. I didn't like that. I really wanted to get rid of that spittle. Maybe they thought I was crazy, but I didn't want them to think I was frothing at the mouth. I wiped my cheek on the tar-seal. Unsuccessfully.

'Let me go,' I said, hoping someone would hear me above all the talk.

'Oh no,' said one sweaty face. 'You're not going anywhere, mate. You're staying right here, fella.' He stood up.

'I've got to get to Rolleston,' I pleaded.

'What?' He came back down crouching. 'Hey shut up you guys. What'd you say?'

'I've got to get to Mount Rolleston.'

'What for?'

'I've got to climb it. The Otira face.'

He shook his head sorrowfully. 'Jesus,' he said.

I had to laugh at that one, and I could see they thought it was crazy laughter. They just didn't know. Some children arrived, and that made me cry as well. Then I remembered about being tied to the towbar, and reasoned that they wouldn't drag me with children watching. I stopped laughing and crying and timed how long it took another dribble of spittle to drop from my cheek to the road. Naught, one thousand; one, one thousand; two, one thousand; three, one th . . . Three and a half seconds. And in the space of that same three and a half seconds I could collect and register pain messages from every part of my body. Interesting. I remembered my father explaining about messages of pain being sent by the nerves. Ancient dinosaurs were so big, he had told me, that you could hit their tail with a hammer, and run behind a tree before the message of pain reached their brains.

There wasn't enough pain yet. Perhaps if I made them angry again they would do it. But not too much. I didn't want to die. I had to find Mount Rolleston.

'Stand back. Stand back.' That just had to be a policeman. He would have come from Otira; summoned by radio. Hah! If these people only knew how logically my mind was working they wouldn't have me tied up like this.

He added his handcuffs to everything else holding me down. I don't know how he found space on my wrists. There was a lot of chit-chat between him and the rangers. Then he bent over me again.

'Now look, mate. It's no good being tied up like this, on the road, is it?'

I agreed with that. Just the barest nod.

'Fine. Well, we want you to be untied too, and we're not going to harm you. I'm going to keep the handcuffs on you, but we'll untie everything else if you promise to behave yourself.'

I nodded again. He was really laying on the Mr Nice Guy

approach. But I wasn't falling for that line, no sir. I'd go along with it and wait my time.

I was dizzy with pain immediately after being untied, and there were men three deep around me, hoping I would make a break for it. Not that they seemed angry any more. The atmosphere was more like that of an unexpected holiday.

The motorcyclist was still around too. Why didn't he take the helmet off? And let his head cool down. Heh, heh . . . that was a good one, too . . . they just didn't know how logically my mind was working, these people.

It was no good trying to escape now; but the cop had promised that the handcuffs would be removed once I was safely in the police car returning to Christchurch. That would be the time.

However, the Christchurch police weren't keeping any promises made by the Otira police. They were wary. They allowed me just one concession before bundling me into the car: I stepped through my arms and brought the handcuffs out front.

'That's alright,' one said. 'You're allowed to do that.'

Why did they treat me like a child? They'd see how much of a child I was when we got under way.

But it was futile. I had one try at unlocking the door and falling outwards, but I was much too slow. I was beginning to slow down. The policeman on my right was half my weight again. He showed me the error of my ways.

All I could do was gaze wonderingly at the handcuffs, or crane my neck to look back at the fast receding Mount Rolleston. So much for God, I thought: on the summit near the sun was the view that encompasses all views. But God saw my pain and said, 'It is not good for this man to suffer.' And He took away my mountain.

We made one stop at Darfield. After some palaver outside a private home, I was taken into a kitchen. The woman gave everyone a cup of tea, including me. She looked at me closely, and her eyes were crinkled. Would I like some cake with my tea? Yes. Every time I took a sip of tea I waved the saucer around. I didn't think to abandon it and it didn't cross my mind to fling the tea in anyone's face. My brain wanted to lie down.

A red-faced traffic-cop came in the back door, greeted the policemen and threw his cap on to the bench. Without taking his eyes off me, he crossed the kitchen, sat on a chair, accepted a cup of tea, and sipped it a couple of times.

Everyone watched him watching me. Except the woman. She gazed out the window with the tips of two fingers of her left hand touching the little finger of his right hand.

'You could have killed me,' he said quietly. 'You know that, don't you?'

He didn't say anything about the other people I'd forced off the road. And I didn't answer him. My brain was trying to lie down on the floor.

On the outskirts of Christchurch, a girl with skates was speed-wheeling loops around a lamp post. A complicated manœuvre. She had just enough room for one skate between the post and the gutter, and she was whisker-hugging the post on the narrow side of each loop. As the police car rolled past, the girl slipped. As she fell, she bashed her nose on the post.

'Stop!' I called out. 'That little girl's fallen over.'

The two police up front glanced at each other and went back to silently gazing forward. That was more than they'd said to me the whole trip.

'She's hurt herself,' I insisted. 'She's hurt her nose.'

Silence. I twisted round for another look.

'She's crying,' I added, feeling the girl's tears exactly in the top left centre of my head.

'Don't you worry about her,' said my giant guard. 'She'll be just fine.'

At police headquarters I had one last attempt at escape. My handcuffs were removed in the cell block, so that's where I tried it. I found out later that my screams were heard right out front in Hereford Street.

A large group of dark uniforms broke over me like a wave of warm, blue-black sea.

'Bastards,' I screamed. 'Murdering, fucking bastards. What about the little girl?'

'We should put him in a padded cell,' panted one as they carried me jerkily along the corridor.

'We haven't got one,' panted someone else.

But they did have a cell with just a narrow peep-hole. The handcuffs had been bad, but they were nothing compared with this totally enclosing featureless, too smooth, too bright cell. I backed into the corner where they couldn't see me from the peep-hole. I curled up to the size of a rat. I thought to myself that rats could walk through concrete walls if they could learn to get the first paw started into the concrete.

'Michael,' came a voice. 'Michael, it's Doctor Patterson here, I want to give you something to relax you.' He'd been a friend of the family before I was born. He'd delivered me in the Chatham Islands. He'd been a friend to me, and now he had come to treat me in a police cell.

The police were close by when he injected me.

'You're going to commit me, aren't you?' I murmured later. I had to have two shots.

'Yes Michael,' he said. 'I'm afraid so.'

7

I floated, just under wakefulness. Tremors reached down from the ripples of the world, but they passed through me unknowing. I was too small to disturb their path. I was curled, head to knees; an apostrophe on a soft white page that is glanced at and forgotten because there are no words printed there.

The tremors strengthened. I began to feel warm. I didn't want to feel warm. I didn't want anything. But the warmth cuddled with me, between the too hot and the too cold. Sheets whitened my eyelids. I began to apply effort to staying asleep. Somewhere, slithering outside the grey mindscreen, there was a terribly important reason for staying asleep.

The blankets helped. They held me lightly, but firmly, the way it always felt when mummy tucked me up after the bedtime story.

Tell me some more, daddy. I want to know what happens when Peter William McPherson McLazybone gets found out. Does he get a whalloping?

Not now, Michael. Time for sleep.

How old are you, daddy?

Me? I'm a hundred and seven.

Bounce me, daddy.

Alright. Rrrraaaarrrraaaarrrraaaarrrraaaarrrr!!

Shrieks of laughter.

Daddy, why do you go like a lion when you bounce me?

Because you ask so many questions. Go to sleep now, you'll never wake up in the morning wake up in the morning wake up.

No.

Daddy, how big is the sun?

That's enough. Goodnight. I'll tell you in the morning when you wake up.

'Wake up.'

No! My forehead pressed hard against my knees.

'Come on, Michael, up you get.' A woman's hand pressed my shoulder the way mum's used to when she and dad left me to sleep. But the woman didn't know she was supposed to go away.

'Time we got you something to eat, Michael. You must be

starving.' The tone was too reasonable, too matter-of-fact. It crawled through my right temple and insisted its way around the inside of my head. It carried with it the assumption that obedience was a certainty, only a matter of time.

It was over. The refuge had gone. The apostrophe became a series of dots rattling across a movie screen. I uncurled, turning slack cheeks and dull eyes towards the owner of the hand on my shoulder. The face was two feet from mine, smiling.

'Good man,' the face said. After a hesitation, its body stood up. It had carrot hair, a bright red cardigan over a nurse's smock, and carried a pink dressing-gown over its arm. 'Your pyjamas are on the chair and here's a dressing-gown. You put them on, I'll be back in a moment.'

They *were* my pyjamas. I recognized them before I could stop myself. I didn't want them. I sat hunch-backed on the edge of the bed, rocking backwards and forwards, hugging my chest. I was still wearing my shirt and underpants. The shirt had tar stains on it, and looking at them made my chest hurt.

Mental hospital. Every breath sucked in was that of a mental hospital. The sluggish molecules stirred around my face, sticking to eyes and cheeks. I closed my mouth and breathed shallowly through my nose. Then I had vague recollections of lying on this same bed, watching a stethoscope that tapped and tapped relentlessly on the back of a pale hand. The movement had stopped only to allow the instrument to spray another abrasive jumble of words, then the tapping had started again. It had been possible to unscramble the words. Some of them had translated into things like, 'How old are you?' and 'Do you know what year this is?' But the questions had not been relevant to me, so there had been no need to answer them.

The sunlight bounced unreasonably round the room, warming the varnished wooden panels and the gleaming cabinet. Flowers on the dresser burst into applause, admiring themselves in the mirror. They didn't know I was in the room.

The nurse returned.

'Come on, Michael. Look, it won't take much effort. Are you going to start, or do you want some help?' I didn't want any kind of communication with her, but had to shake my head to avoid contact with her hand. Insidious, I thought. Insidious, the way she had manoeuvred me into moving my head. When she had gone, I slid into the pink dressing-gown. Ghost flesh into night attire. Wake the dead and restore them to the pink of condition. Roses outside the window mismatched the gown with a different shade of pink.

I shuffled into the corridor. I couldn't see a thing, apart from the wall opposite the door. Accustomed to the brilliant, sun-lit bedroom, my eyes saw the mental hospital as two black holes, stretching unknown distances in opposite directions.

There was something unpleasantly familiar about the blackness. I took two steps down the corridor, keeping close to the wall. Still I could see nothing. I took two more steps. Then, a doorway opened far down the corridor, creating a point of light in the blackness. Swampy waves of memory heaved in me. My God! The tunnel!

No! No! Just a corridor. The light's from a doorway; take a grip on yourself. If it was the tunnel, there would be that evil formless shape between me and the light. No. No. It's okay.

Scared, I tried to return to the relative comfort of the bedroom. But just before I turned, something did block out the light. My first impression was that the evil something was far away, close to the light. Then it was right in front of me. The rush of perspective change brought me close to vomiting. The evil shape gibbered at me.

'Inshnat. Fweeganiwortansbitican. I'll take you along to . . . Are you alright?'

I flattened, against the wall, shaking. She had done it on purpose. She had spoken in gibberish to scare me. They had found out about the tunnel and were trying to drive me insane.

'You *are* in a state, aren't you? Come on. You'd better come back and lie down. I'll get you something to calm you down.'

I wouldn't move. So she went away, returning almost immediately with two men. They took me firmly by the upper and lower arms on each side. It'll be the shock treament now, I thought. They've already probed my mind. Now it'll be the shock treatment. Softening me up for later.

But they hustled me the few steps back to my bed, then handed me a pill with a glass of water. They watched carefully, making it clear that they wouldn't leave until I'd swallowed it.

Hours later, they walked me up and down the corridors, saying that I was getting a guided tour. But we passed the office three times, which led me to the conclusion that they were trying to exhaust me. We walked only in two enormous corridors, with holes attached to the sides. The corridors crossed at right angles, centred on the office; an enormous parody of the Crucifixion. I pictured me and my escorts as termites, walking through a hollow wooden cross.

One of the side-holes contained all the patients; about thirty of them, sitting in chairs. My escorts took me into the hole and guided me to an empty chair. I watched carefully for signs of insanity. Six of them wore pink dressing-gowns. Perhaps we are the sane ones, I thought, imprisoned here by an insane society.

The patients were conducting their own meeting. Three of the men were asleep in their chairs, which I thought was a definite sign of sanity. The woman doing all the talking was organizing a duties roster. She had a firm voice, but she always spoke to peoples' chests.

'This is Mr Brown,' a voice said behind my chair.

Most of the patients gave me a brief once-over, but only a girl with a chubby face looked at me for any length of time. She smiled shyly.

The voice behind me spoke again.

'Perhaps you could make Mr Brown welcome and explain about the roster.'

'Oh,' said the woman to my chest. 'I'm sure we all want Mr Brown to feel at home here, don't we?' She paused. Some of the patients nodded. The chubby girl smiled at me again. The woman continued, 'But perhaps Mr Brown should be left free of duties until he's had time to settle down.' She added, above my head in a slightly admonishing tone, 'That's what we always do for anyone who's new.'

'Yes. Of course.' The voice above me sounded tired.

The meeting was soon declared closed. Almost all the patients stayed where they were. But the chubby-faced girl immediately crossed the floor and stood in front of me. She held a ping-pong bat. 'Want a game of table tennis?' she asked.

I didn't say anything.

'This is Karen,' said the nurse behind me. 'That's a good idea, Karen. Go on, Michael. Do you feel like a game?'

I said nothing. But the nurse came around the front and held out a hand to my sleeve. And I noticed two male nurses near the windows, watching me. They're planning something, I thought. They're setting me up. The girl's a plant.

I stood up and shuffled warily to the ping-pong table. The nurses stayed by the windows, watching me. Perhaps the girl had nothing to do with it, after all. She looked so friendly. I stood opposite her, gazing woodenly at the green rectangle between us. A ping-pong bat was put in my hand.

The girl was smiling again, in anticipation of the game. She smiled a lot. She attempted to serve, but her bat missed the ball.

'Teh, teh,' she clucked cheerfully. She missed twice more, but remained just as cheerful. I waited, thinking about the possibility of hitting the ball when it arrived. I had always enjoyed table tennis. It was extraordinary how much the girl was smiling.

'I've got a brain tumour,' she explained in the same happy manner. 'My co-ordination is deteriorating every day. I'm going to be dead in three months.'

I left the ping-pong bat where it was, in mid-air, and sprinted noisily out of the hole and far up the corridor. Near the main office, two orderlies stepped out to block my path, alerted by my din. I flung myself at the wall, rolled along it, feeling like a tarball, then raced what I thought was left of me back the way I'd come.

The two male nurses from the table tennis room loped up the corridor to intercept me. I found another hole, empty of people but laid out with rows of tubular steel work-benches and chairs. In the far corner, I cast about aimlessly with body and hands, then seized a chair and aimed it at the window.

The two orderlies jostled through the doorway. The chair swung furiously around my body and flew at them. It arched across the diagonal of the room, smashing into the wall beside them, shocking them to a standstill.

Two male nurses appeared at the door. I knew no karate then, but took up what I imagined to be a karate stance. The men waited. I panted, hard and sharp. My body tingled, and my arms leadened. Curious patients watched from the corridor until they were motioned on by the men. Nurses' faces came and went. I thought some of them were very pretty, and I was sorry they were going to watch me being killed.

More men arrived, puffing, until there were about a dozen just inside the door, eyeing me in the opposite corner. A nurse came and went, leaving a pile of blankets. The men all helped themselves from the pile, unfolding each blanket out to half-size. Then they held their blankets loosely and waited. No one tried to speak to me.

A bearded man walked in. He talked to the two male nurses from the table tennis room, then turned to me. He stepped forward.

'Michael,' he said. 'Don't you think it's time to calm down? Let it go? Let me take you back to your room.'

No.

They closed in, holding the once-folded blankets out in front of them. The fight was over quickly, in a frantic, piercingly noisy scuffle. At least, they thought it was over. I was a bit slower coming to the same conclusion. As they bundled me along the corridor, one of them discovered that I could be discouraged if he thumped me in the testicles. Eventually I was pinned down on a floor somewhere by numerous knees and elbows. Then I stopped struggling. Someone told my tormentor to lay off.

Someone else told me to hold still, and I felt a sharp jab at my backside. The needle didn't go in. Nor did it penetrate on the second attempt. A woman's voice complained that I had the hide of a rhinoceros. She grunted with the third effort, succeeded, then pushed the liquid in quickly.

They continued to hold me. I rotated my head under the hand on my ear, and saw that I was in a tiny room. Everything was being taken out. A bed moved past. Men hopped over and around me, trying to keep out of the way without releasing me. Everyone except those on top of me followed the last of the furniture out. Then, suddenly, all the pressure lifted. Shoes slapped quickly on the parquet floor. The door slammed and clicked.

I dry-sobbed, face down on the cold parquet, shaking in spasms. My knees drew themselves up to my chest. Still curled, I rolled on to my knees, holding my face in my hands, touching my forehead to the floor. The sound of voices made me curl more tightly. But then the sound seemed disturbingly intrusive and I looked around.

I wasn't alone, after all. A narrow, vertical, double-glazed window had been built into the corner to the left of the door. Curtains had been pulled open on the outside. Heads filled the viewing space, staring, staring. In my own wonder, I rose slowly to my feet. Some of the white-coated people outside the window were contorting their bodies in order to get a view, careful not to spoil anyone else's view. Heads were stacked one on top of the other.

At first, I ignored them. I touched the bare wooden walls of my prison, hoping that the sense of touch would contradict the evidence of my eyes. I could not really be locked in a mental hospital, stark naked, exposed to curious eyes.

But the faces were still there when I looked at the window again. They were still shuffling for position when I took a sudden step towards them, silently beseeching with my palms that they draw the curtain. The whole bank of faces started slightly, jolted by the same tremor. Then they came back into position. I was conscious that my genitals had swung with my step forward. Still facing them, but unable to move, I sank my chin down to my chest, and stared at the chilly sweat drying on my stomach.

I don't know how long I contemplated my stomach. But, during that time, the lunatic made a conscious decision to become sane.

Nothing, I told myself, could be worse than this. It wasn't possible to get lower than I was now. There was no comfort beyond the breaking-point, no hidey-hole; only a screaming void. From here on, I had to head the other way. I had to go back to the other side. I had to drag up every social skill I knew to convince the authorities of my sanity.

And I would not be content with release. I would keep going until I discovered the meaning of my dreams. But I would be careful, this time. So careful. Yes. That was it. It would be like sailing on an ocean, using all my resources to make sure I never sank again. This time, it wouldn't matter if I never found harbour. I would have to be content with the sailing and with the learning of the currents. That way, the harbour would always lie across peaceful seas.

Of course, I decided, my present life, outside the hospital, would have to be abandoned. Marriage, family, teaching job: that would all have to go. That way, I thought, my keel will not drag me under again. But, my immediate concern was to show the authorities that I was sane. I had to be seen to be sane.

With that decision came the relief of having direction and purpose. I raised my head. The curtains had been closed. I had privacy when I didn't want it. But I would have to wait: if I shouted or banged for attention, I could just be adding locks to the doors. From now on I must show patience and quietness. I must talk with as much reasoned intelligence as I could muster. I would have to show a sense of tragedy at my own situation, a sense of sober reflection on what I had done. Perhaps, also, a hesitant touch of wry humour. And, surely, if

I was now sane, these things would take care of themselves.

A horrible thought occurred to me. Perhaps I had injured someone on the road to Arthur's Pass. I could even have killed someone! That was a bad moment. But I clung to my resolve, knowing that no matter what I had done, I couldn't go back into that screaming void.

Sometime later, the curtain at the viewing window twitched back. A nurse glanced in and disappeared. No time for communication. I sat on the floor, in as modest a position as I could manage. In a few minutes two faces looked in. I straightened the fingers of one hand, in rueful acknowledgment of their presence and of my predicament. Then I pointed at the floor, making signals that I wanted to sleep.

In five minutes the door clicked and opened. Half a dozen male nurses crowded around the entrance, one with a mattress, the other with a dressing-gown. The red-haired nurse stood behind them. The white uniforms shifted as the mattress and gown were brought in, and I noticed, for the first time, that my nurse had the rank of sister.

'Sister,' I said to her as the mattress and gown were placed on the floor. I didnt expect her to answer, because my actions must have taken me a long way from such human response. But she did what I hoped. She glanced at me as she backed away from the two men coming out.

'Sister,' I repeated, trying to hold her eyes. 'Did I hurt anyone?'

She shook her head and reached for the door. The men were all behind her now.

'Sister, please.' Careful. Not too desperate. 'Did I kill anyone on the road to Arthur's Pass?'

She scraped a little fingernail on one of her lower teeth. 'No,' she said directly, with her hand on the door.

'Did I injure anyone? Hurt anyone?'

She took her finger away from her tooth. 'No one,' she said clearly. 'You haven't hurt anyone.' The door shut firmly, blocking out the watching circle. The lock turned.

They watched through the window, perhaps to see what I intended to do with the dressing-gown cord. But I was a long, long way from suicide. What a gift. What a glorious gift from whatever God was. To start again from a clean slate. I had stepped across the narrow part at the very bottom of the pit, and now needed only to look upwards as I climbed.

An absurd happiness came to me. But I was careful to keep it to myself. If they saw me grinning now, I'd be back to square one. I lay on my side on the mattress. I slept, then, utterly drained.

8

In the long hours of the next morning, the furniture was returned carefully, piece by piece, from the corridor. The more potentially dangerous items were left to last. But after the replacement of the mirrored dresser, the door remained unlocked. That evening, I was allowed back to my first bedroom. And, by the end of the following day, I had been promoted to the normal 'free range' status within the ward.

Doors to the outside were unlocked during the day, but I had no wish to escape. New Zealand was too small for successful running. And when they dragged me back, I'd be worse off than before. Besides, the thought of heading off across the Canterbury Plains in a shocking pink dressing-gown didn't seem appropriate to my new, self-appointed, state of sanity.

Eventually, I walked unsupervised across the hospital grounds for the first of a series of sessions with a clinical psychologist. For me, they were storm sessions. My calculated plan of action demanded that I not show too much distress. But, in the presence of Ralph Unger, I had no such control: I shivered and sniffled my way through most of each hourly session. He had a nose which didn't even twitch at my red herrings. His expression said, 'Well, we'll take what you've said at face value for now. Go on.' After an interruption by phone he would click back into the conversation, knowing exactly which emotional brick we'd been taking apart, and how much mortar still needed chipping.

I told him about the tunnel – safe enough, I thought – but nothing, nothing, about the dreams. They had left me alone since the night before the car chase, but I had no doubt that they would return. I decided that admitting their existence could land me with the hospital equivalent of a long jail sentence, and with the name of a fancy illness on my file.

'What illness did I have?' I asked him. He acknowledged the attempted cunning with a tolerant smile, but never gave me a one-word answer to the question.

I began to see the staff of Sunnyside Hospital in a different way. They changed from a scheming, homogeneous 'them', to a collection

43

of uniformed individuals. But the change was a gradual one. It was a long time before I saw that the office staff had better use for their papers than as a cover for spying on me.

There were no straight-jackets or padded cells. They had been replaced with drugs, long ago. I was fed chlorpromazine, which made my skin feel infested with the fleas of a thousand camels. Misbehaviour wasn't possible while taking chlorpromazine: it would have used up too much scratching time. I discovered first hand and second hand why one of the nicknames for Sunnyside was 'Monkey House'. After much careful protest, I was moved on to stelizine, a mild tranquilizer.

The patients organized their own dance once a week. There were never more than three couples dancing at a time, but most of the patients came to watch. It was the social event of the week. The music was scratched out of old records on an ancient, portable record-player. The dance hall was the space pushed into the tables of the dining-room.

Old Hilda couldn't dance, but she liked to stand with her arms around people, and cuddle them while the music was going. She was so small and bent that when her arms were around me, her head pushed on my stomach. And she was so crooked she had to hang on tightly to one side of my dressing-gown. But, in her head it was cuddle; and I put my hands on her back in response.

'Are you the doctor?' Judith asked me, as soon as we took our first quick-quick-slow. She askéd the same thing of every male she could pull on to the dance-floor. When she had tried every man once, she started a second round. As long as the record-player squawked, Judith kept up her anxious hunt for the doctor that never came to dance with her.

Tony wouldn't dance with anyone. He wouldn't normally have come to the dance at all. But the indoor bowls had been locked into the games cupboard in an attempt to get everyone to the dance. This was Tony's second stay at Sunnyside, and his time between, out in society, had lasted just one eventful night. He was a dry alcoholic, wanting to return to normal life. He'd been dry for years when he left Sunnyside for a long-planned evening at home with his wife. But his wife wasn't at home when he arrived. She had left him a piece of paper on the kitchen table, held down by a bottle. The bottle was full of gin, and the paper said, 'Enjoy yourself'.

Karen, the girl dying of the brain tumour, had almost given up dancing. She loved trying to move in time to the music, but every now and then one of her legs would forget to support her. She told me over a nerveless lower lip that she used to dance a lot; that she used to play many sports, but that now she could only manage table tennis. Karen was happiest at table tennis. But her co-ordination had deteriorated noticeably within two weeks, and she hardly ever hit the ball. During our last game she fell against the end of the table, knocking her face on the edge and trapping the bouncing ball with her long, fair hair. Then she carried on cheerfully trying to hit the ball, as if nothing had happened.

After that game, I lay on my bed for hours, frustrated and helpless, remembering my healing dreams. If only it were possible. Then I made myself move about the ward for the rest of that evening, aware that if I stayed out of circulation for too long the fact would be noted and recorded. But, that night, the dreams returned. Not just the healing dreams, but all of them. The sun, the earth, the water, the hill, the healing and the cross. I woke as if I had not slept.

Still, I dared not confess. Instead, I told the psychologist about the tunnel and the light, which, for some reason, had not appeared in my dreams at all. And I spent much of that day wondering about the difference between sanity and insanity. I came to the conclusion that I was sane if I could cope with my condition. Whatever that was, and whoever I was.

My wife, Anne, brought Stuart to see me. He was eighteen months old then. And Anne was nearly full term with the new baby.

The visit was a failure. I could hardly speak. When I looked at Anne, I was only aware that she would be bringing up two children on her own. When I looked at my eighteen-month-old son, I could only think that he would be growing up without a father. The baby inside Anne . . . also without a father.

I couldn't pick Stuart up. I couldn't even touch him. I spoke in monosyllables, and eventually closed my eyes behind my hands. I didn't tell Anne I would be leaving. I didn't have the guts at that stage. When they left, I went to the nearest toilets and vomited.

In group therapy I was told to try to give a shape to the monster in the tunnel. A snake-like creature rose out of the plasticine; similar to that of a king cobra poised to strike, tensed above the shuffling coils of its lower body. Afterwards, I hurled my monster into the wall with a loud yell. But the walls had been built for such punishment, and the yell didn't count against me. In group therapy they took the wrong kinds of notes if we *didn't* give at least verbal outlet to contained feelings.

In the same therapy session, we were asked to blow up a balloon, make friends with it, then do what we felt like doing with, or to, our new friends. One woman cried over her friend, cuddling it on the floor in the corner, until someone else put a pin through it.

After several weeks, I was released. I expected a visit from the police, but they never came. I found later that no charge had even been laid, as was usual for the criminally insane before they were taken to Sunnyside. I didn't understand why I had been spared. And for that, as well as for the lives of the people on the road to Arthur's Pass, I could only be grateful.

I handed in my resignation from teaching, and applied for entry to journalism school. I launched anew into collecting skills, but found that I now got much more from learning about people. So, I studied people and social interaction.

I left Anne, Stuart, and Andrea. The dreams continued.

I lived in a flat in the company of smooth criminals. I learned massage from massage girls, and later taught others as they came into the profession. Usually they learned it as a front for the oldest profession. My boss said on the phone, 'No sir, the girls do not do extras.' To me, he said, 'Any of my girls who can't open up a bit of poontang won't last long with me.'

I left that venture when I could stand the self-punishment no longer. And I took up karate at the same time, because it was impossible to leave the massage boss without falling out with him.

When Stuart was old enough, I took him to one of my karate lessons. I explained before I went on to the floor that all the fighting would only be pretend-fighting, like a dance. But, during the lesson, when he thought I'd been hurt, he came running to me through all the frenetic bodies. Afterwards, in the changing-rooms, he spoke to me with tears in his eyes: 'Daddy? Me love you.'

And on the way back to his mother's flat, he said, 'Daddy? Can me come to stay at your place?' A few seconds later he said, 'It's alwight daddy. Me will only stay a vewy little bit.'

A year and a half later, I was sitting on a bed with Julie, explaining why a man, trying to stay sane, would need to go into the Andes Mountains to find a place to put on a robe.

She sat up with me.

'Thank you for not stopping me,' I said.

She gazed at me, long and direct, seeing me naked inside. 'You still have the dreams?' she asked softly. 'You still dream that you are Jesus Christ?'

How terrible finally to hear that statement in words, on someone else's lips. 'Yes. More often now, and more vivid.'

She kept on looking at me, holding my eyes up to hers. And I felt safe. After a while, we lay very close and slept.

9

I trod lightly through the following days, with secret shared and purpose set. Everything I touched returned me meaning and pleasure. Sometimes I found Julie looking at me strangely, but it wasn't the expression of the sane regarding the insane, rather the new workings of her own life. Somehow there seemed to have been a perfectness about the last days; a sure sign, I thought, that the abbey was my one and only chance of survival. Find it, and my dreams would be explained, to be forgotten or acted on. Fail to find it, and insanity would swallow me, and this time anchor me to the bottom of the abyss. No, I would not fail.

We loved, we slept, we talked. How much we talked. Julie asked more of Sensei, then went to him herself and came back deeply reflective. She read the book about the abbey. 'There's a note, between the lines,' she said. 'It echoes in me. It's like part of a tune that seems familiar, but that I don't quite recognize . . . as if it has always been in and around me, and I've been too sleepy to notice.'

She knew the next step was up to her; if for no other reason than the coincidence that she had planned to travel to South America anyway. But it was many days before she said the words I longed to hear: 'If you'll have me, I want to come with you.' It was as well her decision took that long, because by then it was clear to both of us that she wanted to find the abbey for her own sake. Not because she wanted to be with me.

By the end of that week, we had a departure date set for a few months away. And we had a plan, of sorts. Once in Lima, the capital of Peru, we would travel slowly across Peru to the area to the north of Lake Titicaca, asking for directions to the abbey. We saved every possible cent of our wages. Peru was going to be cheap to travel in, but expensive to travel to.

We began learning basic Spanish, and forced ourselves to speak in Spanish whenever possible. We discovered that there are two ways to say, 'I'm hot', to a Spanish lady in front of her husband. There is the right way, and there is the wrong way.

We sent many letters, within and without New Zealand, trying to get a head start on clues to the location of the abbey. We concentrated particularly on organizations which could know of the brotherhood, and on climbers and other individuals familiar with that region of the Andes. Some letters were never answered, and some were returned unopened. But a few returned from Peru with general information about the area. Those letters warned us not to travel into the interior without firearms and guides, both things that we would not be able to afford. They warned us of the extremes of terrain: most of the area was either dense jungle, or a type of very high, often snow-covered, plateau called altiplano.

The information itself affected both of us the same way: it sobered us, yet somehow made us more determined. But after a while I noticed that Julie was troubled, particularly at times when I had been speaking passionately about the coming journey. One night, over a candlelight dinner at her flat she brought the problem out in the open. Oriental chicken, bamboo mats, light dry wine, and Beethoven. Julie twirled a generous fall of pepper on to her plate, frowned at the rising steam, and tackled the subject head on.

'Michael, there's something I have to tell you.' Her tone was so serious I put my knife and fork down again. 'When we do get directions through the mountains, I may stop at the last town and leave you to go on by yourself.'

'I don't understand. Are you afraid? So am I. We both know that . . .'

'I'm afraid alright, but it's not that. I'm sorry, this is going to be rough, but we have to put this on the line between us.' I sat back, with no idea at all, what she was on about. 'I want to find the abbey. You know that. I *want* to. But you, in your eyes at least, *have* to find it. It's become all or nothing to you.' She looked down, then up. 'You're afraid that if you don't get there, you're going to cut loose again, perhaps killing someone this time, ending up in a mental home for good.'

Extraordinary to hear those inner fears coming towards me in words. 'Yes. I . . . Yes. But I don't see how . . .'

'You're fit. You're determined. You're already very, very intense. If the way is as difficult and dangerous as it looks from here, then you're going to drive yourself far beyond what I could do.'

I began to speak, but she stayed me.

'Also, you're experienced in the mountains. I'm not. We can't afford more supplies than we can put in our packs, and we can't afford a back-up team – so we'll probably get just one shot at this. You've said so yourself. So this is what I want to ask you: what happens if we're in the middle of nowhere and I can't go on?'

The full import of what she was saying passed me by at first. Then I stared at her. 'You're thinking that if I have to turn back, that . . . that . . . that I'll go insane right there.'

'I don't want to . . .'

'You think I might harm you? Go on without you, maybe?

Abandon you in the snow?' I turned away in bewilderment.

'Michael. Please. Look at me.' She reached over and took my hand. 'It's not a matter of you abandoning me. But I'm going to take every care not to end up holding you back. I must: if finding the abbey is everything to you, then I can't take such a risk on my shoulders.' With her other hand, she pushed the candles aside, fumbling slightly, then she had both my hands in hers.

'Michael. I want to get to the abbey. And I want to walk down that llama trail with you. But please understand – when we know what the route is, if there looks to be any chance that I might cause you to turn back, I'm not going to start the last leg.'

10

'You won't find the abbey just by asking the right people for directions across Peru,' Sensei said. 'Whether or not you're given those directions is going to depend on your state of readiness. You must prepare by opening yourself to what is around you now.

'Don't talk only to me. Everyone's path is different. If I express a truth, my words are a screen through which you see one thing, and someone else sees another. No one person, or book, or religion or philosophy can give you all. But many contain fundamental truths that you must recognize before you can advance.

'Go and talk to others, to people who have found inner peace. Ask them what their answers are. Go to bookshops, libraries; when a book catches your eye, open it at random and read. Listen to the radio, watch television; if a line of thought, a philosophy catches your ear, find out who gave it and track him down.

'Don't completely accept, or completely reject, anything. Don't judge what you find in terms of right or wrong. Watch it all pass by. If you're ready for a particular truth it will reach out from behind its words and strike a chord in you as it passes. As you go on, you'll find that these fundamental truths are not isolated, and that the essence that binds them together cannot be expressed in words.

'Your path is not laid out for you in advance. You don't follow a path; you make it as you go. And it's when you take conscious part in the creation of your path that you can reasonably ask it to lead you to the answers. Once you begin that, you'll discover that the answers come down that path to meet you. Seek, and you'll not only find, but *you* will be found.

'But to build paths, you need materials. Don't shut yourself off from your resources. You've decided to solve your particular problem by travelling to Peru to find an abbey. But that journey is one tiny part of a much greater journey for which you have chosen to live in this world. Don't reject the world. You need it and it needs you. Expand. Reach out.'

11

In the remaining months, Julie began to work on her physical fitness. I spent considerable time trying to prepare mountain equipment that would also serve us in the jungle. It had also to be planned so that, if necessary, basic equipment could go into one pack.

Julie took a higher paid job with another paper, and I began work as a television reporter. Just as well; the saving had been slow.

We expanded our hunt for organizations and individuals, tracking down even the most obscure if there seemed any chance of finding something helpful. We studied every scrap of religious thought and philosophical doctrine we came across. And, constantly, we tried to sift meaning out of the mountain of thought and dogma, in order to prepare ourselves. Those weeks were exhausting, exciting and frustrating.

Someone called the newsroom and asked if we were interested in two old ladies in Stanmore Road who seemed to have a hotline to God.

'A what?'

'A hotline. If you ask me, they've got His unlisted number. They're just pensioners, and they're turning an old empty house into a rehabilitation centre for addicts. They pray for something one night, and next day it arrives, bingo! I've seen it; they send God a shopping list. Paint, wallpaper, toilet paper . . . you name it. Even the rent.'

When I arrived with a camera crew, Jessie and Rosie were standing in a clutter of beds, wardrobes, paint tins, cutlery, and linen. They had just spent an extra session on their knees, they said, thanking God for the three hundred dollars He'd sent them for the mini-bus.

'Mini-bus?' I asked, not at all sure of the sanity of the sub-editor who sent me on the job.

'Last night we prayed to the Lord for a mini-bus for the addicts,' Jessie said. 'This morning a man came to the door, and he had *such* a funny expression on his face, didn't he, Rosie? He was holding the cheque for three hundred dollars . . . and he said the Lord told him to bring the money to this address, and it was to be used for some sort of transport. He had *such* a funny expression, didn't he, Rosie? Praise the Lord.'

51

'But the city social services know about you, don't they?' I objected. 'You ask them for these things don't you?'

'Oh no,' they said. 'All that comes too, but if we need something we just ask God.'

God had a sense of humour, according to Jessie and Rosie. A few days earlier, they had decided that the addicts would need two institution teapots. But there was only storage space for one. The two ladies had sent that problem also to the heavenly supermarket, and had taken delivery of God's solution the next morning. They brought it out for the camera – one institution teapot with two spouts.

It made me wonder what would happen when the ladies completed the house, and started praying for the addicts.

With closed eyes, the palm reader ran long, pale, delicate fingers over my palm. Then, with eyes intently directed, she traced a fingertip along the creases. Her white poodle scrabbled out of her lap, and high-stepped across to the sofa, miffed at the loss of attention.

'Yes,' the woman said, after much study. 'You have been to Australia four times, and you have two children. Your wife is Australian, perhaps.'

'That's right,' I said, astonished.

'You were married in Australia.'

'That's exactly right!' I frowned at my tell-tale hand.

'The oldest child is a girl, and the younger is a boy,' she continued dramatically. 'And you and your wife have just taken them to Australia for a holiday.'

'No,' I said, disappointed. 'That's not right at all. I'm separated, and the children are round the other way.' It puzzled me that she could be so right one moment, then completely wrong the next.

'Beware of mysticism,' a well-known and respected Christian man told me. 'I understand why you want to go and find this abbey of yours; it means that you're searching within yourself, and that's wonderful. But don't be trapped by mysticism. The devil often appears in tempting guises.'

'How would I recognize the devil?'

'Simply be on your guard. He could be in any guise: even that of Jesus Christ Himself.'

'Oh,' I said, caught off-balance. 'In that case, how would I know?'

'By familiarity with the real thing. Read about Him in the Bible. Get to know Him. There's your answer, you know. Read the Bible properly, and you'll find that you don't really need to go to this abbey of yours; you don't even need to leave Christchurch.' He pulled two versions of the Bible from his bookshelf: the standard version, and the modern one called *The Way*.

I opened the modern version at random. On page 353, it said, 'God must feel slightly sick staring down into our cruddy world.' Being more interested in a God with perfect health, I opened the standard version. On page 892 it said that before curing a man of his blindness, Jesus led him out of town.

Every individual, every organization, and every written page gave us different words. The more we studied, the more variety we found in doctrinal form. But, as we progressed, we began to feel that something subtle held them all together, something indefinable by us. As the feeling grew stronger, the abbey increased its pull on us, and we became more determined to be prepared when we began the hunt for clues across Peru.

12

'Everything is connected,' Sensei said. 'Each of us is connected to every living and so called non-living thing. The universe is a vast living network, of which we, in the physical plane, see only the tiniest segment.

'Each action radiates out like ripples into a living sea. Each of our actions returns to us. No one is immune from his own actions. We take ourselves with us wherever we go, and eventually we all open our eyes and face ourselves.'

13

One month before leaving New Zealand, my dreams began to push me harder. They were more frequent, more intense. And they changed character: the Crucifixion took over as the dominant dream. It came with more detail and in vivid colour. Some details repeated time and time again: a helmeted soldier who went away and came back; a hooded woman with her eyes to me, and her face to the ground.

One evening, when Julie was away, I prayed, on my knees, for the first time. I knelt by the end of the bed, as did children I had seen in old movies. I pictured my father and flushed with shame and embarrassment. But I made myself go ahead.

'Please God,' I started, then faltered, shocked by the sound of my own words. 'Please give me a sign that you exist.' I waited, eyes closed, but nothing happened. 'What are the dreams for? What am I supposed to do?' Still nothing. I switched to praying to Jesus. 'Please Jesus. If you show yourself, I'll know the dreams are meaningless, and they'll stop.' I went on to suggest that He appear on the fuzzy grey thing I called my mindscreen. But still nothing happened, until I got blanket dust up my nose and sneezed.

For a week, I spent a lot of time on my knees in empty churches. And still, the answers I chased directly were not given. Ministers, finding me alone in their churches tried to encourage me to talk. But the questions I could put to the Deity were somehow not repeatable to his deputies.

In the last two weeks before we left, I gave up on direct prayer, and studied reincarnation. I ignored my particular concern, and tried to understand the various concepts of physical rebirth.

When Benjamin Franklin died in 1790, he left this for his gravestone:

The Body
of
Benjamin Franklin
Printer
Like the Cover of an Old Book

Its Contents Torn Out
And Stripped of its Lettering and Gilding
Lies Here, Food for Worms.
But the Work Shall Not Be Lost
For It will Appear Once More
In a New and More Elegant Edition
Revised and Corrected
by
The Author

Some of history's most remembered people also claim to have been recovered: Mozart, Plato, Pythagoras, Edison, Emerson, Goethe, and many others. But, in spite of such respectable involvement in the theory, and in spite of my attempts to keep my problems separate from the study, I didn't research reincarnation with much peace of mind. I knew I had to keep learning, just to stay sane. But I couldn't avoid gut-stab feelings that any action stemming from the dreams was the beginning of delusions of grandeur.

And besides, there were many others in the same queue. Becoming Jesus was one of the 'in' reincarnations. Mental hospitals abounded with Jesuses; and with Gods, and Popes, and Napoleons. There is a joke:

A psychiatrist on his evening round of the dormitories came across a patient he hadn't seen before.

'Well, who have we here?' he said to the patient.

He was answered with noble dignity and restraint. 'I, sir, am Napoleon.'

'Who told you you're Napoleon?' asked the psychiatrist.

'God did,' was the reply.

And then a voice came from the next bed: '*I did not!*'

And I was always aware that I didn't feel anything like the stuff of Jesus. I sympathized with a Sunnyside patient who couldn't decide whether he was Jesus, or the King of Rock, Elvis Presley. When Easter loomed, he decided that he was Elvis Presley.

14

For the last time, I walked along the training-room corridor, and clicked the five steps between the end of the carpet and Sensei's office. He was waiting. There was little to discuss, now.

'We leave on Sunday,' I said.

He nodded.

Occasionally, I seemed to be bleating when I talked with Sensei. My words often filled the seconds with muddy water. I wanted to avoid that today. I would think my words through carefully. I took a last careful look around his office, and out into the training area. The kickbag was swaying slightly. Hundreds of bloodstains from skinned knuckles had coated it round the middle with dark chocolate.

I wanted to thank him for the tenuous, still unnamed thing he had shown me. But it wouldn't have been appropriate to thank him. 'Sometimes I won't know what to do,' I said. 'I'll think myself back into this room for guidance.'

He nodded again. 'When you don't know the way, there will be help. Someone will be near you at the right time, as long as you're still looking. But you mustn't sit down and wait to be carried to the abbey. That will never be done for you. The effort must come from you.'

'Will we be safe, then, while we're looking?'

'No. You must be very careful. You're responsible for your own lives. You must keep your eyes open.'

'Apart from directions, is there anything we should look for on the way across Peru? Unless it's important, I don't want to go sightseeing, I just want to get to the abbey.'

'If you make a desert where you walk, you won't reach the end of it.'

'But if the abbey has the Truth, why not go straight there?'

'Each truth taught at the abbey also exists inside you, sleeping. The feeling of recognition you have talked about is caused by the first stirrings of a few of those truths. Each has been stirred by your efforts, and must be fully woken by your efforts. Only when the wakened truth recognizes itself at the abbey will you perceive it consciously as a truth.'

'I have been trying. But it's difficult to know what to look for.'

'The effort you make in overcoming that difficulty is like the effort of weaving a tapestry. Every truth is a thread which you weave into your own tapestry.'

'Surely the Truth has been woven only once, and by one Weaver.'

'You are the weaver. At the moment, your tapestry is small. It looks different from that of other weavers, but only the design is different. All the designs are woven on one fabric. Every person is a weaver and every person uses the universal fabric to create their own unique tapestry.'

15

Anne brought Stuart and Andrea to the airport to say goodbye. Until that day, my children had seen their father only once a week. Now I was to deprive them of their father for at least many months, perhaps years, and, if the worst happened in the Andes, perhaps for good. I didn't try to speculate on the morality of my actions, because I knew I was going anyway. Nothing could stop me.

'Goodbye Stuart. Will you help mummy look after Andrea?'

'Yes. I can do that. That's easy for me. Daddy, are you going to write me a letter?'

'Lots of letters. But sometimes I won't be able to, because I'll be in the mountains where they don't have any post offices.'

'No,' he agreed. 'They don't have postisses in those mountains. I made a butterfly at kindergarten.'

Anne looked softly at both Julie and me. 'Look after yourselves,' she said, and kissed both of us.

Andrea reached up and tugged at my pocket. 'Kiss me too, daddy. Me am two and a half. Me am a big girl now . . . Not too tight, daddy! Me am very little.'

Part Two

1

Julie and I first saw the Andes from the distant comfort of a jetliner. The sight wasn't reassuring. Distance did nothing to soften the insolent contours.

The Andes range is second to none. It plunges and rears almost the full five-thousand-mile length of the west Coast of South America, in a swathe up to four hundred miles across. It thrusts to heights of twenty-two thousand feet and more, within a hundred miles of the Pacific Ocean. And more than a thousand miles of the harshest the Andes has to offer shunts through Peru.

In Peru, the mountains are called the Sierra. On the middle heights, at around ten thousand feet, almost half of Peru's population scratches out a living on poor land. On the highest plateaux, at fifteen thousand feet and more, there is only a sprinkling of remote Indian communities; people physically and psychologically adjusted to the great altitudes, yet the poorest people of a poverty-stricken country. Rivers have criss-crossed the plateaux with canyons, some more than five thousand feet deep with a tropical climate at the bottom. Somewhere in one of those canyons, Julie and I hoped to find one of the mystery schools. The abbey.

To the east of the ranges is the Selva, a carpet of forest and jungle that feeds the Amazon Basin. It covers more than half the country but holds less than a tenth of the population.

The economic heart of Peru is down on the western coast, on a narrow strip of seaboard that is little more than desert. Fifty-two valleys have been channelled through the desert, but only ten of them hold water the year round. Fishing once kept the economic heart pulsing, but the off-shore currents had changed, and the fish were going. When Julie and I arrived, Peru was in turmoil.

They say that when there are great contrasts in land, there you will find proud and noble races. Peru is a streaky blend of two once powerful civilizations: the Incas and the Spaniards, each in their time as proud as any in the world.

The meeting of those two races was not noted for the presence of Spanish diplomats. The Spaniards were conquistadors. They had an aversion to saying 'Please'. They enslaved the Incas, and plundered their vast wealth of gold and silver, removing it first to Spain, and then to what is now the capital of Peru, Lima.

Lima stands on a wide, irrigated plain on the desert seaboard. On one side, the plain slides into the sea. On the other, on the very edge of the city, the first foothills begin in the steep climb to the peaks.

In the eighteenth century, Spanish Lima was world-renowned for its splendour, and for the luxury and wealth of its citizens. So much so that it attracted a series of heavily armed visitors, each with a pressing need to remove some of the wealth. The Spaniards, who had a similar approach to life, liberty and the pursuit of money, were remarkably unsympathetic. And their wealth gave them the power to turn away successfully all such visitors.

When Lima did fall, it wasn't to guns, it was to the invasion of liberal ideas from Europe. But Lima didn't fall completely. Even now, the closer a Peruvian is to pure Spanish descent, the wealthier he is likely to be. And rather than merge, the two races spent the next century swirling into a lumpy mixture.

In Lima, that mixture was compressed. Even from the air the contrasts were laid out, seemingly in the broad brush-strokes of an impressionist. There was the dab of grey-brown of the shanty towns, holding millions of Indians and growing fast as the economy worsened. There was the green-terracotta-white patch of the wealthy districts towards the sea. And there was the mottled-grey of the business centre where poverty and wealth jostled together, and where Julie and I began our search for people who knew of the abbey.

Julie, with her blonde hair and fair complexion, could no more pass as a local in Peru than she could claim to be top talent from the Bolivian witch market. And, with my beard, the best anonymity I could look forward to was being shot for perpetuating the memory of Che Guevara.

Beggars, street vendors, thieves and con-men came to us like ants to a picnic. They had a name for us. 'Hey gringo,' they called to me. And to Julie, 'Hey gringa.' They loped out of streets behind us, or moved to intercept us.

When we walked into view, beggar children were instantly gripped by the most imaginative throes of suffering, starvation, and sickness. The street was a stage for the child beggars as long as they held our eyes.

A small boy crouched in front of a temporary wooden fence, which fronted the site of yet another luxury hotel under construction. When he saw us, he lifted his head, uncurled his back, and limped out, firmly blocking our path. He turned up a piteous face and held out his right hand for inspection. It had been mangled in something, and he had been left with massive scars, two fingers and a thumb. With a quick, despairing movement, he used the same hand to push black matted hair away from his face, without manipulating fingers or thumb.

He was about four years old; Stuart's age.

Daddy, daddy, the horse bited me.

There, it's alright Stuart. It doesn't look too bad. You've had a big fright, that's all.

I was giving him the carrot and he bited me. Why is that horse angry at me for?

'Señores, un sol. Sólo un sol.' Only one sol. As the unit of Peru's currency, one sol was worth seven-tenths of a cent. Freely translated, sol meant 'piece of the sun'. The boy knew that a gringo – which meant 'rich' as well as 'non-Hispanic' – would either refuse him, or give him a great deal more then one sol. At four years of age, he was already adept at contributing to the earnings of his family, if he had one. If he had, say, parents, brothers and sisters, they might make their contributions by washing clothes, sewing leather wallets, theft, and street-vending.

Street vendors were experts with their eyes. They used them like manacles; one glance from us at a week-old pair of white puppies held mewing in line with their eyes, and they had us.

'How lucky you are, señores, to be looking at the only surviving pups in South America descended directly from Lassie.' An exaggeration perhaps, because the black pups around the corner were also descended from Lassie. Perhaps she had flown down from Hollywood for a night on the town.

Shopkeepers waited in their doorways for us, needing only a few seconds of observation to see that we were still wet behind the ears. If we could be dragged into their shops, they did rapid, consecutive multiplications in their heads as our eyes went from one object to another. But we had little idea how long it would take to find the abbey, so bought nothing but food. We told most shopkeepers we wanted nothing, thereby shaking the very ground they stood on.

'But, are you not tourists?' some said.

'No,' we learned to say. 'We are travellers. There is a difference, no?' Some understood instantly. Others nodded and smiled stiffly.

'You can't exchange dollars here,' said the bank teller. 'This is the wrong kind of bank.' As we turned to leave, she lifted a phone and spoke into it without dialling. The bank manager intercepted us at the door and herded all two of us into his office.

'Please sit down. A misunderstanding, nothing more. It's only necessary for me to make one phone call and you can change as many dollars as you wish. Afterwards my friend will drive you in my car to wherever you want to go. I have a Mercedes Benz. Very comfortable.' He brought the palms of his hands together and rested his elbows on the desk. 'Now, how many dollars would you like to exchange? We will not concern ourselves with the rate. For friends there is no problem.'

'Ten dollars,' I said.

His smile stayed exactly the same on the left-hand side of his lips, but it sagged on the right side like suet pudding. 'Ten,' he repeated, like the pudding falling out of the bowl. In Peru, every white-skinned foreigner is presumed to be both rich and from the United States. An Americano. 'You are Americanos?' he asked heavily.

'We are from Nueva Zelandia. *No somos Americanos.*'

'Ah, Nueva Zelandia,' he said blankly.

The standard Peruvian world map had unbroken blue where New Zealand should be.

Theft is an art form in Peru. There is the 'money-slider', who acts like any other street money-changer until he begins to count out the soles. At that point, he looks frantically up the street. 'Quickly,' he whispers urgently, 'the police.' He thumps apparently the whole wad of soles into the client's hand and melts away. Too late, it dawns on the client that the police are not coming and that when he glanced up the street, the money-changer slid half the soles under the dollar pile.

There is the 'easy-rider', a sort of mobile, non-stop purse-snatcher. He rides his motorbike past women on street corners, collecting their purses, and weaving away through the snarled, snailed traffic. Women who know, usually walk with their purses round their necks.

In that case, the 'slashers' are waiting, with razors concealed between the ends of their index and middle fingers. If a woman is careful enough to walk with arms crossed shoulder to shoulder, the slasher may treat that as an irresistible challenge to his artistry, or he may look for the younger travellers with lightweight nylon bags slung over their shoulders. Nylon is the slasher's favourite medium. Its texture is perfect for his single movement, slash-and-grab technique.

The 'office-boy', who wears white-capped sneakers, looks for a gringo willing to avoid the bother of walking to a bank to change his dollars. He walks him instead to an empty, two-room office on the third floor of a building just off the street called Jiron de la Union. He stops the gringo in the outer office and says, 'Now you must give me the money and wait here. The boss does not like to be seen.' The gringo who comes this far doesn't expect honour to be the keynote of the transaction, but he allows his money to disappear to the inner office, knowing that he has the stairs behind him. After ten seconds, he hears a pattering sound. After two minutes he discovers a door in the other office, leading to an extra set of stairs. On the door is a poster of the matador El Gallo, who was a bull-fighter famed for his footwork.

When a gringo sits down to a plate of churrasco in a restaurant, he may place his bag next to his left foot, but fail to loop the strap over his knee. Just when he is thinking unkind thoughts about the cook who put too many chillies in with the raw onion, a casually, but tastefully dressed man appears to his right. The newcomer is holding a piece of blank paper.

'Señor,' the newcomer says politely, 'may I use your biro?' Because he is an artist, he asks this question with his face just one and a half feet from the gringo, at the exact distance that demands unbroken attention yet is not quite oppressive. Still close, he scribbles his birthdate on the paper, while his partner walks away on the other side, holding the bag in front of him. 'Thank you, señor,' says the man who is relieved that he will not, now, forget the date of his birthday. 'You are very generous.'

Daniel, also, was a thief, a *ladrón*; helping shoulder the monetary burdens of the rich Americanos. I met him in a store on Avenida Abancay, where I was talking to the owner, trying to untangle a bad patch of 'gringo run-around'.

Sending lost gringos in the wrong direction was second only to football as a national sport. To be fair, some would misdirect me simply because they didn't want to seem unhelpful by saying, 'I don't know'. But most treated the opportunities ignorant gringos handed them as heaven sent. The shopkeeper was a master at handling such opportunities.

'Ah, now I remember, señor. The newspaper *La Prensa* is on Cailloma.'

'Thank you. How do I get there from here?'

'It's better that you don't start from here, señor.'

'But I am here,' I persisted, hoping for mercy. 'Where do I go?'

'Ah señor, it's not possible to get to Cailloma from here.'

A hand tapped me on the shoulder. A young man with dashing clothes and wide moustache grinned at me. 'Come with me, señor. I will show you.' He took me to the door. 'That *imbecil* knows that *La Prensa* is on Union, three, no, four streets that way. Come, I will take you. My name is Daniel.'

He was waiting for me when I came out of the office of *La Prensa*, and he was disappointed and sympathetic when I said that none of its reporters knew anything of the abbey. He knew nothing of the abbey himself, but had many friends who did. I told him I was a journalist, and, by coincidence, his brother was a journalist. I told him I had been robbed of a torch, a parka, and a knife, between the airplane and the customs hall. As it turned out, he had also been robbed last week. 'You must be very careful, Miguel,' he warned. 'There are many thieves in Peru.'

I was curious to see what kind of con he was waltzing, so I didn't discourage him from walking with me. There were people around, and everything of value was in my moneybelt. There were a few small notes in my back pocket, but I was certain that the pocket was tight and flat enough to be finger-proof.

'You want marijuana?' he asked. 'You want cocaine? I can get you plenty. Very pure; only two thousand soles for three grammes. You want a girl? I can get you plenty. Very clean.' He added emphatically, '*Very* clean.'

Two minutes later, he stopped dead in his tracks. 'You see that girl there, with the red hat? She must not see me. We were lovers once.' He gave me a hombre to hombre wink: 'Mucho fuki fuki, you understand. Now I have another woman, and this one she is so angry with me I must hide from her. I will walk behind you, if you don't mind.' He walked two clear paces behind. Then, as the girl came closer, he said quietly, 'We cross the road.' He kept me between the two of them, bumping me slightly on the way across, when someone bumped him.

Daniel wasn't with me when we reached the other side. Nor were the notes that should have been in my back pocket. Daniel was a pocket-cleaner, another artista.

We met Kees a few days after he was mugged on a dark street. He had been lucky because his head had held together, and the muggers had missed his passport. But he was hungry, and waiting for more money to be sent from Holland.

'Now I am eating the hot dogs,' he said in English. 'The thin ones. Without the bread. No sauce.

'It was mine, the fault,' he said ruefully. 'I was going down the street with no lights. They are much more poor than me, but I would like for them to please not hit me on the head.' He frowned thoughtfully. 'Now that they have my money, I wish them luck. Perhaps life will be more comfortable for them now. Living also is for them, I think.' He nodded, satisfied with the way he was fitting his ideas together. Then he chopped his hand sideways. 'But, I think I will practise some more the defence.'

2

Señor Alvarez raged back and forth on the wooden floor. Each time he stormed past the synthetic leather rocking-chair, it trembled. The señor's arms thrashed the air, creating a pleasant cooling effect in his area of the dining-room. His shouts curled through the room in polished crescendos, each carrying with it a warning of the final crescendo to come: the grand climax.

This disagreement was a re-run from Tuesday, which helped considerably with my understanding of the Spanish fighting talk. I continued to sit at my table, where I had been writing a letter. If I left because of their squabble, I would be exhibiting more strange and foreign behaviour than I needed to.

Two afternoons out of three were like this. Soon, Señor Alvarez would begin slapping the tables and persecuting the rocking-chair, which stayed in the guests' dining-room so that Señora Alvarez could rest in it when her legs complained. Which was often. But, at the moment, there was nothing lacking in the señora's legs or her lungs. She stood at full height, tennis-necking so as to score direct verbal hits as her husband windmilled across the floorboards. When Señora Alvarez put her soul into the argument, she could be heard in Plaza San Martin, two blocks away. The señora always put her soul into the argument.

Señor Alvarez slammed the back of the rocking-chair. It whined deeply, then hysterically drummed its feet on the floor. The rocker was going to suffer today; it was about to become the symbol of the argument. And the subject was the laziness of José, their son. The señor was reaching for the peak of his argument now.

'And why? (thump) Because his feet are in his home, where I have brought him up as a son should be brought up, and his head is in the heavens. And why? (crash) Because . . .' His voice overlapped with his wife's. The beauty of such freestyle fighting was in never being obliged to follow anyone's logic but your own.

Finally, the home thrust, the *coup de grâce*: 'And why?' His voice slowed, now, trembling with passion and vibrant with conviction of the truth he was about to reveal. 'I'll tell you why: it is the fault of his mother. How can it be the fault of José, when he has inherited his defects from a mother who sits in this (smash) rocking-chair all day and leaves all the work to her husband?'

Starting at the chin, the señora's face went into a decline and collapse. A long drawn-out wail began to issue from the fallen structure. The wail began on an upcurve, and gathered momentum on the move. When it reached the highest and most piercing frequency possible, the señora threw her tragic face into her hands, turning her crescendo into a flourish worthy of a great opera singer. As the wail began its descent, she punctuated it with brief bursts about such things as misery, misfortune, cruelty, punishment for past sins, and the Virgin Mary. At the end of each burst the wail resumed at the exact pitch it had left off.

Now, it was time to prepare the guests' evening meal. As always, the señor continued shouting for a few minutes. As always, his wife wept her way to the kitchen on the other side of the waist-high partition. There, she sniffled and sobbed, and slapped the fish up and down on the bench, demonstrating that she had been so wounded she was incapable of normal human activity.

Her daughter, Lolita, who had been preparing soup, shoved her mother unceremoniously aside and did the job herself. Seventeen-year-old Lolita was the undeclared boss of the family.

'Where *is* José?' I asked her when she brought knives and forks to the table.

'Accch,' her mouth pulled down at the corners in mock disgust. 'He is outside, playing. Eighteen years old – playing!' But she smiled too, because she was very fond of her brother. They were a close family. They fought hard and loved fiercely.

On the day they took us to the beach, Lolita had come howling along the sand with a sea urchin spine in the end of her big toe. From two hundred yards away she sounded like a fire siren. Her mother inspected the toe, sucking breath sharply through her teeth and rolling her eyes in sympathetic pain. Lolita howled that she was close to death, but broke instantly into wet smiles when the spine was removed.

Shortly afterwards, Señor Alvarez had collected his own spine. His performance made his daughter's effort seem like a mouse complaining about the cheese. He sobbed. He blubbered. He thrashed around. He flailed at the sand with his fists. Whenever his wife attempted to touch the spine, he beat her about the ears. Soon, also howling, she dropped his foot so she could use both her hands to beat him on the head. Lolita and José came to join in. Anyone who wasn't thumping someone, or yelling abuse, was shouting orders. The tide went out.

Julie and I had expected those close to pure Spanish descent to be less accessible than the Indians. But the Alvarez family was a bonus for us, because they were recent arrivals from Spain. They knew nothing

70

of the abbey, but gave us at least some understanding of the influence the Spanish conquistadors brought with them when they originally came to Peru. And the Alvarez family ran a cheap, friendly hotel.

Ten minutes before dinner, Julie slumped wearily into the chair beside me. We touched fingers on top of the table.

'Nothing?' I asked.

'Nothing,' she replied. It was the same story every day. No organization knew, or would tell, about the abbey. The only difference between inquiries in Peru and in New Zeland, was that here people said things like, 'This author, Brother Philip, perhaps he is sick in the head, yes?'

An alarming thought occurred to me. 'It's not beans and eggs night is it?'

Julie blanched and showed the whites of her eyes. 'Oh,' she said throatily. 'Oh, I surely hope not.' She thought about it some more. 'I don't want to offend the señora, but if it's beans and eggs, I'm going to eat out.'

Our stomachs had taken to the señora's beans and eggs the way a twenty-foot ketch takes to a fifty-foot swell off Cape Horn. On the evening of our first introduction to the delicacy, forty people had eaten it with us. And the hotel only had two toilets. What with the bug and the extreme heat, there had been a lot of fast flesh in the corridor that night. The alimentary canal is said to be a continuation of the outside of the body. One woman had glared at me because I found her sprinting along the corridor wearing make-up and panties. I thought that unfair of her, because I wore even less. But I didn't want to stop and argue the point because she was bigger than me, and obviously in a dangerous mood. I flattened against the wall as she thundered past, cutting me to pieces with her eyes. An ambitious salesman could have kept his mistress in roses and lace for a year, just by stepping into the hotel that night with a few chamber-pots.

The streets of Lima still had us confused, but since that beans-and-eggs night, we could have given any newcomer an informed tour of Lima's toilets. It was a major achievement to find one in working order, and an impossibility to find one with paper. We started to give each toilet a grade out of ten: 'Now here's a unique little water choset. A cheeky little number, pleasant in aspect, but a little presumptuous considering that it has no seat, the bowl is broken, there's no paper, the flush doesn't flush, and the pan is half full. The bouquet lingers, but its delicacy could be improved . . . five out of ten.'

Señor Alvarez patted his wife's bottom, picked up two plates and headed for our table. We were the first to be served tonight. Please, anything but beans and eggs. Anything.

The señor launched the plates dramatically and simultaneously in front of us both, then stood back and waited for the applause. Beans and eggs. Plus whole-baked fish with eyes glaring upwards.

'Ah, señores,' he said, noting our pale faces. 'You have been sick, yes?'

'*Un poquito*,' Julie said, carefully. 'A little.' The señor's voice was so loud, it was foolish to answer health questions truthfully.

'A little? A little?' He sprayed laughter-peals all over the table. 'Ah yes, you have been sick just a little, and now I must repair the toilet, yes? Ah señores, it is the Coca-Cola. So many of the tourists come here and drink the Coca-Cola when it is hot. Then they get sick.' A helpful thought came to him. 'But don't worry, señores. You can be sure that this abbey of yours has no Coca-Cola, yes?'

He chuckled back to the kitchen before we could think of an excuse for leaving the dinner uneaten. He explained the joke to his wife, who looked across at us and grinned. Three tables away, the lady who had nearly flattened me in the corridor said something to her husband and three children, jerking her hand emphatically in our direction.

3

The wheat bowl of Peru is a shallow pan, slightly tilted as if to swirl for its gold. The long, wide valley is so delicately sloped that the train from Lima winds mile after mile with engine almost silent, slowly and respectfully approaching Huancayo. The town sprawls freely, rolling easily with the placid undulations of the valley, overlooking land that feeds wheat to nearly half of Peru.

The valley has such a gentle aspect that by sight alone, we might not have suspected that we were walking around at an altitude of ten thousand feet. But our lungs and legs were in no doubt. Walking at that height was like walking knee deep in a vat of oil. For three days, our first flirtations with high altitude led us, again and again, back to bed. And even after that time, a walk of more than half a mile turned us into gasping lowlanders.

After yet another midday rest, I went looking for Julie.

She was sitting in front of the bull-ring, on the bottom steps. And, at the moment I saw her, a swarthy thick-set man sat on the steps behind her. His movement must have disturbed her, because she turned and glanced at him. Even from my distance I could see his burning stare, which proclaimed, 'I lust for you.'

Julie faced front again, but not before she had arranged a look of indifference on her face. Foreign women on their own had a reputation for immorality and willingness for the conquest. That meant that a man filled with the passion of the conquistador looked at gringas and thought, 'This woman is a foreigner. Foreign women on their own are known to open legs for *anything* resembling a man. Therefore if she does not do so for me, it is an insult to my manhood.'

Julie stood up.

'Hey,' called the man behind her. 'Hey, gringa, I have money.'

As Julie walked away, she mixed a little contempt with the indifference. Not to do so could be treated as a come-on. But it was a tricky game; she also had to be diplomatic. Already one Don Juan had slapped her face, and another had physically dragged her along the pavement, saying that he was going to buy her a drink. That one she had hit in the stomach.

She and the would-be lover saw me at the same time. She angled

73

her walk to meet me; he spread his hands, shrugged his shoulders, and raised his eyes slowly from me to the heavens. '*Es la vida.*' That's life.

Julie had no wish to cling to me. But her insistence on independence had made life difficult for her as soon as we left the relatively international atmosphere of Lima. A shapely, fair-haired woman in Peru needed a compensating thick hide. Most men stared. Many prodded, poked and tickled, some with practiced and accurate expertise. Others shouted, 'What beauty!' and 'Are you white all over your body?', and a favourite, '*Que pechos!*' What breasts! Most assumed she wouldn't understand Spanish. The rest obviously didn't care.

Even in the relative shelter of a bank there was little respite: when she fronted into a corner to delve into her money-belt, there'd be a quarter-circle of interested male eyes around her by the time she'd finished. The only place of complete privacy was in a toilet.

But walking with me was no guarantee of immunity. And the couple-front had its disadvantages. Street vendors loved gringo couples and applied special techniques to suit. An Indian flower woman would shove a carnation down Julie's sweater, a polo-necked sweater, and hold a hand under my nose. 'So pretty,' the flower woman would say. And with a straight face, 'Pretty lady. Only twenty soles.'

Only the Indian men were more reserved. They called out mild compliments, and limited their groping to touching her hair. Mostly they just stared.

At the Huancayo bus station, we bought the last two places on the Friday bus to Ayacucho. No one at Huancayo had the slightest knowledge of the abbey, so it was time to go one stage closer to Lake Titicaca.

'Take care with your baggage when you come here,' said the manager of the station. 'There are many thieves around this building.' He grinned hugely, in an odd fashion: so odd that although we shrugged it off at the time, we didn't forget it.

A teenage girl angled in on Julie as we returned to the hotel. 'Señorita, give me money from your country for my collection?' It was one of the favourite ploys.

'Sorry, I don't have any,' she answered. 'Everything is in soles.'

'Señor?'

'The same.' And for me, it was a lie. I had two or three New Zealand coins in the bottom of my money-belt.

As the girl walked away, Julie gave me an approving nod. After all this time in Peru, I was beginning to bend. In the first week I had projected my dream ideals on to my behaviour with such intensity that they far outweighed my strength. My bearing had proclaimed unprotected manna, and the gringo hunters had descended on me relentlessly and endlessly, from the first day.

To refuse a person in need was to betray my dreams, but to solve the dreams I had to find the abbey. And to achieve that I had to protect my money and goods, at least for now. There was a contradiction there that must have a solution. But it would have to wait for the abbey. For now, I had to accept the selfishness in myself, take the middle road, and give to some and not to others.

As we continued back to the hotel, I felt an absurd light-heartedness.

Our room was three floors up, overlooking a courtyard as wide as a barn. The yard was entirely surrounded by three floors of hotel rooms. Normally, it was no more pleasant looking into the brick courtyard than it was pleasant looking at our dirty little room. But the harsh midday sun had gone from the metallic courtyard bricks, and had been replaced with shade . . . and with five boys playing football. From this height, they looked like five pairs of scissors, snapping at a white circle. It was siesta time, but the boys played on, their shouts echoing frantically off the walls and slapping into the bedrooms.

I gazed upwards. The flatness of the rooves around the courtyard was broken on the side adjacent to our bedroom. An Indian shack perched shabbily amongst ten washing lines loaded with the hotel guests' washing. Under one end of the lines was a washing basket, perched near the edge of the roof, no more than twenty feet away. It was occupied by the dog that guarded the washing. Perro, as we had dubbed him, had already paraded up and down the roof, sniffing suspiciously at the boys playing three storeys below. But as always, after his patrols, he had retired to his matted hair and filthy grey body in the cane basket. He never seemed to sleep; he basked in the sun with his left eye open.

But, now, Perro had noticed that he was being watched. Slowly, he opened his right eye, and carefully raised his head one inch, so as to review the situation more clearly.

I couldn't resist it. I puckered up my face and scowled in Perro's direction. 'Woof,' I said flatly.

Perro's eyebrows rose to form gothic arches. His head rose too, but his body stayed in the same position. 'Woof?' Perro blinked, unable to believe the impertinence he had just seen and heard.

Then it registered. With a howl of outrage and fury, Perro thrust on his front legs so fast they lifted off the base of the washing basket. While still airborne he pitched his first round. When he came down, he tore out of the basket, dashed around the shack summoning reinforcements, then returned to the edge of the roof. There, he scrabbled on the edge, giving his most remote ancestors full throat, tensing for the twenty-foot jump across the three-floor drop to our bedroom. But seeing that staying alive was marginally more important than tearing out my throat, he raced left and right along the edge of the roof, howling with frustrated, murderous rage.

That performance pulled a trigger in me that I didn't know I had. The mechanism opened an unused gate. For a few minutes, I was helpless with laughter. I rolled around making snorting noises, and putting my hand over my eyes. 'Woof?' I kept mimicking through the tears, 'woof?'

Julie watched me in delighted wonderment until her own laughter subsided. Then she lay on the bed, and I lay face down beside her with one arm across her stomach. Every few seconds my shoulders went into a shaking spasm, preluding more laughter. Each time, Julie touched my hair, smiling.

I hopped off the bed and crouched down at the bottom end so that just my eyes showed. Grinning, Julie watched over her poised letter pad. 'What on earth . . .' she began, then my face shot into full view and launched at her a deafening, and very bad, imitation of an outraged dog.

When I stopped, there were no more sounds of football outside. Perro had started up another verbal hate session, and a boyish voice floated up from the courtyard. 'Hey gringo. Much noise.'

When everything was quiet outside, we closed the shutters and the windows and lay down again; this time, very close. Julie whispered, 'Thank God. Thank God.' She turned my face to her and said, 'Welcome back, darling.'

4

Every brilliant colour imaginable could be found somewhere in the crowd that stretched between the Huancayo bus station and the edge of the footpath: sharp turquoise, lolly pink, vivid-green – often tumbled together on the same garment. Some of the Indian women could have understudied a paint company selection chart. For every ten colours intending to board the bus, there were a hundred to wave them goodbye. Suitcases, sacks and bundles, surfaced out of the rainbow sea and climbed towards the luggage rack on top of the bus. Already, the first luggage lined the road side rail of the platform.

Through the crowd strode the station manager, shouting. 'Take care. Take much care of your luggage. There are many thieves about. *Cuidad.*' Most of the crowd ignored him because they had nothing a thief would steal.

The manager was enjoying himself. He had the strut of a man who has been awarded both the bull's ears and the tail. And, as he strutted, he was grinning, shouting, and casting about with his eyes, looking for something. When he spotted Julie and me, his grin widened and pulled his ears out of line. He strode to our sides and beamed at our packs, tied together at our feet. 'Ah, señores, now your luggage must go on the bus.'

'We'll leave ours until last,' I said. 'We're getting off first at Huanta.' Huanta was a pretty village we'd heard about, a few miles short of Ayacucho.

His grin vanished. He hesitated, then cheered up. 'Ah, an unfortunate mistake, señores. The bus does not go through Huanta. It goes to Ayacucho by another route. *Que lastima.*'

That made no sense to us. As far as we knew, there was only one route . . . through a hundred and sixty kilometres of mountains, gorges and passes up to fourteen thousand feet, then down through Huanta into Ayacucho.

We said so. The manager trotted away and returned speedily with a bus driver in tow.

'The bus does not go though Huanta, señores,' said the driver. 'It goes by a different route.' The palms of his hands were eloquent.

They never came above his waist, they seemed to be flapping at our packs.

Well, we would have to give up on Huanta. The important thing was to get closer to Lake Titicaca. We would go, we told the manager, and all his joyful teeth came back into view. He was so sorry, he said about the misunderstanding. *Es la vida*, you understand.

Within three minutes our packs were safely on the luggage rack. In spite of the delay, it happened that there was still space at the rear, against the roadside rail – exactly the right space, in fact, for two packs. Once they were in position, we regretted leaving our knives in them. I had bought a new one in Lima to replace the stolen one. It had a picture of a boy scout from Sweden on the sheath. The picture was embarrassing, but the blade was beautifully balanced. I'd become so used to wearing it, I felt uncomfortable without it.

'Five minutes,' shouted the manager.

Julie boarded. I wandered out round the bus to check that our packs had been covered by the huge tarpaulin. They hadn't. In fact, they were the only pieces of luggage uncovered. The man on the roof had one hand on Julie's pack and the other hand on mine. Directly below him on the road was a tattered, elderly Peruvian with an empty street barrow.

The traffic was detouring to get round him and his barrow. He was scratching at a sore through a hole in his jacket sleeve. Then he saw me out of the right corner of his eye and the scratching movement stopped. He shot a glance up to his partner on the roof.

The light from the barrow man's eyes seemed to take seconds to reach the man on the roof. And it took more long seconds for the light to drift from the tarpaulin man's eyes, down to me, and back up to him. He stayed frozen over the packs. His unbuttoned striped jacket hung down on both packs.

The barrow man pushed away along the street. His partner also came to life, and pulled the last corner of tarpaulin over the packs. Except for one glance, snapped across my face, he kept his eyes on the roof.

'Two minutes!' The manager beamed at me from the sidewalk. His beam said, 'Well done gringo, you outsmarted them.' And it said, 'This is a good game, yes?' Then he moved back into the crowd.

I felt pleased with myself. He was right. It was a good game now that chance had handed me the win.

A nagging doubt put me last in the boarding queue. Even then, I turned back at the door and started round the bus for a last check. Before I reached the rear end, a shoeshine boy bounded in front of me.

'Very cheap, señor. Only twenty soles to clean your beautiful shoes.' The shoeshine boys always referred to my dusty sandals as beautiful shoes.

'My socks will get dirty,' I answered, and made to walk round him. We had a little dance as he kept up a hard sell.

'No señor, look, I will take them off. Very clean. Very cheap.' He reached for my sandal straps. I'd seen persistent shoeshine boys before, but this one could have sold fire insurance in the headwaters of the Amazon. He was a bit too good. I almost leapt over him in my haste to reach the end of the bus.

Déjà vu. The tarpaulin had been pulled back, and once more the roof man stooped over the packs. Once more the barrow man waited beside his empty barrow. The sore on his arm showed an angry red through the hole in his sleeve.

Once again the tattered man and his barrow pushed leisurely away down the street without looking back. His partner on the roof stayed momentarily frozen, but this time when he straightened, he did it slowly, deliberately, and with a look at me that made the grey afternoon harden with the chill. I waited until he'd tied the tarpaulin.

The manager appeared at my side, and he wasn't his usual fun-loving self. He waved his arm curtly at the bus. 'Get on,' he said abruptly. But I waited until the bus roof was clear.

The shoeshine boy leaned against the station wall. He was about eight years old. He had the stillness of an adult and an adult's impassive face. A thin face.

Daddy, please can I have more stew?

That's your third helping, Stuart.

Yes, and I'm going to eat lots and lots and lots. Then I'll be a big boy very fast.

'What's the matter?' Julie asked as I sat down.

As I started to explain, the tarpaulin hand climbed aboard and the door closed behind him. He spoke rapidly to the driver, who glanced furiously in our direction. The engine was thumped into gear, and the bus started off to Ayacucho with a savage jerk. As it rolled past the last houses, the man from the roof extended his angry conversation to include two more men; one sitting on the engine cover, and the other on the nearest passenger seat.

How many of them were there? I looked carefully round at the passengers. There weren't as many Indians as I'd expected; but at the same time there was no one in expensive clothes. In a confrontation, there would be little support for rich 'gringos Americanos', and it was already too late to stop the bus and get off.

There were two other gringos on board. A timid-looking couple, but gringos nevertheless.

I pointed them out to Julie.

'We stay?' I asked her. She nodded.

As the bus climbed into the darkening foothills, I left my seat and spoke to the other couple. They came from California. I told them that their luggage wasn't necessarily safe on the roof, and I pointed to the roof during the explanation.

As I returned to my seat, there was a buzz of animated coversation up front. One of the four company men seemed to be explaining to the others what I'd done. He was using his hands even faster than his lips, jerking them up and down, expressing varying degrees of anger.

There is a story about the Peruvian who was looking after his friend's house when a gang of robbers arrived. The robbers bound him to a chair and demanded to know where the money was. When the bound man didn't tell them, they wrecked the house; found the money, and departed. The friend returned, freed the Peruvian and looked around in despair.

'My house is ruined,' he said. 'Why didn't you tell them where the money was?'

'I couldn't,' said the Peruvian, 'the sons of bitches tied my hands.'

From then on, the four men up front made no effort to conceal the stony hatred they worked up for our benefit. Julie and I remembered gloomily that this area was infamous for its well-organized bandits. It occurred to us that the set-up back at the bus station had been beautifully organized. And the sense of humour back there had missed the bus, so to speak. The atmosphere up front, right now, was about as funny as four helpings of biftec smothered in cyanide sauce.

Outside the bus, a fox-like animal bounded up the hill into the darkness. Julie watched it dispassionately. It might have been a garden snail. 'It's going to be a long night,' she said.

Two hours after dark, the bus pulled up outside a cafeteria under the only street lamp of a small mountain town. The lamp glowed in the narrow space between the bus and the cafeteria, sending bright wings into the shadows at each end.

'Everyone must leave the bus,' called the driver. 'Dinner.'

The passengers funnelled gratefully into the warmth of the cafeteria. The four company men went too, leaving more exhaled breath glowing yellowly under the street lamp.

I kept first watch while Julie ate.

Two dark figures stood in the shadows on the far side of the road. They were keeping watch on the bus also . . . on the ladder side. One was fat, the other thin. The thin one was bending over his boot, perhaps tying his lace. I couldn't see them well; the bus blocked off the light all the way across the road.

Julie returned. 'Do you mind if I walk a little, first?' she asked. 'I want to stretch my legs.' I pointed out Laurel and Hardy in the shadows. 'I won't go far,' she said. 'They're probably just interested in the bus.'

As she walked down the road, along one of the wings of light, I realized that the thin one had been bent over his boot for at least ten minutes. I experimented: walking round the bus as if to enter the café. After half a minute, I walked straight back. Laurel and Hardy were half-way across the road towards the bus.

They stopped abruptly. The fat one went back to the far side of the road. But the thin one started to walk – not slow, not quick – in the direction Julie had taken.

I couldn't see Julie any more. If only it wasn't so dark. This could all be imagination. If I started yelling, I could be creating an unnecessary scene. If I went after the thin one, I'd be leaving the packs for the fat one. I dithered, then started to move in Julie's direction.

In that same moment, she came back into sight. She was in the middle of the deserted road, and the thin one had reached level with her in the darkness on the far side. I could see him, but Julie had her face to the light and couldn't see much else.

Then he dashed out into the road, straight for Julie.

'Julie, get back here!' I yelled, and sprinted at the same time. Then the three of us were running. Me at top speed towards them; Julie towards me, and the thin one towards Julie.

My knife was in the pack!

But the thin one had been unnerved by my noise. He swerved like a footballer to avoid Julie, and continued into the darkness. By the time Julie and I met and stumbled to the bus, the fat one had disappeared also.

We must have already been at a high altitude. Our gasping sounded thin, especially after the thump of our feet on the clay road. We stayed by the end of the bus as our breath reluctantly returned. Julie was still shaking when the Californian couple came out of the café.

'Gee, that's real bad,' said the girl. They offered to stand watch for a while with Julie. They looked a little bewildered, as if they couldn't quite believe it.

'What town is this?' I asked before I went inside.

'Pampas,' they said.

Julie and I looked at each other in shock.

'Are you sure?' I asked.

They were sure. We were, after all, on the high mountain route through Huanta. No doubt about it now: the manager, too, had been part of the gang. His little story about the different route had been concocted to ensure that our packs went, as planned, to the vulnerable spot on the roof rack. We might have admired the man's ability to think on his feet. We didn't.

In the café, I walked past the counter where the bus driver was using the phone. As he caught sight of me, his lips stopped moving, and he turned further into the corner. The other three company men had nothing on their table, not even a drink. They didn't speak as I moved around them, their faces were set and cold. They looked steadily at a point on the table in front of an empty fourth chair.

All the hot food had gone. I went back to the counter to buy anything going. The driver had returned to his seat.

'Chocolate, por favor,' I said, when it was my turn.

The café owner didn't acknowledge my existence in any way. He served someone else. I waited.

'Señor, chocolate, por favor,' I said more insistently.

He twitched his eyes at me once, then away, coldly. Three more customers came to the counter and he served them. The passegers were all leaving for the bus, and I still hadn't eaten. When the three customers had gone, the café owner picked up a glass and started cleaning it with his finger.

'Señor!' I said unpleasantly.

He looked over my shoulder, then raised his right index finger up to just under his left ear and looked me full in the eyes. Then he drew his finger across his throat, slowly at first, speeding up at the end with a sudden, jerked stop under the ear. The sound he made matched the motion. His face was not that of a man who wishes the stranger a pleasant and safe journey.

Cold wavelets rippled around my forehead. I looked for the joke in his expression. But it wasn't a joke. I spun on my heel. Except for the two of us, the café was empty.

Julie appeared in the doorway. I didn't think she'd seen the performance, which was just as well, she would not have felt like applauding. She beckoned. Yes, we would be safer on board. At least on the bus there were two more gringos. But we had better not be last to the bus door.

5

The bus headlights slashed from side to side as the road twisted in tight agony into the mountains. On the open stroke, soft grey slopes hung faintly over carbon-black canyons. On the return stroke, the two beams ran in lock-step across vertical rock, illuminating projections as cancerous growths.

More often now, the bus inched through a tight curve only to catch on the safe-side rocks. Three of the four drivers clambered in and out, comparing the proportions of the bus with its distance from the rotten rock at the edge. Each cry of *'Arre! Arre!'* was followed by groans of metal on rock as the bus continued its turn on a complicated sixpence. Some light bounced reluctantly back into the bus; enough to show that most of the passengers preferred to close their eyes rather than watch. A few, probably regulars, were asleep.

My eyes ached. The atmosphere between us and the drivers had become vibrantly cold, keeping us on a highpitched wakefulness. Even though we were seven rows back from the drivers, and all four men were often busy with the bus, the pungent hatred rolled constantly back to us.

For two hours, as the bus moved steadily deeper into the mountains, we waited, hoping that the frustrated thieves were retaliating simply by giving the gringos a sleepless night. But after that time, though they had taken no overt action, the atmosphere forced us to come to another conclusion.

'They're spinning it out,' Julie said to me. 'They're waiting for something.' I agreed. She scratched the side of her knee, speaking with a flat kind of anger. 'What kind of bus trip *is* this?'

At two-thirty in the morning the bus stopped on a high bluff. The canyons formed a black, crescent moon, enfolding us on three sides. No real moon. No stars.

'Dos minutos,' called the driver. *'Para orinar.'* Toilet stop.

Of all the passengers, Julie was the first on her feet. She hopped over my legs and stepped quickly towards the front. *'Estoy enferma,'* she said as she passed the drivers. 'I'm sick. I need pills from my pack.' All four men rose to their feet, but she was down the steps and climbing the ladder to the roof before they could think or act.

She was sick, but with fear. We had to get a knife from one of the packs. And she had to be the one to get it. If she was still up there when the toilet stop was over, then I stood a better chance of preventing the drivers from giving a gringo an air-conditioned ride through the freezing mountains.

I moved outside with the other passengers. We were assuming that the showdown wasn't intended for this stop. But even if we were wrong about that, our move must have thrown such plans out of kilter. All the same, I waited to see that no one had gone up the ladder after Julie. Then, satisfied, I walked to the other side of the narrow road to relieve myself. I reasoned that I could put my back to the mountain and watch the top of the bus at the same time. But it was so dark, I couldn't see any sign of Julie on top of the bus. The rear end of the bus was too close to a spur for me to walk closer to where she must be, so I waited impatiently, zipped up my trousers, then returned to the door and ladder side. Passengers were starting to return to their seats.

As I reached the door, I heard the unmistakable sound of a man's voice coming from the roof. Only three of the bus drivers were on board. I cursed myself for a fool, and leapt up the ladder, shouting, 'Julie, are you alright!'

In my burst of anxiety I was totally unprepared for what happened next. More than forty people were still outside, adjusting overstrained plumbing. My shout silenced their chatter. So, from all around the bus, floating up to me, Julie, and the company man, came the sounds of steamy urinating. Someone was retching, and someone else sounded as though he had taken a dose of the señora's beans and eggs. Instead of an answer, all I heard from Julie was a burst of hysterical laughter.

A man's voice snarled, '*Rapido, rapido.*' Then both of them were scrambling back across the icy tarpaulin towards the ladder. Julie reached the bottom gasping with fatigue and cold, but stumbled on to the bus immediately and took her seat.

'I didn't get it,' she said harshly. 'I didn't get it.' She stabbed a finger forward. 'He made sure of that. I couldn't do more than open one strap.'

The bus drove on.

'Look,' Julie said much later, 'they surely won't harm us themselves, not while we're on the bus they run, and not in front of all the other passengers. The only way they could do it would be to have someone outside the company come aboard somewhere along the way. Before dawn.'

'You're right, and they'd have to phone ahead for that. They *must* be having us on.'

Her head turned. 'Didn't you say the first driver made a call?'

I took a slow, deep breath, remembering the driver's odd

behaviour at the phone back in the last town. The packs, surely, couldn't be this important to them. But we had stopped them twice, perhaps three times so far, and we had pointed out their dishonesty to others in front of them. Perhaps revenge was more important than the packs.

I went through everything we had on us, looking for the best weapon. And the best seemed to be a stainless steel camping fork – perfect protection against rampant cutthroats. My heartbeat felt amazingly slow. Each beat, instead of thumping sharply, seemed to surge like a small wave.

'The map showed just one village between here and Huanta,' Julie said. 'Assuming the map's right, that will be the place.' All I could see of her was the darkest of silhouettes, but there was a stillness about her which betrayed her fear. 'We won't get to Huanta till daylight,' she continued, 'so if no one gets on at the village, we'll be okay. I haven't seen any farmhouses on this road.' She knew as well as I that it was too dark to see farmhouses anyway. But it seemed reasonable.

I leaned across the aisle and tapped the shoulder of an Indian who had chewed coca leaves non-stop since Pampas. 'Señor. A question. How far to the next village?' The chewing stopped, the man's head turned to me, then turned away again. The jaws went back into action. Maybe he didn't speak Spanish; many of the more isolated Indians spoke only Quechua. Most of the passengers knew what was happening now, but, in the uncertain light, expressions were impossible to read.

On the far side of the village, at four in the morning, the bus stopped. Three men stepped across in front of the driver's window. Julie gripped my arm, then let go as I pulled the fork out of my pocket. The bus was silent but for the idling motor. Not a word from any passenger.

'Huanta?' called one of the three outside.

There was a moment's silence. 'No,' called the driver. His silhouette moved jerkily, as if making urgent hand motions. He had given himself away. He must have thought we were still ignorant after falling for the original story about an alternative route.

'Half stand up, then sit down,' I said to Julie in English. She caught my meaning and did so quickly without overdoing it, while I wriggled as if pulling something out of a pocket. The present driver had gone down the first step to exchange a quick word with the three men outside. Another of the drivers was on his feet looking down the bus in our direction.

I brought the fork round to my left side, on the aisle. I slid it into my pocket, trying to make sure that, on the way, it angled to reflect light towards the front, and willing the watching man to notice the action, grateful that he couldn't possibly see what was reflecting the light.

As he watched, the present driver returned to his seat and the three newcomers boarded. The bus jerked into gear and ground noisily into the first curves beyond the village. The three stayed up the front for a few seconds, and I couldn't hear or see what they were doing. All I saw was the moment they began to walk slowly down the aisle.

I shuddered in a long breath, pulled out the fork and laid it on my left thigh with my right hand over it. I pictured Sensei telling me to focus the blow two inches behind the target, which would have to be the eye. I shifted a leg quickly in response to tensing muscles, then stilled.

With one seat to go, the leader's movement slowed. Then he regained his pace, with the suddenness of quick decision. As he passed us, my head moved of its own accord, no more than ten degrees, but enough to see him pass beyond arm's length. My head returned and went through the same motion with the other two newcomers, as if fixed on a self-controlled coil. As the last one went by, I turned enough to see all of them safely into the blackness at the back of the bus.

As I faced front again, a looming bank on the road returned enough light to the bus for me to see that almost every near face was turned in our direction.

When the light passed, I savagely punched the air in front of me. 'You okay?' I whispered to Julie.

But it wasn't over. Now we had to watch our backs. I had visions of black figures creeping forward and gently passing knives under my chin, and of the bus rolling into Huanta after dawn with blood turning sticky and red in the first light.

Half an hour later, I felt a light touch on my hair. I gagged and threw my body upwards. The fork went half-way to a passenger's eyes before I stopped it. The passenger was from two seats back, walking forward to speak to someone. He stopped for a moment in the semi-darkness, looking with an unseeable face at me, unseeable, beside him. Then he walked on.

Every ten minutes after that, I patrolled the front half of the aisle, afraid of falling asleep, and wanting to demonstrate that we were very much awake.

At the beginning of dawn, the bus pulled up in the centre of Huanta, and the three men disembarked. Somehow we weren't as keen to see Huanta as we had been. We stayed on board. The bus rolled on without the drivers announcing the name of the town, and daylight crept through the bus, bringing long, drawn-out, release from the night.

At Ayacucho, followed by the still hating eyes of the four drivers, we caught a *colectivo* taxi to the airport. In two hours we were off the ground, and heading for Cuzco.

The flight was packed with an American group, one of whom was a comedian. He stood in the aisle, practising his act, while the rest of his party admired the mountain ranges out to port. His hair toned perfectly with the orange-red decor of Aero Peru's aircraft interior colour scheme.

'Hi there,' the comedian drawled. 'This here's y'r cap'n speakin'. Yo'all c'n call me Mel. We appear to have a dozen or so aircraft between us and the strip. Well, f'r sure, that ain't gonna be no problem. We'll be upstairs in less time 'n it takes to run over a couple o' them Cherokees. Then we c'n break out the booze.'

He paused. He was getting an unprecedented, bonanza response from the haggard-looking pair sitting forward on the right. Those two had done nothing but cuddle each other since they boarded. Now, they were laughing so hard they were almost off their seats. Tears in their eyes!

The comedian bowed to us, and gave of his best; 'Hi there. It's me again – Mel. Now, yo'all 'll notice that the seat belt sign is turned on. We'll jess ease on down 'n play kneesies with a couple o' them storm clouds. Then yo'all c'n get right back into the booze.'

6

On the eastern side of the Andes, just a few miles from the Urubamba which feeds the Amazon, is Cuzco. The jungle is close, but the valley still belongs to the Andes: the wide, twenty-mile-long valley slopes only gently away from Cuzco City at eleven and a half thousand feet. The city is folded into one side of the head of the valley, mostly on the flat, but partly spilled up the side, towards the fortress of Sacsahuaman that once protected it. Its grey and terracotta colourings merge easily into the haze of browns and golds of the valley. Cuzco is a quiet and very old master of its surroundings.

The Spaniards went to a great deal of trouble to find the city, and with good reason. Cuzco was the capital of the Inca Empire, the heart of one of the greatest empires the world has seen. It lasted from the eleventh to the eighteenth century, and within that time took in a planned, efficient society that stretched from Argentina to Ecuador. It boasted ten thousand miles of roads, suspension bridges and tunnels through the Andes.

The Incas had their own social security system, for which the price was personal liberty. They used the decimal system to bring economic efficiency of a high order, and that efficiency required that no one be allowed to quit his home or work. The Incas even anticipated modern totalitarian societies by making compulsory practically everything that wasn't prohibited, and by rewriting history to suit itself. To ensure that this highly tuned empire lasted, the Inca rulers instituted something which, for that era in the world's history, was surely a stroke of genius. Each Sapa Inca, Son of the Sun, made the secular and religious élite about him open to talent, whether or not that talent came from a conquered people.

Ruled from Cuzco, the empire co-ordinated the skills of those conquered peoples. When it fell, it left behind an archaeologist's paradise, the results of six centuries of highly developed expertise in textile weaving, ceramic making, stone building, and metal working.

The Spaniards were rather impressed by the metal work, which happened to be in large quantities of gold and silver. In fact, conquistador Francisco Pizarro was so impressed he offered the Inca Emperor Atahualpa an exchange: Pizarro would give

Atahualpa his life, if Atahualpa would give Pizarro and his men a room full of gold. The gold was collected. Pizarro, naturally, was grateful, but found himself unable to overlook a charge that Atahualpa had committed treason against Spain. For that crime the mandatory punishment was burning at the stake, but Pizarro generously allowed Atahualpa to be garotted instead.

However, the treasure that lasted best wasn't made of gold or silver. It was made of stone. The Incas built with artistry and they built to last: Cuzco is a living museum. To walk through the city is to hear an echo of the heartbeat of the Inca Empire. And it was from the Inca stone builders that Julie and I found the first clue.

We arrived with great hopes of Cuzco. The book on the abbey had talked of both the Inca Empire and of Cuzco. It had talked of the Incas' descendants living in the valley of the abbey. And, in particular, the book had specifically mentioned Cuzco's Temple of the Sun. Surely, we thought, we must begin to get answers there.

But we were still adjusting to altitude. Cuzco was the highest city we had yet come to. So we kept clear of the temple for four days, wanting to be at our best for the crucial visit. When we weren't resting we wandered the city, learning as much as we could of the Inca system. Almost every street in the city centre had remains of walls, arches, and doorways. Many streets were lined with the original stonework, so secure that much was used as the foundation for modern buildings. And all the while, as we walked we didn't realize how close we were to the clue.

Then we collected our concentration and went to the Temple of the Sun. And, at first, the visit seemed a total failure.

'A hidden valley!' said the guide, gripping my arm in excitement. '*A secret abbey!* Is this true? Here in Peru? In Cuzco? And our temple is in your book? . . . Nooo!' His mouth rounded out to match his eyes.

Nor did the priest from the now Christian part of the temple know of the abbey. After a long, careful scrutiny of corridors, rooms, and all traces of writing, we still had nothing. The guide took all our disappointment to his own shoulders.

'This is *horrible*, señores. The evidence must have gone. But that is Peru, no? There are many mysterious things in Peru's past that will remain mysteries because all the evidence has disappeared.'

Thoroughly gloomy at this dampening of his day, the guide pointed out that there were many interesting things to see around Cuzco. Why, for instance, didn't we walk up the hill to the ancient fortress of Sacsahuaman?

For the first two hours we clambered over the fortress, wondering at its sheer size, and at the mysteries of its construction.

The main wall is eighteen hundred feet long and sixty feet high, rising from the arena in three tiers. Many of the stones are six feet thick, three times the height of a man, and weigh two hundred tons.

No mortar was ever placed between the stones, but most of the walls are still intact after centuries of earthquakes that tumbled almost all Spanish structures. In spite of the violence of Peru's earth, most of the stones are still so perfectly fitted together it's impossible to push the end of a human hair into the cracks between them.

'No one knows how it was done,' the guides say. 'The Incas didn't discover the wheel, so had no way to transport blocks of such size. They had no iron to cut the stone, let alone any tool that could produce such smooth, perfectly-matching, irregular shapes. Each stone fits snugly against its neighbour right back to the full depth of the stone. Each cut is so smooth, there is no mark to indicate the kind of tool used.'

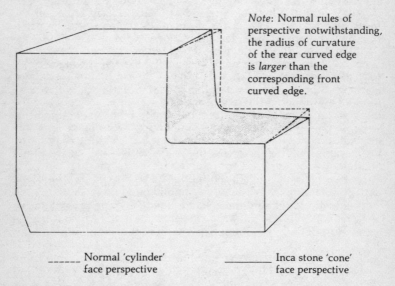

Note: Normal rules of perspective notwithstanding, the radius of curvature of the rear curved edge is *larger* than the corresponding front curved edge.

_____ Normal 'cylinder' face perspective

_____ Inca stone 'cone' face perspective

In the mid-afternoon, near the north end of the second tier, Julie and I lay back on a patch of grass to rest. Altitude still tired us easily. Four or five paces away lay one of the smaller stones – about four feet long, three feet high, and three feet thick. It had recently been levered away from its position at the top of the tier, newly exposing one of its uniquely shaped faces cut into the top of the right-hand end.

For a while, I took no notice of the stone. But my eye began to come back and back to it as I became aware that there was something odd about the shape of the newly exposed face. The curve of the face seemed in some way to be 'pointing' at me.

The face was almost side-on, so I moved around for a better view. The pointing effect disappeared. I shifted around on the grass, experimenting. The effect was only noticeable from my original viewing position, within a radius of about a foot.

'Feeling alright?' Julie inquired. In my present position I must have looked as if I was worshipping the ground she lay on. Either that, or she thought I was about to break into more dog imitations.

'Yes,' I said absently. 'Something funny about this stone.' It bothered me that, front on, there seemed nothing special about the cut face, no reason for the sideways pointing effect.

I pulled the lace out of one of my boots and took it to the end of the stone. At first I didn't know exactly what I wanted to do with the lace, so I pulled it taut and held it in various positions on the curve. I found a place where the taut bootlace touched stone all the way across: a straight line across the curve. The bootlace pointed back to my original viewing position. Then my memory hit the right cog, and I had the answer.

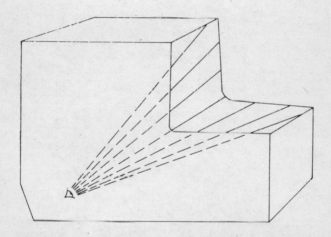

'Julie!' I dashed back to my spot. 'I've got something!' I manœuvred her into the right place, then bounded back to the stone. While she watched, I found three, then six, then ten places where the face was perfectly straight at right angles to the curve. Every point on the face had a straight line of stone running through it, and every straight line pointed at Julie. It was a bit like one segment of a wavy-sided funnel, with the surfaces all sloping to one point.

Then Julie had it too. 'The book!' she breathed. 'The stones of the abbey! This is the same. It's been cut with some kind of beam!'

We spent much longer at the fortress, looking for more exposed faces that hadn't been too pitted by weather. All of them had been cut the same way. If those smooth faces had been cut mechanically, the saw would have needed a pivot arm at least fifteen feet long, and it would have needed a wide, continuous running blade capable of turning tight corners.

No. The cutting tool had to be a beam of some sort, from a technology that has been lost. It would be like a 'torch', attached to a fixed mount a few feet back from the stone, but free to swivel about on that one spot. Each 'cut' of the torch down one end of a stone, would be duplicated exactly on the matching neighbouring stone by using a simple, movement-constraining jig fastened to the torchmount.

The discovery both delighted and confused us. It was the first direct confirmation of anything in the book; and yet we had originally dismissed the book's reference to stone-cutting with 'the primary light source' as being nothing more than esoteric enthusiasm. And as yet the discovery gave us no way to narrow down the search area north of Lake Titicaca.

But it was the beginning.

7

Within hours, we were strike-bound to Cuzco.

'No. There is no way out,' said a travel agent we had come to know. 'It's a general strike. No trains, buses, or airplanes; not even private cars. Some motorcyclists will offer to take you out to Pisac, but that is a dead end. And if you don't take double the agreed price, they will leave you there, or ride over a rock to make you bounce your bums on the road.' The agent had spent two of her training years in the United States, and was proud of her clipped colloquial English.

'What's the strike about?'

'If you ask these agitators who started it, they will tell you it's because the government has nearly doubled the price of petrol. If you ask the teachers, they will tell you it's because they have to whistle with seventy dollars a month, compared to the *militares* who get between a hundred and fifty, and six hundred . . . You want to ask me what I say?' she demanded.

'What do you say?'

'It's because Peru's economy is nearly dead. The strike starts today because revolutions and strikes never start on a weekend: it starts this week because soon is the fat tourist season. It happens at this time every year; but this year it is the end – all the money in Peru is walking around in tourists' pockets. Now, those motherfuckers of agitators will stop the tourists coming and make our economy completely slice out the Hari Kari; and the point on the sword is here – Cuzco.' She ceased breaking the point of her biro on the table, and spread her arms. 'We are not Argentina. In that country also, they try hard to suicide the economy, but the land is too rich. Here, they will succeed; this year, they will succeed. It will be revolution. Usually, there are only a few thousand people killed, but this year there will be quite a few.' She brushed her hands resentfully down her sleeve, smoothing away non-existent wrinkles.

'Who are "they"?' Julie asked in the unexpected silence.

'The workers. The people. They do not like the military government. They say the military administration exploits them, but they can't accept that Peru will always be poor. Now that the sea current has changed, even the fish are gone. Our only major resource is mining the pockets of rich gringos.'

During that first day, the atmosphere on the streets was little short of that of a fiesta. Soldiers with bayonets fixed to rifles guarded every corner and government building, but their presence had no effect on the football games that rolled up and down the carless streets. The greatest concentration of both people and soldiers was in the plaza, where the crowd played a different game – soldier baiting.

Each soldier baiter was the matador in his own bull-ring. Instead of darts, he hurled insults; some of such Spanish ferocity that a soldier out of uniform might have responded instantly with a knife. Each pushed a chosen soldier towards snapping-point, approaching the climax with such delicate skill that the victim never knew which matador was his principal tormentor. Audience participation was essential to the skilled baiter, even for one with years of experience behind him.

But the soldiers were under constant and careful control by their officers. And their tormentors were never well co-ordinated with each other. Time and again, before an individual soldier could be driven to injure or kill, an entire squad would reach a semi-controlled snapping-point first. When that happened, a complete area of the square would be cleared with a sudden bayonet sweep, in which the baiters were certain of survival provided they kept out of stabbing range.

After the first few hours, the officers allowed their men a controlled outlet. A water cannon rolled around the Plaza de Armas, soaking as many of the laughing, fleeing people in the icy water as it could.

Ten wet men pushed a concrete block into the path of the water cannon, then stood back to see what would happen. They had no sooner taken their places, than one of the crowd weaved out towards the blocks, so tingling under the influence of the local raw spirit that his feet moved with a kind of palsied fandango. He didn't, at first, see the soldiers, or the crowd, or even the concrete block: he had eyes only for the imaginary woman on the end of his lips until he blundered into the block. The collision caused him to unpucker his lips, thereby losing him both his woman and his peace with the world. He leaned on the concrete obstacle, muttering poisonously as he considered possible courses of action. Then he came to a decision. Staggering back half a pace, he drew himself to full square-shoulder height, raised an imperious arm, and commanded the onlookers, 'Bring me fifty soldiers, *immediately!*'

The poetic probabilities of this order were not lost on the crowd. They burst into prolonged applause, sustaining it until the soldier-manned water cannon rolled to a stop ten feet from the concrete block. Perhaps understandably, the would-be 'general' didn't appre-

ciate the free cold shower that followed. Not only had he been sup-
plied with fewer soldiers than required, but they had shown a
sobering lack of respect for his authority.

At the bottom end of the plaza, a section of the crowd developed a
different game with a particularly patient squad. While the soldiers
sat miserably in their truck, the civilians ripped up a wide swathe of
the beautiful road-bricks that pave Cuzco's streets. Then they stood
back, expectantly. A gloomy and tired looking officer ordered his
men out to replace the bricks. They did so under the taunts of the
crowd, then climbed wearily back into the truck. After three such
performances the soldiers surrounded their repair work with slanted
bayonets, and with faces set cynically at the uselessness of their own
action. The crowd applauded the initiative, then set-to to rip up the
next section of bricks, opposite La Compania de Jesus.

Within hours, the new game spread. Cuzco's polished brick streets
became ugly, rubble-strewn gaps between buildings. The army
trucks continued to patrol, but with great difficulty, jolting across
the uneven surfaces, and stopping to clear broken bottles from ahead
of the tyres.

More than any other part of the city, the market was the place of
the people. For that reason, no roads were torn up in the area, and,
within a radius of two blocks, there was little of the usual
destruction. All the outside stalls had been abandoned, but the
trading continued – just. Indians squatted in the main street, selling
various foods from blankets laid out on the bricks. Stalls inside the
main building still traded, but anxious men guarded the iron doors,
ready to slam them at a moment's notice.

An army truck straddled the highest point in the market area,
overlooking the main street. Soldiers lined both sides of the trailer
with their backs bent to the world; all silent, heads bowed, staring at
the floorboards. Their rifles leaned beside them, sloping long bayonets out to the sky and turning the truck into a bereft porcupine.

Julie moved towards the indoor section to buy vegetables. I
walked downhill from the truck to find oranges. As I walked, the
atmosphere changed: backs stiffened, hands reached out across blankets, rearranging the food displays for a reason that wasn't immediately apparent. I turned to face the direction I'd come from, looking
for the cause. A heavy gauge machine-gun had been mounted on the
cab of the truck. A man sprawled behind it, legs splayed for pur-
chase, training the gun on the crowds around me.

Many of the customers walked quickly into side streets. None of
the vendors moved, but all their displays were now ready for a fast
decamp. Time to go. I delayed at the nearest fruit blanket to buy
whatever was going. Mandarins. '*Cinco*,' I said to the woman,
noticing that a second truck had begun to roll down towards us,
under the cover of the machine-gun.

'*Treinte soles*,' the woman responded, glancing at the approaching truck. As she picked up one of the traditional, balanced piles of five, a small metallic object flew out of the truck, twenty feet away. People exploded outwards from the object, screaming. Tear gas!

Within four heartbeats, the woman beside me snatched at the corners of her blanket, swung all the mandarins on to her back, and hobbled away. Bulging blankets bobbed frantically outwards from the cannister, many of their owners with tears pouring down their faces and coughs jerking at their bodies. In the centre, three displays of fruit lay abandoned, and the cannister continued sighing its white gas into the thin, greedy air.

Distressed children howled for their parents, one not knowing which direction to go in to get away the hurt in his lungs and eyes and nostrils. A woman ran back to snatch him away, but had to grope through her own tears before she reached him.

Julie was clear; she had been fifty yards uphill. But I had caught enough of the gas to set a dozen knives to work in my lungs, all anchored beyond the reach of the deepest cough. My eyes burned for a few seconds, then ran with blinding tears. As Julie and I walked back to the hotel, my condition did much to improve the general air of festivities. Even the normally stolid Indians smiled hugely at my discomfort. Some smiled in sympathy, some with sneers, and others with delight that a gringo was joining in the fun.

As I rested near one of the last stalls in the area, an Indian woman trotted over the road towards us. She squatted near us for a moment, then stood, leaving a neat mound of excrement next to Julie's feet.

'No hay pantalones, eh?' Julie said dryly.

'No,' the woman sneered, and trotted back across the road.

When we passed a machine-repair workshop, a thin, tall man stooped out of its tiny interior. 'Eh! Señores, you want to change American dollars?'

We shook our heads without stopping.

'But I will give you a hundred and thirty soles to the dollar!'

Julie turned, intrigued by the amount offered. 'But that's less than the offical rate,' she said.

'Ah but, señora, the banks are closed.' He grinned sideways at me, noting my streaming eyes.

'What about that one?' Julie said, pointing directly across the road to a bank that was, incredibly, open. Almost certainly, it was the only large business open in Cuzco.

The enterprising mechanic shrugged, spread his palms and beamed his acceptance of the failure of a potentially superb joke. Es la vida.

Most of the union leaders were rounded up that night. The following morning, we saw one of the remainder frogmarched out of his home. He was drawn in the face as if from a confrontation. But of the dozen family and neighbours watching, not one made a sound or single movement as he was bundled into the can of an army truck. General strikes happened every year.

Fresh troops came from Lima. Jets rolled showily over the city. Rumours crackled through the city, almost all unfounded.

Newspapers were useless: at the height of the general strike, headlines said, 'Oil Possible From Mexico', and 'President in Oil Talks'. Our best source of information was an Argentinian, Harry, with access to short waves BBC broadcasts.

On the fourth day, food shortages became critical. Looting started, and the Indian women were the most efficient emptiers of large locked foodstores. In one of the smaller, open shops, a frantic Indian woman held aloft the single can of condensed milk she had been given. 'But I have ten children!' she shouted at the girl behind the counter. The girl shrugged and turned to me.

'Sugar,' I said. She poured the standard ration into a cone-shaped roll of newspaper and gave it to me in that. Another assistant handed two single-teaspoon sachets of sugar to an old woman next to me. The old woman whined, holding out a one sol coin. The assistant gave her one more sachet, grimacing.

In the following days, the Plaza de Armas became the heart of an organism driving itself to catharsis and release. Strikers heaped intimate personal insults on soldiers they had never met, and on soldiers they knew well. Between refills, the water cannon squelched continuously. Bullets leapt into the sky leaving the sounds of the shots to slap around the plaza. Baton and bayonet charges swept resilient crowds again and again into side streets. Tear gas hissed more frequently for less immediate cause.

A favourite place to lob the silver cans was into the middle of a crowd listening to a political speech. That was the most interesting place to throw tear gas, because the flash of bright metal dropping down into a tight press of people produced the most spectacular results in terms of human dynamics. And that was always the safest place to throw tear gas, because there were some strikers who followed the trucks, cherishing the hope of being able to throw the can straight back on to the truck.

Sharp stones whipped savagely into foot patrols, always one stone at a time, always from behind, and always from the middle of a crowd.

By the steps of the cathedral, a complete road-brick was thrown from behind a squad on bayonet sweep. It crashed past the feet of a soldier no more than eighteen years old. He swung, growling with fear and aimed his rifle at the crowd, which scattered. A shouted command stopped him firing, but his lips were curled back and his face white as the others fired a volley into the air. Then he walked rigidly as the sweep resumed, holding the rifle in an exhausting pose. The man to his right swore at him for having swung the point of the bayonet too close for comfort.

On a quiet street off the main plaza, a boy of about ten years threw a stone from the top of the steps of the church La Merced. One of the passing squad doubled over, holding the side of his head. The boy turned parchment white. He began to walk towards the halted soldiers, crying out, 'I didn't mean it! I didn't mean to hit you!' One of the squad moved to meet the boy, grasped him firmly by the arm, and walked him to the hurt man, who straightened, wiping at a small flow of blood. He and the sobbing boy looked at each other while the squad and the crowd waited, all quiet. Then he held out his hands, the two of them put their arms around each other, and the boy sobbed on the soldier's chest.

8

The strike continued. Six days.

We were sitting in a restaurant. Jean-Paul wasn't interested in the conversation. He lounged three feet from the table, his slim body so relaxed that the spartan wooden chair might have been custom built. His blue eyes gazed lazily about the two-table restaurant; every view framed by his blonde, shoulder-length hair. He said nothing, but his teeth played dazzling one-upmanship with his lips. His cheeks hinted at a smile. He sat in the classic, aggressive-male style – legs wide apart, and hands cupped in front. But the posture wasn't staged, nor was the display of masculinity necessary: regardless of how his limbs arranged themselves, Jean-Paul carried himself with the poise of a man who knows, as a pleasant and inescapable fact of life, that he is devastatingly attractive to women.

One of that species came through from the kitchen to take the orders. She was about twenty-two, still with a girlish tweak in the dark complexion. But plumpness had already overwhelmed her teenage figure, to a degree beyond that normal for an Indian woman of her age.

'*Que quieres?*' she said from behind Jean-Paul, looking at me.

'Two *tostados* with butter,' I ordered, momentarily forgetting a courtesy word. 'Please,' I added, and Jean-Paul frowned at the effort.

'One of the same, with coffee please,' Julie said. Jean-Paul reacted again to the courtesy, shaking his head in disapproval. He rearranged his limbs, placing his feet on an empty chair, and gazed upwards at two flies mating on the ceiling.

The woman moved to where she could see him. Her eyes started on his face, travelled to the miniature nature display on the ceiling, then went back to his face. She swallowed, '*Que quieres?*' she repeated, with her voice pitched a full tone higher.

Jean-Paul looked at her as if she had crossed piranha-infested rivers and cut through dense jungle to bring him this invitation to eat. 'The complete breakfast, my beautiful,' he said in perfect Spanish, and smiled, rewarding her efforts. Her mouth opened. She turned her head, but her eyes wouldn't leave his face. She moved her lips silently, turned her whole body, and headed back to the kitchen.

'Hey! What about me?' The fourth guest slapped the table irritably, stopping the woman. 'The complete breakfast for me, too. And a glass of milk.' The woman whisked through curtains separating the kitchen from the dining-room. 'If you don't mind,' Miles Hannah added sarcastically in the direction of the curtains.

'You see?' he said to us, exasperated. 'He confuses them. He only needs to look at them, and they go weak at the knees.' The beefy, rugged-featured Londoner grimaced at Jean-Paul in what was probably good-natured disgust; his expressions were usually difficult to read, because most of his face was hidden by a luxuriant beard. He was balding on top, but claimed not to be losing any hair – just transferring it. Miles had met Jean-Paul in Peru a month ago and had travelled with him ever since, as a friend, and at the slightest excuse, as a talking archaeologist. In that month, Miles had attempted to discover Jean-Paul's secret of success. But, without result. And in the last two days, a week after we met them, he had taken to expressing his frustration to us.

Now, he leaned across the table, eyeing us, but making finger-stab motions in Jean-Paul's direction. 'Let me tell you something about this French-Canadian upstart . . .' As always, when Miles became earnest, his huge shoulders hunched forward. He said it was a habit from his childhood. Whenever he expressed his opinions too freely, his father had beaten his head and shoulders with an old canary cage, which became smaller over the years.

'I', Miles said dramatically, 'have travelled on every continent in the world. I have met some characters in my time. But him? I have never seen anything like him.'

Amused, and slightly bored, Jean-Paul inspected a Tumi hanging on the wall. He leaned forward and scornfully fingered the poor quality fabric that supported the design.

'This country is an archaeologist's paradise,' Miles continued. 'This city has seen emperors who wouldn't give Caesar the time of day. This street . . .' he waved to the open doorway. 'This little street has seen more gold and silver running around in one day than the care-taker at Fort Knox ever dreamed about. This very restaurant is built on the stones laid down by the original Incas.'

Now, he looked pleadingly at Julie for understanding. 'Do you know what this guy . . . this . . .' two fingers jerked compulsively in the direction of Jean-Paul's throat, 'this island-unto-himself does to all this priceless history around us?'

'Tell us,' prompted Julie. Jean-Paul winked at a tiny gap in the curtains. The curtains fell straight.

'He pisses on it,' Miles said huskily. 'On the streets, in the plazas, on the sides of buildings . . .' He paused, allowing the enormity of Jean-Paul's crimes to sink in. '*And*,' he added, raising his arm to restrain our knife hands, 'he cannot distinguish between the old and the new. This alley out here – those stones were laid more than five hundred years ago. But does that restrain Jean-Paul? No. Is it because of his inner traumas and tensions? No; he doesn't have any. He is the most relaxed gringo in Peru. And that's also true of his urinal sphincter.'

Jean-Paul dipped his head graciously, acknowledging the compliment, but tilting his eyebrows at Miles's transparency.

Julie sniffed at the smell wafting in from the alley outside. 'But that alley is the local toilet anyway,' she said to Miles. 'Like any street. Most of the population does the same thing. They wouldn't object.'

Jean-Paul chose to contribute to the conversation. He waved a hand vaguely in Miles's direction. 'Miles is not really talking about where I go to relieve myself. What he is meaning is not what he is saying.' He shrugged at his friend in easy apology for the frankness.

Breakfast parted the curtains, in the hands of the woman and her husband. She wore dignity like pancake make-up, feigning indifference to Jean-Paul's presence. But as soon as Jean-Paul found a plate of buttered toast in front of him, he bit enthusiastically into a piece, causing a gob of melted butter to run down his chin. Helpless, the woman was forced to glance at him. And since he chose that moment to flourish the butter away with the back of his hand, she was unable to dignify her glance with brevity.

Her husband, on the other hand, only removed his eyes from Jean-Paul's face when he had to. Eventually, however, he turned full attention to pouring four coffees from a pot-shaped container made of encrusted food.

'Not for me,' I reminded him. 'I ordered manzanilla.'

'*No hay manzanilla, señor.*' There isn't any. '*No hay*' was the most often heard phrase in Peru. He continued to pour coffee.

'The manzanilla was for my stomach,' I explained.

'Your stomach is bad?' He snatched the coffee-pot away, out of my reach. 'Ah, señor. You must *not* have coffee. What you must have is a boiled sheep's head.' He stood still for a few seconds, regarding Jean-Paul, then walked towards the kitchen. At the curtains he turned. 'We don't have sheeps' heads, señor.'

As the kitchen curtains fell into place, a six-year-old girl appeared in the alley doorway with her hand outstretched. She was filthy, tattered, and looking for the most likely gringo. She made a bee-line for Jean-Paul.

He didn't seem to notice her at all, so she whined and pushed her little hand right up in front of his nose. Normally, restaurant owners sent beggars away with food, rather than let them disturb the prize customers. For that reason, the girl had waited for the owner to leave the room.

Jean-Paul noticed the hand. His face transformed into that of an Old Testament God contemplating Gomorrah. A dreadful sound came out of his mouth. 'Grrrroooooaaaarrrrrhhhhh!!' He seized the girl under the armpits, tossed her upside-down over his head, and landed her only just on her feet, on the other side of his chair. He accomplished that feat without moving from his chair, so was in a position to calmly help himself to more soggy toast.

For five seconds, the girl was transfixed. Then mewing sounds came out of her throat. She backed away from him, then sidled past the curtains behind him, and backed the rest of the way to the alley door. She vanished, but reappeared half a minute later and hovered in the doorway, quivering at Jean-Paul with fear, respect and reverence. Then she went away and didn't come back. A guinea-pig ran out of the kitchen, across to the alley door, and disappeared in the same direction as the girl.

Miles was the first to speak. His throat was hoarse, so he abandoned his first attempt and took his first swig at the milk. His moustache swigged too, and he came out of the glass like a lactating walrus. Then he spoke thoughtfully, spacing his words for emphasis. If nothing else, a walrus has emphasis.

'Jean-Paul is, without a doubt, the rudest, most arrogant bastard ever to goose-step his way across Peru. But, of all the gringos I've seen in this country, do you know who they love the best?'

Julie and I looked dutifully at Jean-Paul.

'Him. They worship him. One moment he tells a woman, in front of her husband, that she has only to look at the church bells and they will ring of their own accord in acclamation of her beauty. In the next, he shouts at her husband to bring more coffee. And, do you know? The coffee is brought to him as if he were El Presidente.

'I thought . . .' Miles frowned hard at the table, where someone's portion of estufa had filled up a substantial portion of the gap between two of the boards. 'I thought, at first, that they loved him for his pretty head. But it's not that. It's something more. I've even seen a pickpocket try his talents on Jean-Paul and end up buying him a drink. This French-Canadian, cast-iron, Kahlua-and-milk has some kind of secret weapon that compels people to kiss his sandals. He walks around acting as if he knows something to everyone's advantage, but won't tell them.'

For the first time, Jean-Paul's face lost the hidden smile. He became entirely serious, and thoughtful. 'It is true,' he said to Julie and me. 'But I am not wanting to talk of such things, only because it is not possible to explain. I have tried.'

'What's true?' I asked. 'That you know something?'

'Not know,' he said. 'Feel. But I cannot explain.'

Julie and I pressed knees under the table. 'Please, can you try?' Julie said. 'We're interested.'

'But it is impossible. It is a feeling that fills me up to here . . . but not with words. Many times I try to explain, and always people say, "What? What? What are you talking about?" It only means to me because I looked for it to put inside me. It took a long time, many years of learning.'

'But you have to describe it in some way.' I objected. 'Or people won't know what to look for. You must have a name for this feeling of yours.'

An expression of amused resignation came over Jean-Paul's face, as if he had been through this scene many times, and it had never been productive. 'What could it be but God?' he said. 'It is the Spirit of God.'

Miles, who had been taken aback at the turn of the conversation he started, became irritated. 'If you're overflowing with this Spirit of God, would you explain to me why you flirt with married women, and piss in the street, and throw beggar children through the air and send them away without money? Explain that!'

Jean-Paul touched fingers to temples, further expressing his conviction that explanations were so much wasted breath. 'It is that I am having no rules for my conduction. Conduction? Conduct. Yes. Many, many people live all day in rules. They say I must, every day, do this, and this, and this. Usually it is because of their religion. But they do not see that the Spirit behind all the religions is the same. They come to another country and they bring their religion with them, and they use their religion to say that this is of God, and that that is not of God. You understand?' He waved a hand about him in an all-embracing gesture. 'But it is *all* of God. *Nothing* is not of God. So, I come to another country, I meet someone, I know he is a piece of God like me. That way a man can go anywhere, he can talk to anyone, even when he speaks a different language. That is the best communication. Is it not better than bringing rules from another country? And sometimes the best thing is not in the rules.'

He fell silent. Miles said nothing, realizing that after a month of trying to find out what made Jean-Paul tick, he had got as much, at least in words, as he could expect.

'How did you start?' I asked. 'How did you start looking for this feeling?'

'That is what I can't explain. I just wanted to, so I looked everywhere. And, anyway, you should not listen to what I say, because I always make mistakes.'

'Throwing that little girl about,' Julie said, 'and sending her away without money . . . was that a mistake?'

'No,' Jean-Paul said.

That night, Julie and I walked through the Plaza de Armas. In Inca times, on feast days, mummies from the Temple of the Sun had been carried to the plaza on Indian shoulders to be arranged in neat rows alongside the reigning Inca. In Spanish times, the Plaza was the execution place for unsuccessful revolutionaries – both Inca and conquistador. On the east side, still overlooking the execution place, in Cuzco's most beautiful church, the Spanish built La Compañía de Jesus. The Society of Jesus.

A statue of Jesus swayed into the plaza on the shoulders of six Indians. Some fifty people bobbed around it, a few attempting to keep time with the brass band in front. But that was difficult; the musicians seemed to be in the same parade by chance, perhaps because each had to pick out an individual path through the rubble and cobblestones scattered by the strikers. Jesus meandered above them, bearing a face of immense suffering, yet clothed in purple and white satin, gold and silver that could have been the envy of many an earthly king.

This evening the strike had left the plaza alone. The walkways were filled with Peruvians taking the evening stroll. That was one of the national pastimes: *tomar el fresco* – to take the fresh evening air.

A mime artist held greatest sway in the plaza. He had a crowd of more than a hundred attached on invisible elastic to the ends of his fingers. When we passed, he was sobbing in passionate silence because his invisible balloon had been broken by one of the audience. The innocent accused was a small boy – so taken in, that he looked about him for the dead rubber. He didn't know whether to laugh or cry, but he had a wet sparkle on his cheek.

Jean-Paul had left for Bolivia, along with Miles.

Just outside the Pizzeria, near the cathedral, Julie and I came across one of the shish-kebab stands. The usual shish-kebab consisted of three lumps of meat and one lump of potato, skewer-roasted over a small barbecue.

Until then, I'd given up on shish-kebabs. Invariably, the cook would hand me the fattiest, gristliest, dirtiest lumps of meat that could be dragged up from the bottom of the pile. And not because of any lack of politeness on my part: I had always sprinkled Spanish versions of 'please,' 'thank you' and 'a bit chilly tonight' into the conversation.

I stopped giving Julie the benefit of my imitations of the mime artist, and made sure that I was grinning when I turned towards the shish-kebab stand. The instant my eyes fell on the sizzling meat, I changed my expression to one of scornful disdain.

'*Uno*,' I said with indifferent flatness. And I turned my head away slightly, as if the sight of the meat made me nauseous.

She handed me the skewer she had just removed from the hottest part of the grill. Out of her endless layers she dug up eighty-seven soles change for the hundred soles note. The difference was half the price I had paid last time. The woman allowed her expression to twinkle; just slightly.

'*Que les vaya bien*,' she said as we walked away. May you go well.

9

Two days later, the strikers made a single concession on public transport: they allowed trains to run on the short, no-exit line to Chaullay. It was a concession that would change the whole nature of the search for the abbey.

Fifty-five miles from Cuzco, the line passes the beginning of the Inca Trail, a centuries-old foot-trail that winds five days through the Andes to the deserted, ancient city of Machu Picchu.

For Julie, the opportunity for a 'trial run' at the mountains was too good to miss. While we had to be based in Cuzco, she might as well cut her teeth on mountains close to civilization and on a clearly defined trail. Nor would the hike be wasted on me; my mountain experience didn't include any altitude work above ten thousand feet. The Inca Trail went up, at one point, to just under fourteen thousand feet.

But it was another reason entirely that capped our decision. What the abbey was to us, Machu Picchu had been to the ancient Incas. It had been the spiritual centre of the empire; remote, hard to reach. There was something alluring about the prospect of walking the Inca Trail before going to the abbey, even though Machu Picchu had long been deserted. And, we thought, we might even learn something on the way.

The second-class train from Cuzco to Kilometre 88 doesn't go 'clickety-clack, clickety-clack' like normal trains. It shudders, it screams, it groans and it heaves. It regularly slips into crisis-breathing with little hope of being put out of its misery. It has been scalded out of its cell at five in the morning, force-fed with passengers, and dragged indigesting up the zig-zag out of Cuzco and towards the mountains. Once over the ridge, it grinds through the valleys and then the canyons, running deeper and deeper, tortuously to the north west. As the bush in the canyon floors merges to jungle, the mountains rise more aggressively, refusing to bow to the very beginnings of the Amazon Basin.

There are one hundred and twenty passengers in the carriage, playing unmusical chairs with forty-eight seats. Newcomers to the game are treated the way an automatic watch is treated: innocent, random movements are taken advantage of, and exploited. Move your foot just half an inch the wrong way, and that half inch is half-inched instantly, never to be regained.

You discover that the hefty leg most to blame belongs to the innocent-looking woman sitting on her potatoes in what was originally the aisle. Her son is sitting in your lap. He dribbles on you steadily while your limbs become trapped in impossible positions. If you don't make your own unmusic you leave the train at Kilometre 88 the way a meat pie comes out of a mangle.

It is possible to reach the toilet. With extreme rudeness you can make it there in ten minutes. Of course, there is a queue squirming in the chaos, but you won't know how long it is until you try to get past it. Then it will let you know. It's better to start moving the moment you've finished your drink of chicha, or your potato roll, or whatever else you foolishly bought on the train.

Every Indian family has at least four bundles of merchandise laid out on the luggage rack, under and between the seats, and in the aisles. This makes it difficult for you to place your feet on the floor as you assert your way towards the privy. In one respect, that's a good thing because those rare patches of visible floor have been thoroughly peed on by small boys. But it's risky climbing on peoples' bundles because you are probably turning their hard-won produce into fruit salad and potato squash. Or, if the bundle stops moving once it's been stood on, you have killed either two chickens or a turkey. Occasionally, a free floorboard can be seen close to the aisle, under a seat. But it's a mistake to insert a leg in your desperation for secure footholds: there is a hobbled, but unbagged, turkey under the seat who believes that the space immediately around him is his territory, and he is willing to prove it. In any case, it's not wise to concentrate only on footholds: chickens stuffed in the luggage racks become restless for some reason, and periodically fall, thrashing and squawking, about peoples' heads.

Half-way to the toilet, you see that one of the numerous babies is being treated to a rare bottom cleaning. In such conditions the event is a feat of ingenuity and endurance, so you pause, momentarily, to join the admiring audience. The baby's waste is collected on paper and thrown out the window, but a trick of the wind sticks it to the outside of the glass, where it will stay for the rest of the journey.

You reach the end of the queue and shut yourself gratefully into the toilet, leaning against the inside of the door. Perhaps you should have let that frantic-looking woman go first. You open your eyes. You began this venture so long ago, you may not remember which specific intention you started out with. But now the decision is taken out of your hands: once you see how imaginatively the floor and walls are decorated with urine, faeces and vomit, you want to do everything. First, though, you make a frantic, unsuccessful effort to open the window. Then, while deciding which end of you has priority, you roll up your trouser legs as high as they'll go. Now it's just a matter of finding the right position for the feet, holding the door against the woman who's trying to force her way in, and avoiding, just like the plague, any contact with the pan.

We were to have two companions on the Trail. Dave Fredrikson and Jackie Hays from Washington, USA. We had met by chance in a hotel, discovered a common purpose to walk the Inca Highway, and pooled our resources. They were experienced hikers and climbers, and they were both outgoing and cheerful. To be in their company somehow lightened our purpose.

They were playing a card game called crazy-eights on a sweater that lay on their knees. Dave was just feigning a yawn of boredom at his run of good luck, when two thieves came down the aisle. There could not be any doubt that they were thieves. They were walking proclamations of their profession, from the tips of their respectable pointed shoes, to the peaks of their white cloth, cocked-over-the-eye caps. One carried an empty sack, the other an empty bag.

Dave's lower jaw, in the middle of his yawn, stayed down. He stared in disbelief. He plucked at Jackie's sleeve and pointed, whereupon Jackie's jaw also disengaged. She tossed her right hand towards her shoulder, palm up, then flipped it forward and down at the two men. This, we soon learned, was her way of indicating that she had discovered yet another wonder of the world.

Dave's large, muscular frame rumbled with laughter. As the two thieves moved past him, he clapped the leader on the shoulder and encouraged them both in a loud voice. He spoke in English, but followed with a guffaw, a thumbs up, and a wink, that were unmistakable in meaning to anyone within a distance of fifty feet – had they been listening. Each of his victims promptly developed a face like the end of a glacier, and continued to negotiate the aisle.

Half an hour later, a storm of shouting and movement erupted at the far end of the carriage. A furious Indian man bulldozed up and down, searching frenziedly through the chaos, mashing bundle after bundle in his way. 'Mi maleta. Mi maleta,' he hissed. He had been the only Indian on the carriage with a suitcase. Long after he gave up searching, he sat hunched forward in his seat, taking one hand up and down from his eyes.

Julie, with no mountain experience, had begun the day determined to prove herself to herself, and was nervous. It was a critical stage for her, not the time for anything to go wrong. But it did. The worst thing that could have happened did happen. She fell ill on the train.

Had the bug hit her with its hardest punch immediately, we would have returned to Cuzco on the next train. But it began slowly, apparently just another slight variation on the mild upsets served up in many Peruvian restaurants. There was one difference – Julie felt hot and cold at the same time. But we put that down to the stifling conditions in the carriage, the hot stench of bodies combined with the cold draught from the door.

One of the vendors on board waved a roast pig's head under her nose. 'How tasty,' he said hopefully, and the head grinned at her out of its bath of half-congealed fat. Shortly afterwards, the man sitting behind Julie stood up on his seat and added impressively to the already rich variety of gases in the carriage.

Julie rolled her eyes, shut them firmly, and turned a delicate shade of off-white. 'What happened to that woman selling lilies?' she murmured.

Dave and Jackie made it clear that they wouldn't mind returning to Cuzco, if Julie wanted to postpone a day or two.

'No,' Julie said. 'We'd still be in Lima, if we stopped for these things. Don't worry. It always goes in a few hours. We're almost there. A bit of fresh air, and I'll be back to normal.' At the time, there was no reason to think otherwise.

Over the back of Dave and Jackie's seat, an Indian woman unwrapped her baby from its cocoon of swaddling clothes. Like most Indian babies, it had been unable to move legs, arms, or wrists for long hours of the day. The freed baby stared woodenly across its mother's shoulder. It was a year old – a girl, we thought.

I made faces at her, but she didn't see me. I passed my hands in front of her wide, beautiful eyes. They didn't respond in any way. I put my index finger in her palm, while the mother smiled shyly, pleased at the attention her baby was earning. Over a period of about five seconds, the palm closed, so slightly that my finger was just as free to move as before. A normal newborn baby will hang safely from a horizontal bar, or from two adult fingers, if given the chance. But not this baby. There would be little metamorphosis for her when the cocoon came off for the last time.

'*Que linda*,' Dave said to the mother. Isn't she a lovely baby. The mother gave him a proud smile, but turned her head away again, overcome with shyness.

Jackie shook her head slowly, and said nothing. Her job, back in Washington, was to train retarded people. She tried to motivate them to develop skills and interests, to increase their range of sensory experience. Touch, taste, texture, sound. Movement. Julie hardly noticed the baby. She kept her eyes shut, trying to cope with her rebellious body.

Another child and his mother sat in the same alcove as the retarded baby. The boy, about four years old, perched on his mother's knee. In the last two hours he had been totally absorbed in the world passing by outside the window. With each new sight, his eyes rounded and his mouth opened.

Suddenly, he pulled his nose off the glass frowning as if he couldn't believe what he was seeing. Then he turned to his mother with one of the expressions that make children, the world over, one species.

'*Maaaama, miiiira!*' He swivelled his head back to the window, '*Un burro!*' Muuummy, loooook . . . a donkey!

His mother gave a silent chuckle and tousled the back of his head. '*Si,*' she said, conscious that her son was being admired. '*Que chiquito con más suerre.*' Yes. Aren't you a lucky boy, then.

10

The train left us, taking with it the noise and stench of the carriage. It grumbled away down the right-hand bank of the Urubamba gorge, the heavy rattling taking minutes to fade to a faint, almost musical hum. We were left, for the moment, in complete silence. Then our ears adjusted. Our hearing sense pushed outwards to meet the contracting circle of birds and cicadas striking up the interrupted song.

We had been dropped in an area of low grass and scrub, with sparse bush in the middle distance. Kilometres away, the jungle began; a tossed green blanket that, further east, would subdue and close over the mountains that now thrust out of it so arrogantly. We were standing at the confluence of two rivers; the powerful Urubamba on its way to the Amazon, and a small tributary whose valley yawned away from us across the gorge before leaning to the right and disappearing. The Inca Trail would begin in the mouth of that valley.

At the edge of the gorge, our hearing adjusted to another drastic change. The Urubamba boomed from far down the rockfaces, roaring its objection to being squeezed through the gorge. The Incas had used a suspension bridge for this crossing. But recent civilization had replaced the bridge with something even more nerve-racking; a pulley-slung, hand-pulled platform. Once launched over the frantic water, the device gave its occupants an excellent impression of a matchbox.

That was Julie's introduction to the mountains. But whatever she felt on the way across the gorge, she didn't let it show. On the other side, when we had all swung packs, she looked back at the platform with an expression that said, 'Got you, you bastard.' And in the short time since the train she seemed to have recovered from whatever had ailed her system.

With packs bobbing unevenly at first, we settled into our individual gaits, and began the Trail. .

The first day should have been easy. The Trail stuck to the valley floor all the way, rising so slowly that the going was little more than a stroll. The valley walls trapped the air, and the sun baked the hard clay, turning the valley floor into an oven. But the Trail followed a

110

cool stream which had laid a ribbon of grass and low bushes from one end of the valley to the other. Ripe stands of maize softened the landscape with dry yellows and browns. We saw no farmers, and missed them, knowing that this valley would be the last with people and farms. But, in the early afternoon we saw a group of fifteen or more, working a field on the far-side slopes.

I picked four maize heads from a field next to the Trail, than stood on a nearby rock wall and shouted to attract attention. The sound easily carried in the still air. I held a couple of maize heads high, and pointed to them, and then to a prominent loose rock on the wall. But, as I placed a few soles near the rock, one of the workers broke away from the group and started across the valley towards us. So much for not interrupting them. I told the others to go on, noticing at the time that Julie was looking pale once more.

It was an old woman that joined me, walking steadily but slowly, only slightly disturbing the faded black dress that hung limply about her legs. Her bare feet were deeply cracked and callous-hard, yielding little to the iron clay they walked on. She was long past the age that turns wrinkles into furrows. Yet she was only slightly stooped and seemed not at all tired by the walk across the valley.

She spoke briefly in the Quechua tongue, the language of the Incas, then, seeing that I didn't understand, made hand gestures that asked why I didn't take the maize stalks. She cut one of the stalks I had left, and tore round the outside of one section with her teeth stumps. When a few inches of its inner section were exposed, she handed me the result.

'Sweet, sweet,' she said in uncertain Spanish. I wished I had tackled basic Quechua.

And it was sweet. Also, though not a liquid, it was refreshing. Soon I had eight stalks strapped across the top of the pack. But when I attempted to put the maize heads into the pack's outer pocket, she stepped forward and tapped one of them. She passed an arm slowly across the sky, east to west, then made a negative gesture at the end of it. I took the heads back out and gave them to her. If I understood her, the only way to cook this type of maize was to put it in a pot with a stone, and take it out when the stone was soft and tender. . . .

I hoisted the pack, thanked her, and began to walk. I turned again, almost immediately, wondering what it was about her that bothered me. But she was still looking at me, so I went on my way, feeling unaccountably carefree.

That feeling disappeared the moment I caught up with the others. Dave and Jackie were sitting gloomily on a rock by the river, a few steps off the Trail. A sun shelter had been rigged beside them – forked sticks covered with clothing. Underneath it, was Julie. Her eyes were closed, and she was making small muttering sounds. Hallucinating. The illness had caught up with her.

'Julie?' I knelt beside her. Dave and Jackie had put a wet handkerchief on her forehead. She was pale. She was sweating, and her temples were hot.

Her eyelids opened, twitching, and her eyes cleared. 'I'm so sorry,' she murmured distinctly. She closed her eyes. Shortly afterwards her lips began to move again, though she made no more sounds.

I joined Dave and Jackie, who told me that they had given her sips of water just before I arrived. For now there was nothing to do but wait. The nearest doctor was in Cuzco, and there was no way to get Julie back to the gorge in time for the evening train. Lying in the shade, on cool grass, she was in as good a position as she could be for now. The three of us ate a few rations, crackers, cheese, honey, trying to weigh the alternatives.

After an hour, her lips stopped moving. She began to smile; not a humorous smile, but a wondrous one, as if she had encountered something inexpressibly beautiful. She was sweating even more now, so I dripped more water on to her forehead and temples. Without opening her eyes she murmured, 'Such a marvellous thing.'

I was about to attempt to talk to her, when there was a snorting sound behind me. Two black pigs were snuffling and foraging in the scrubby bushes round the Trail. On the Trail stood the old woman who had shown me the maize stalks. She was just standing there, looking at Julie. The pigs, obviously the old woman's, were making full use of the time on one spot: they rushed from one bush to another, trotters clacking on the patches of bare clay, routing food from every possible source before their mistress moved them on.

The woman nodded at Julie's form. 'Back soon,' she said cheerfully, using the feminine ending on the word for 'return.'

I blinked. A pig was trying to drag away one of the maize stalks, which were still attached to my pack. Jackie discouraged the attempt with a flapping arm and without taking her eyes off the pig's guardian. Obviously we had not understood. The old woman stepped off the path and pointed emphatically at Julie. 'Not here,' she said firmly, 'back soon.'

She then walked past the four of us, climbed a rock wall, and hunted around in a patch of low shrubs. She returned with a handful of a plant with a tiny, dull-green leaf. 'Later,' she said, again nodding at Julie. She pointed at Dave's billy and made drinking motions, then spoke sharply in Quechua to the pig who was making a more determined bid for the maize stalks. The porcine privateer wheezed huffily and wheeled away.

The woman walked back on to the Trail. I called out my thanks, as did Dave and Jackie. And before she walked away with her pigs, the woman glanced back and nodded to us. I saw then what it was about her that had bothered me.

She wasn't just being kindly to strangers. There was a radiance coming from her that was like an embrace. It wasn't directed at us. It simply included us. A contentment surrounded her, a compassion;

tinged with a distant dry humour as appropriate to animals, plants and the earth, as it was to people. It had been there all the time. How could I not have noticed before? I wanted to go after her, but knew that I couldn't. I watched her and her attendants until they disappeared around the next corner.

In half an hour, Julie woke and asked for a drink. The fever had gone, though she was pale and weak. Another twenty minutes and she was walking about, testing her leg muscles. She asked how much further it was to the village at the turn off to the next valley, where we had originally planned to shelter for the night.

There followed a great deal of argument about the wisdom of moving anywhere, let alone further up the Trail. But the village was only two hours away, and she was certain her illness was over. Extraordinarily certain. I decided she was keeping something back.

We were under way in ten minutes, all of us watching Julie closely. She sweated again, this time with physical exertion. She was dizzy and sometimes nauseous. She walked very slowly, but with gradually increasing strenght. She was obviously in pain, but cheerful in spite of it. Underneath all the suffering, she was excited and deeply moved about something. I waited until Dave and Jackie were out of earshot.

'Alright,' I said. 'Out with it.'

'There was a woman, wasn't there?' she said. 'An old woman and two pigs.' And then she explained. It took a while, because she had to conserve her energy with long periods of silent walking. But by the time she had finished, a small part of my invisible carriage had become visible.

What she said boiled down to this:

'I was out of my body. I was standing there looking at it, and you three talking about me. It was so clear, so vivid, unmistakably real. I went away to a place I knew, a restful room that contained a table with two chairs. In one chair was a man in late middle age, brown-skinned, with short, white hair. He said he was my guide, my teacher. And I knew I had sat and talked with him in this room many times before.

'I asked if I should try to continue towards Machu Picchu. He answered that he could not make decisions for me. He said that he placed situations in my path, and that I must decide how best to deal with them. Each situation, each problem, he said, is an opportunity, containing a lesson that can be accepted, or rejected and learned later in a different way.'

A hallucination, I thought. It had to be some kind of weird hallucination from the fever. We were well into forest by now, under the shadow of the western side of the valley. It was very cool, very quiet. So still, that, when we stopped for rest even the birds seemed to have stilled to listen to the forest breathe.

Julie continued. 'Suddenly I was back in the valley, this time look-

113

ing at you three, and my body, and the old woman. She was just leaving, and I saw you notice in her what you had missed before. I understood that you noticed it because you chose to accept it, and I knew that I was meant to see exactly that.'

I expelled air from my lungs in the way that breath goes when you are trying to cope with conflicting emotions. No, no: it was too neat, too symmetric to be real.

She went on. 'I returned to my teacher and told him I had decided to continue to Machu Picchu. I asked him if you and I were going to succeed in finding the abbey, and if so, what we could learn there. He said he wasn't going to tell me either of those things, but that he could tell us we were already enrolled in a mystery school with an excellent reputation, and that we had been attending classes for some time.'

At the village we were invited to stay in the valley's one classroom. Children and adults from the village's four huts turned up to watch as we began preparations for eating and sleeping. Pigs, dogs, two horses and a donkey joined the curious faces lining the window and door holes in the walls. One small, male pig tried to take advantage of the fact that the large female pig beside him was distracted by us. But he was bitten for his efforts and fled squealing into the evening.

Julie, aching and exhausted, laid her sleeping-bag out on the earthen floor, where Jackie and I scraped hip and shoulder holes. She clambered into the bag under the close, serious scrutiny of a small boy whose curiosity had dragged him all the way in.

'Goodnight,' she said to him in Spanish.

'*Si*,' he beamed in response. Yes.

But Julie knew one word in Quechua; the word for beard. She pointed to the boy's smooth chin. '*Shapu*,' she smiled.

The boy retreated a step or two, taken aback. He inspected my beard carefully, then pursed his lips and glared at Julie, silently accusing her of gross misconduct.

11

The third day. Just after dawn, I woke before the others. Around me were the remains of an ancient shepherd's hut, with walls now three feet high and less. Sitting up, I still couldn't see much, so I slipped quietly out of my sleeping-bag, pushed reluctant feet into frozen boots, and walked the hundred yards to the bottom lip of the valley – the highest and smallest on the Inca Highway to Machu Picchu.

Clouds stretched away from the edge, a vast cotton-wool sea, rolling away from a lumpy, green and brown shore. Distant peaks held their tips out of the sea, glinting gold, white, and black in the coming sun. The earth, somewhere below, was connected to my valley by the Trail, which tongued up out of the cloud and flopped over the lip. If I were a condemned man, I thought, I would ask to die at dawn.

By the time we had drawn the scattered camp into the packs, the sky had begun to look peculiar. For many weeks we had seen nothing but blue skies. Now, today of all days, the weather was going to turn on us. We moved quickly, apprehensively, eyeing both the sky and the ridge that reared at us from the end of the meadow-like valley. On top of it lay the highest pass, just under fourteen thousand feet.

Just before the bottom of the ridge, we stopped. Dave unwrapped his bag of coca leaves and offered it around, along with lumps of the catalyst. He Jackie and I wrapped chunks of leaves around pinches of the catalyst, and stuffed generous wads into our mouths. Julie turned it down. The after-effects of illness had left her stomach with a violent dislike for the leaf.

According to legend, Manco Capac had brought the coca plant to earth as a gift from his father the sun. According to orthodox history, Indians of the Andes had used the drug for the last two and a half thousand years, combating hunger, cold, weariness, and oxygen starvation. Saliva, with the help of the catalyst, extracts cocaine from the leaf and passes it into the bloodstream.

While we stood there, the sky showed what it had in mind for us. A bank of steel-grey cloud rose from behind the peak immediately to the east and moved steadily, decisively, up and over towards us. We were jittery, nervous. We had to move fast while we could, but now

115

discovered that Jackie's rain gear had been stowed at the bottom of her pack. Experienced though Jackie was, she took some persuading to make it more accessible. There were some sharp words between her and Dave, and then we started to climb the pass.

In twenty minutes, Dave, Jackie and I had our rhythms worked out, and, perhaps because of the altitude, the coca worked better than it ever had for all three of us. Even when the storm cloud took up a third of the sky, gleeful yells rolled around the ridge, boasting about our various states of weightlessness. But, Julie stayed very quiet. She placed one foot steadily in front of the other and spoke only to say that she needed all her energy for climbing. Yesterday, without the benefits of coca, she had climbed seven thousand feet while still recovering from her illness. But today we were into altitudes that would sap anyone's strength. It was ironic that she, of the four of us, should have to do without the help of the coca leaves.

The storm clouds reached the pass, and began to roll down the ridge to meet us. The breeze became a wind. Small stones began to blow loose and roll down the slope, knocking others and creating miniature slips with a dozen stones or less.

After two hours, Julie began to fall back. She didn't have the co-ordination she had yesterday. She attacked the slope unevenly, too slowly and then too fast, ending up at a standstill and gasping for breath. She heard our advice but couldn't seem to work it into her movements.

The wind doubled in strength and the temperature plummeted in seconds. The cloud consumed Dave and Jackie and reached long streaming tentacles down to collect us. Julie began to spend too much time doubled over, sucking in air through curled back lips. She knew the pass was still more than a thousand feet away, but that it would take long hours to get back to the relative safety of last night's campsite. The thought of retreating just a thousand feet short of the highest point on the Trail dismayed her, and she became angry with herself.

It was a vicious circle. Her anger and anxiety took away her co-ordination, which sapped her strength. Eventually she sank on to the Trail and hunched forward, head between her knees. Never in her life had she faced such a gruelling physical test. For a full half hour we sat together while she recovered, watching the grey stone mix into grey cloud just a few feet away. Soon, time would force a decision on us.

But, after a while she went through an important mental change. If she stayed anxious, she was going to lose what little strength she had left: she must have known that, and she must have decided that her one chance of making it to the top was to take a grip on her emotions. She didn't say anything, she was reluctant to talk at all, but I could see the change on her face. At the end of the half hour she stood, and this time she moved with none of the erratic jerkiness of before.

'Could you count for me?' she asked, and I wondered why I hadn't thought of it before. It was a trick I had learned in the army, years ago. A kind of self-hypnosis. After a long period of concentration, the count had the effect of forcing the feet to move with it.

It took some getting going. 'Start with the left foot. Slowly. *One*, two, three . . . Okay, start again. *One*, two, three, four. *One*, two, three, four. *One*, two, three, four . . .' Eventually she locked on to it, and we were under way.

I began to leave out the 'two' and the 'four', if for no other reason than my own exhaustion. I wondered how Dave and Jackie were getting on. Next I left out the 'three'. I left out every second 'one', then every third, until we trod steadily upwards for long periods without any spoken count.

Then the numbers pushed into a kind of automatic gear that clicked through both our heads, whether or not we were climbing or resting. No matter if it was a stumble or a long sit-down rest, when we resumed both of us heard precisely the same count and began on the left foot on the first 'one' that spoke in our heads.

On top of the pass, we found Dave and Jackie huddled behind their packs. Both were grey with exhaustion. A freezing wind howled around us, whipping fat snakes of cloud back down the way we had come. We hardly spoke to each other. Apart from our exhaustion and shortness of breath, it seemed ludicrous to be standing at the highest point we have ever been on the earth, and yet to see nothing but cloud and twenty feet of Trail.

Jackie made some insulting and unlikely comments about the cloud's origins. It responded by increasing its speed yet again, and then it unloaded a hail storm on us.

But the worst was over. Julie's trial run at the mountains had succeeded. As the hail stones cracked viciously on the backs of our hoods, she put an arm between my pack and my lower back. We put our heads together, and she grinned, grinned at what she had conquered in herself.

12

The fifth day. In the ruins where the trail begins to return to the Urubamba, there's an ancient Inca fountain. It's not decorative; the Incas built it as the water supply for what was then a village. They diverted a stream, passing it through a constant level reservoir. From the reservoir, they drew off water into a small tunnel cut through stone. On the other side of the stone, the water came out as a simple jet, arcing down into a pool.

That fountain still runs. And because it was built as a constant pressure system, the jet hits the collecting pool at exactly the same place as it did centuries ago. In all that time the jet may only have wavered for wind and earthquakes.

Just after sunset, I walked from the fountain down a stone staircase to a rampart wall overlooking the Urubamba valley. A stone dropped from the edge of the wall would fall hundreds of feet before bouncing. If thrown hard, it would fall a thousand feet. The Incas had the knack of perching their towns in magnificent and impregnable positions.

The valley, below and around, was beginning to sleep. Animal and bird noises tailed off as the valley drew together, hushed for the evening. Many tendrils of mist hovered below the Inca outpost, suspended layer upon layer throughout the valley by the approach of night. Far below them, pieces of the Urubamba river ribboned through the jungle, fine silver on deepening green. Only once was the silence broken, and the sound that threaded thinly, mournfully up through the layers of mist lifted the hairs on the back of my neck. A train whistle. That would be our train, a ghostly reminder of civilization, still two days and many thousands of feet away.

Then nature presented me a play, a silent, half-hour sketch. No preamble, no credits, no curtain-call. But it had an ending that taught me more than I had ever learned from a stage.

Almost above me, a small section of cloud softened, lightened, then parted. I had walked two days with dense cloud just above my head; I had walked two days with the whole world below me, so I just wasn't prepared for the sight of a massive object above me. The grey cloud formed a window. From the darkening mountainside. I looked ancient Inca strong...

The window in the sky closed. But, in the meantime, the western sky had been breaking up near the horizon, and now took on a delayed glow of sunset. Some of the red gold light reflected down from the cloud on to the mist hovering below me in the valley. Each layer lit up with a different shade of red-gold, and each tendril began to glow against a background of deep green, now almost black, jungle.

As each shape pulsed and changed in the altering light, it was as if the whole display was saying things to me. Then I seemed to expand. I felt intimately connected with the flowers by my feet, and with the bushes at the end of the ramparts, and I suddenly realized that all the different life forms in the valley were different cloaks worn by one life. One life, I thought. We are one life. We are one person.

My sense of time expanded: the interval I called my life shrank. The image came to me that my life was like the single wingbeat of a bird in the valley. One lifetime, one beat of the wings.

It was as if I played the prompt and called the cue. Ten, then a hundred, then uncountable numbers of birds flew through the valley just above the mists. They flew down the valley towards the Amazon. Each bird was visible only when the tops of its wings reflected the falling light. At any given moment, each visible wing reflected a unique shade of red-gold. Each colour, once gone with the fall of the wings, came again from the same wings, but was subtly changed from the time before. Often groups of colours vanished and reappeared together as the flock followed the river towards the sea.

13

There is a place in the Urubamba where a ridge with almost vertical sides distorts the valley, forcing the river to surround it on three sides. Slung over the ridge, like a tattered grey blanket across a horse's back, is the ruined city of Machu Picchu. The Incas' secret city cannot be seen from the valley floor, and is protected from invasion by the river, a seething, natural moat, two thousand feet below its walls.

The city's centre-point, the spiritual focal point of the Empire, is an asymmetrically-shaped altar known as 'The Hitching Place of the Sun.' During winter solstice, astronomer priests tethered the sun, preventing their principal deity from wandering too far north and becoming lost to them. Spread out around the altar, for those spiritual aspirants who found the city, are the plaza, shrines, fountains, theatres, lodgings, and farm terraces.

The Spaniards never found Machu Picchu, which may explain why the city is the most perfectly preserved remnant of the Inca Empire. For centuries, they moved up and down the Urubamba under the noses of those still living in the city. The invaders' communication with the Indians may have been lacking, Spanish records don't mention Machu Picchu even as a myth. But, of course, the conquistadors aren't remembered for their sensitivity to the races they conquered, or, for that matter, for their conservationist principles.

The conquistadors may have wondered why they captured few of the Inca nobility after their invasion in 1533. According to legend, the nobility fled to their secret city in that year, bringing, with their luggage, the Virgins of the Sun. That 'home-away-from-home' legend received some scientific support after Machu Picchu's discovery in 1911: skeletons were dug up in the ratio of ten females to one male.

But even if the Spaniards had heard of Machu Picchu, they would not have found it easily. The only entrance, then, was via the Inca Trail, which slips down into the city from the mountains behind – four passes, five valleys, and many ridges after its inconspicuous parting from the Urubamba.

The last of the passes is less than half an hour from Machu Picchu. It's so narrow that only two men can walk through it at once. It's fortified against attack from one direction, and laid out as a scenic viewing platform overlooking the city in the other direction.

The four of us unwrapped the last of our mouldy cheese and crumbled bread, and looked down at the old city in silence. It was an empty shell. But to Julie and me it echoed of the abbey that still waited for us somewhere north of Lake Titicaca.

14

We walked into the town of Aguas Calientes on a kilometre of the railway track that is the town's only link with the world. We drooped under the weight of six days of walking, but plodded with determination, anticipating the comforts of civilization.

Dirty Harriet met us on the outskirts. She was, without doubt, Peru's ugliest and dirtiest turkey. With an ominously lowered head, she waited until we had approached to within six feet, then snaked her head from side to side making regurgitation noises. She looked as though she washed regularly in bilge water, and had recently been rejected from a bacteriological warfare laboratory. 'Greetings,' Julie said. But Dirty Harriet turned her back and proceeded to gobble into a weed growing close to one side of the track.

It started to rain again, heavily. Five Indians ran out of town towards us, one swinging a hatchet in his right hand. But none of them had designs on us; they ran past with no more than a curious glance in our direction. 'Where are you going?' I called to the hatchet man.

'There is much driftwood in the river, señor; it has come down with the floods.' And they ran on. A woman trotted past us in the opposite direction, carrying so large a load of driftwood that she ran half crouched. We sloshed into town after her.

Half-naked children played in the cold rain, some splashing in and out of the sewer. The children were only outnumbered by the dogs who were mostly male and mostly randy. A pig chewed at a banana skin, flopping it back and forth across the wet tracks until a dog came sniffing from behind. Two roosters began a deadly fight, attracting a crowd of men and boys. As the roosters tired and slowed, self-appointed handlers picked them up and threw them at each other, renewing the slashing, pecking and gouging. Human and animal faeces blotched the main street; the area created by the railway track. On one side, tiny eight-foot-square shacks housed families with up to five children.

The population of Aguas Calientes was about three hundred. There were seven restaurants and three hotels. With an unflinching desire for luxury, we hunted out the best hotel; its rooms were barer than New Zealand prison cells, but the beds had mattresses. And one of the beds had sheets.

'Señor,' I said to the owner, pushing my luck. 'There are no sheets on the other bed.' Julie and I had decided that our most urgent need was to sleep.

'There are sheets on this bed, señor.'

'But there are two of us.'

'You want to use both beds?' He was incredulous. 'Why?'

'To sleep. We need two more sheets.'

He collected two more sheets, making it clear that he would play along with our little game, but that if he ended up with four used sheets we would have acted in defiance of natural law.

'How long will you stay, señores?'

'One night,' I said innocently.

'Ah, but tomorrow there are no trains, señor.' He waited, enjoying himself.

'Why?'

'Because a landslide has pushed the track into the river. It is the rains.' He smirked at the bed nearest Julie. 'Perhaps you will sleep for many days, señor.'

'But this is the dry season, no?'

'Si, señor.' He smiled, amused but unruffled by the vagaries of life.

He left, ducking the rain which tipped sloppily out of the gutters. And we might have slept if it hadn't been for the parrot perched on a ledge outside the door. And the bird wasn't satisfied with anything as simple as 'Pepita want a galleta.' Some enterprising and talented woman had kept the feathered memory bank in her room during many passionate encounters. The parrot's repertoire extended all the way from the sweet nothings to the shrieks of ecstacy. After half an hour we gave up waiting for it to repeat itself, and left with Dave and Jackie to find the town's hot springs. Fifty yards up the main street we could still hear the parrot developing a pre-climax series of deep throated moans.

The pools were half a kilometre up a side valley. For a while, we lost ourselves in the dark and rain; but two men appeared out of the blackness with candles in tin reflectors. Their eagerness to conduct us personally up to the pools was unusually considerate, but it was exceeded by our eagerness for a hot bath, so we thought nothing more of it.

The main pool was occupied solely by gringos, five of them, shimmering pale in the steamy light of one candle. Three proclaimed themselves Frenchmen by their accents. The other two were known to Dave and Jackie from earlier in their travels, so the air warmed with many greetings and much friendly abuse. It looked as if we would be sharing the hot pools with three Frenchmen, a Texan, and an Eskimo.

'Señores,' said one of our guides, through the hubbub, 'se prohibe *banarse desnudo; la policia.'* Nude bathing prohibited. Having done their duty, the guides generously placed both their candles by the poolside and appeared to walk away into the darkness.

But none of those in the pool wore swimsuits. And we four had imagined this swim for too many aching days to give up bathing nude. We stripped and immersed ourselves, emitting groans of happiness as the warmth closed over our skin and muscles. The heat soon sapped what little energy we had, leaving nothing for conversation. Soon, the only sound was that of the rain, and the stream beyond the pools.

'Hey,' said Jackie. 'Those guys are watching us.' The two guides had been so intent on watching the naked gringos that they had moved too close to the candlelight. Within a second, Jackie and Julie became conspicuous by the insignificant amount of their bodies showing above the waterline.

There is a story about the playwright George Bernard Shaw, who, with a male friend, bathed nude in a country stream. When a boatload of picnicking women came chirping downstream in their Sunday best, the friend seized a towel and wrapped it around his waist. G. B. Shaw wrapped his own towel around his head. 'Why did you do that?' asked the friend afterwards. 'Well,' Shaw replied, 'most people know me by my face.'

The guides retreated. Julie looked thoughtfully into the darkness. 'I think it will be some time before they call the police,' she observed. The Frenchmen shook their heads at each other and made comments of sad disapproval about the guides, disheartened by the inherent sinfulness of man.

Within a few minutes, all except the Frenchmen arranged to find a restaurant in town and began to leave the water. Julie was the last out, of the six of us, because she had been practising her French. But she didn't stay long; she had difficulties with the submarine division of the French navy.

Peruvian restaurants are a kind of free-range zoo. Up to Aguas Calientes, Julie and I had known restaurants with chickens cackling under chairs, guinea-pigs pattering between tables, rats knocking pieces of straw from the rafters, and the usual assortment of mice, flies and dogs. If we wanted to remind each other of a particular restaurant, we referred to it as 'the parrot place' or 'the cockroach place' and so on.

The restaurant we chose for our first meal back in civilization seemed, at first, to be free of livestock. But no sooner had my dinner been placed in front of me, than I heard a solid double thump from down to my right. Unwilling to distract my tastebuds from the long awaited orgy, I glanced down. Beside my chair were the feet and haunches of a dog. With my knife poised above the churrasco on the plate, I ran my eyes up the legs, the stomach, the chest and the jaws of the new arrival. Especially the jaws. The dog's eyes gazed sternly at me from about the level of my armpit.

'God!' I said, inadvertently reversing the correct word.

'Would you look at the size of that thing?'

'Now even the dogs are robbing us. Maybe they have a school for houndrels around here.'

'Mmmmff,' the dog rumbled, nodding its agreement.

'No hay,' I said firmly, reasoning that any dog smart enough to pick out a gringo table would understand basic Spanish. I turned away and cut into the steak, lifting the first succulent piece towards my mouth.

A hefty paw thwacked my lower right ribs. Had the meat morsel reached my mouth, I might have choked. Fortunately I was only winded. The dog shifted its weight from one back heel to another, pushed its chin forward, ran its tongue around its lips, and gulped pathetically. The subservience was abysmally feigned, the dog uncaring that its act was transparent.

'Not a chance,' I muttered, outraged but cowed. 'I earned this.'

The dog stopped playing games with me then. It growled deep in its throat, and followed up with two fast straight-legged rights across my ribs. It was like being hit with a baseball bat. The monstrous eyes looked pained that I could be taking so long to understand a simple request. I threw down a piece of bread, playing for time. But, without shifting its feet, the dog intercepted the scrap six inches from the floor. Clack. Scromff. Then it looked hard at me, and rasped its opinion of the bread through slightly open jaws. It patience was almost at snapping-point. I gave up – I gave up a large chunk of steak. And, then, like any expert extortionist, the dog went away, knowing not to kill the goose.

'The mafia could give that animal a kind home,' said the Texan. 'I've heard tell they're partial to pumas with a bit of dog in them.'

The Texan's name was Tex. And he looked good for the part; his leather hat wouldn't hold ten gallons of anything, but the way it hung over his swarthy, lined face gave the fleeting impression that he might be packing an iron somewhere. His jeans were so tight, his paunch rode high. Snake-proof jeans were presently in their second bonanza; so Tex was now back in fashion, having bought his pair in the early fifties. He wore ankle-length pointed boots, despising my rounded ones: 'Man you cain't kill no cockroaches in the corner with them sledgehammers.' His red bandanna would have looked good riding drag on a cattle train, but his sheepskin-lined waistcoat might have earned him a showdown with a real cattleman.

According to Dave and Jackie, Tex had a wife and daughter in Dallas. He bought large quantities of presents for them both, attempting, against all advice, to send the parcels by Peruvian post. He ran a car-wrecking firm employing a Puerto Rican who usually gave most of his pay back to Tex because his own family tended to spend it. And when his employee drank himself into the gutter and into free transport across the border. Tex would close the yard, leave Texas, and bring the man back.

He would share anything he had with anyone he took a liking to.

'Could you figure that guy?' he was saying to the Alaskan. He turned to us. 'Here we were in our room, havin' ourselves a party with jest about every gringo in the hotel, an' this Swede guy comes in askin' for the time o' day. Now I knew f'r certain that he had a bottle o' rum hidden in his bag. But he jest stands there, drinkin everybody's Pisco, fair splashin' in his tweeds to blast me with this Texan joke he heard. Sumpin' about a Texan who went to Australia an' shot his mouth off about how much bigger everythin' was in Texas, until he saw one o' them Australian grasshoppers with a baby in the pouch.' He scowled, lifting his hat off and then replacing it. 'That Swede guy was real ugly to me.'

Alaskan Mike, as he called himself, shook his head in wonderment at the memory. 'You sure do find 'em a long way from their mamas.'

Alaskan Mike wasn't completely Eskimo. He had a streak of middle-shelf, white, protestant American in him, but enjoyed acting ashamed of the fact. He was handsome, about thirty years old. A headband made from a rolled up red and white bandanna pulled his hair back from a smooth brown complexion. Peruvians always mistook him for a Red Indian brave. He never wore jeans; rather, pale-blue, faded, heavy cotton trousers. His poncho stood out in a country of ponchos, because it was in the Mexican style – a fringe, and black motifs on white. The flowing garment did little to hide his athletic agility. He was used to a freewheeling life, much of it while working the railroads. He was confident in himself, but had been known to blush; which, for someone of his complexion, was a memorable event. He had poise, as opposed to social poise. He was easy going. His invariable answer to questions concerning time was, 'In about a half hour.' But that habit was nothing more than an eccentricity; Alaskan Mike was not short on incisive intelligence.

He had travelled a long way with Tex. They were a complimentary pair in many ways. Alaskan Mike's Spanish was easy and fluent; Tex's Spanish was often more easily understood if he spoke it in English. Alaskan Mike spoke very little; Tex did most of the talking. In any other pair of travellers, that combination would have been a drawback. But not for this pair. Peruvians usually chose not to trifle with them. Usually, but not always.

Tex tagged the passing restaurant owner.

'Cerveza, señor. Two bottles.' Beer.

The restaurateur hardly looked at Tex. 'No hay.' And with an indifferent shrug he passed on.

The normally gentle Texan slammed his knife on the table, rose to his feet and spoke with rising tone and increasing volume. Every word, except one, was in English.

'You come right back here you goddamn son-of-a-bitch when I'm speakin' to you.' Pause. 'Now get me a fucking *cerveza.*' And, miraculously, beer was found in full crates stacked six high behind the counter.

Unwisely, an Indian woman chose this time to try to sell something to Tex. She stepped up with a pendant, wrought artistically from copper. 'Very cheap, señor, very good quality. Very unusual. Only two hundred soles.' It was unusual, in that most items sold by the pedlars were garments made of wool from an animal called an alpaca.

But Tex was in no mood to appreciate the pendant's rarity or quality. He held it up to the light, showing it to Alaskan Mike. 'Pure alpaca wool?'

'Pure alpaca,' agreed the Eskimo, admiring the intricate copper.

The woman was astonished by such ignorance. 'No señor, it's not alpaca – it's copper! Metal!'

'Pure alpaca,' Tex affirmed. 'Beautiful.' An uncertain smile wavered on the woman's face. Such idiocy was impossible even for Americanos.

Alaskan Mike pointed to the woman's baby, which gazed solemnly at the roof. 'How much?' he asked. The smile vanished, leaving a look of blank incomprehension. 'How much for the baby?' Mike persisted, patiently.

'For my baby?' She shook her head vigorously. 'No, señor. No! My baby is not for sale.'

'A hundred soles,' Alaskan Mike offered flatly.

Tex shook his head at his friend's unscrupulous offer. 'The baby is worth more,' he said, and turned to the woman. 'One hundred and fifty soles,' he offered.

'A hundred and eighty,' Alaskan Mike shrugged. 'No more.' For two days, no trains ran. During that time, no one tried to sell anything to Tex or Mike. No one tried to cheat them, steal from them or inconvenience them in any way. Many attempted conversation with them, and Tex, in spite of his reluctant Spanish, set up a poker group in a restaurant off the main street. He and Alaskan Mike were the most respected of the nine gringos in Aguas Calientes.

After three days, trains were sent to the landslide area from both ends of the line. Exchanging passengers carried themselves and their luggage across the violently disturbed earth between. Theoretically, the trains were to arrive at the landslide at the same time. In fact three hundred Indians, Tex, Alaskan Mike, Julie and I, waited two hours on the far side of the slip for the Cuzco train. Dave and Jackie stayed in Aguas Calientes intending to take another look at Machu Picchu.

Tex and Alaskan Mike sat with Julie and me on the track attempting to pass the time with a quiet game of poker. It was anything but quiet; the Urubamba roared past the nearby slip in full flood. Nor was it inconspicuous; word of Tex and Alaskan Mike had spread swiftly through the three hundred passengers.

'Apache,' they grinned, pointing at Mike. *'El es Apache.'* Most of the three hundred pairs of eyes investigated his clothing for evidence of a knife. Others checked Tex for pearl-handled six guns.

'Raise you two,' Alaskan Mike said. And to Tex he added in Spanish, 'That's the last time I let you take my tomahawk out at night. You've got no self-control.'

At the time the first rumble of the train was heard, Tex and Alaskan Mike were sitting on the tracks, with Julie and I just clear. Julie and I were cleaned out of matches.

'The train, señores,' half a dozen Indians shouted helpfully.

'Your deal,' Tex grunted to Alaskan Mike.

The train appeared round the bend, two hundred yards away.

'Señores, the train. Quick, it is coming,' yelled twenty Indians.

'That's the third load of shit you've dealt me,' Alaskan Mike remarked conversationally to Tex.

The train bore down on us, with its drivers leaning out the sides, yelling frantically at the two men still blissfully absorbed in their poker hands.

Most of the three hundred Indians still in view screamed and stamped at the two fighting Americanos who were going to be killed by a train. When it was no more than twenty feet away, one man leapt to Tex's side and physically forced him to notice the train.

'Goddamn it,' grumbled Tex as he ambled off the track. 'An' I done had me a good hand there.'

15

Part of Peru's navy carries out its manoeuvres more than two vertical miles above sea level. That's not a figure of speech, or an
exaggeration. Nor is it the result of spectacular technology. The ships
are supported by the waters of Lake Titicaca. It's the world's highest
navigable lake – two thousand five hundred square miles of deep
water in the heart of the Andes, between Peru and Bolivia.

The town of Puno is Peru's customs port to Bolivia. It squats on a
strip of flat land on the lake's western shore, backed by a ridge of
granite. It's a grey town, dull in appearance, only saved from glaring
ugliness by the sameness of the surrounding countryside. In both
town and country, there's not a single tree to be seen.

When we arrived, even the mood of the town was depressed. The
general strike was still bitter in peoples' mouths, and the teachers
were still striking and marching through the streets. It didn't look at
all promising. But we were depending on Puno; if we got nothing
here, we would only have one smaller town to try, further north,
then we would be moving at random.

For the first three days, we did little but tramp the streets looking
for people to question. In that time, we found many people but no
answers; although it occurred to us that, throughout Peru, not one
person had played 'gringo-runaround' after being asked about the
abbey.

Almost laughing at ourselves, we tried the most obvious yet
unlikely organization – the ministry of tourism. We found a surly
civil servant with brows beetled over a too-busy desk. He listened to
our questions with poorly concealed impatience, then dismissed us in
clipped tones. 'I have no information.'

'Have you heard anything at all?' I pressed, as he bent his forehead
to his papers.

He twitched his shoulders but didn't raise his head. 'No, nothing. A
man came here, but he told me nothing.'

I straightened like a string slung to a bow. 'A man? What man?'

'A gringo. He said he stayed at an abbey, but he told me nothing.'

He softened the game, intrigued by my eagerness. 'He did not tell
me, señores. When he first came here, he said he was going with a

friend to look for an abbey on the high altiplano . . .'

'Yes,' I breathed. 'To the north?'

'Yes. It was to the north. But I do not know if he went to the altiplano: when he came back he said he could not say, because it was a secret abbey.' He moved his mouth and spread his arms, 'A secret . . .'

'That's the one!' I interrupted, talking fast. 'He told you nothing more? Please, señor, tell me what you know. There is more altiplano in Peru than there is land in my country. Do you know where this man is now? Or his friend?'

He leaned back in his chair. 'He asked me how to get to Taquile Island. But I don't know if he went there, and it has been many weeks.' I stared at him in a haze of frustration and joy. Taquile Island lay in Lake Titicaca, just a few miles off Puno. Expecting to find our man or his friend still there was a long shot, but better than heading aimlessly for the high altiplano. It would have to be tried before we moved on to the next town. I glanced at Julie, who nodded, then back to the man who had given so much hope with so little information. 'We go to Taquile,' I told him.

'Señor,' said the civil servant. 'I do not think this abbey exists. The other gringo is crazy.' He waved at folders and documents scattered on his desk. 'If the abbey exists, then where is it in my papers? Where? It does not exist except in his head.' I was directed to navy headquarters for general information and topographical maps of land areas around Titicaca. Some of the time on Taquile could be spent familiarizing ourselves with the contours of the northern areas.

The naval commander and his aides were fascinated by our purpose, but unable to help. 'This is a fine thing that you do, señor, but we cannot help you. Here, we don't know of this abbey. Our maps are useless to you because they have no detail for land that isn't immediately adjacent to the lake. If the abbey is ancient, and under the lake, then we can help you, *verdad?* No, for maps you must ask the army at Tarabamba. That is where you go next, yes?'

'Yes. After Taquile.'

'Now I will have one of my men take you where you want in Puno.' He opened the office door and sprayed orders into the corridor.

'Thank you,' I said. 'I need to find a doctor.'

'Ah, but that is easy. We have doctors in the navy.' He spoke to a seaman now standing in the doorway. 'Take the señor to the surgery.'

As I left he said, 'Señor. I think your source of information, your book, is wrong. But who can be sure? There are many parts that have never been explored in those mountains. So, I wish you well on your journey, you and your friend. It is a mission, *verdad?* If you find the abbey you must come back and tell me. *Suerte.*'

So far, in Peru, our stomachs had suffered bouts of Montezuma's revenge, the Aztec two-step, the Lima cleaner, the Huancayo shuffle, and the Cuzco curse. Now, I had started on the Puno punishment; which by way of variety, gave me severe abdominal pain and a cough.

I described the problem to the navy doctor. He took a considerable time examining my body, looking in every orifice but the one that most concerned me. Every now and then he said to himself, '*Si, si.*' Possibly he was satisfying himself that gringo bodies were correctly structured.

'It is an infection,' he announced, after some thumping and tapping. 'You have a friend?' He used the feminine form of the word friend.

'Ah, ah, yes, but . . .'

'You must get your friend to inject you in the bottom with this antibiotic. She can buy a syringe from any chemist.' He handed me a phial. More than anything I was struck by the number of things I wanted to say all at once.

'What kind of infection?' I started.

'It is a simple infection in the throat. Not serious.'

'*Gracias a Dios!* But don't you do the injection?'

He shrugged. 'If you prefer, I will do it. But you must go first to buy the syringe.'

I did.

When I came back, there was a mechanic in the surgery. He was pulling a spanner and two screwdrivers from oily overalls, laying them on the examination bench. The doctor filled and tapped the syringe, then instructed me: 'Your trousers down, please. Stand by the examination bench, facing the window.' The mechanic watched vacantly, with one hand dropped in an oily pocket.

I released my trousers, and made to grip the edge of the bench. The doctor handed the syringe to the mechanic, then frowned at me. 'Face the window.'

'Who gives the injection?' I asked.

'He does. Turn around.'

There was the consolation that backsides are not easy to miss with a syringe. But I eyed the mechanic's dirty tools on the bench next to my trembling hands, and speculated silently about union demarcation lines in Peru.

Three fast hand-slaps hit my left rump, which had also been trembling.

'When are you going to start?' I asked, wondering if the mechanic had an adequate sex life.

'It is finished, señor.' And it was. The area immediately around the needle mark ached slightly. It was the most unobtrusive, skilfully administered injection I had ever known.

'Incredible! You are an *artista*! How did you do that?'

'It is easy, Señor. The bottom is confused. The needle goes in on the third slap, but the bottom does not know.' His smug grin widened.

'The needle is better than Casanova, yes?'

I fastened my trousers, thinking about that comparison. Then I picked up the spanner, holding it in both hands. 'A joke, eh?' I said to them. Both men looked hurt. The doctor placed his hand over his heart. 'Señor,' he said reproachfully. 'A joke? No, we do not joke with you.'

We found a sail boat, the twenty-foot *San Martin*, and pushed off late the following afternoon with twelve Taquile islanders.

As daylight fled west, sufficient air slid eastwards to slip the *San Martin* a few silent kilometres off shore. But when the light was gone, the air stood still.

There were oars on board, but the islanders were in no hurry to use them. The mast tip drew smaller and smaller patterns on the brightening stars, until it shivered with the message from one faint star above Sirius. The sail died, becoming its own ghost; a pale apparition over the men of the lake. Each star twinned into the water, the effect placing the *San Martin* as a capsule into the milky way.

The islanders, and we, listened to the lake.

> *Our Father the Sun, seeing that men lived like wild animals, took pity on them and sent to earth a son and daughter of his, in order that they might teach men the knowledge of our Father the Sun, that men might know how to cultivate plants and grains and make use of the fruits of the earth like men and not beasts. With these orders and mandate, our Father the Sun placed his son and daughter in Lake Titicaca.*

So says the legend about the first Incas. But in terms of chronological history, the Incas arrived to find another race already living literally on the surface of Lake Titicaca. The Uru Indians built their homes on floating islands of totara weeds; living on fish, birds, and, in both senses, on the reeds. Many spent their whole lives without stepping on to land. And yet all were afraid of the water, fearing that if they fell in, they would die. They poled their reed boats gently so as not to wake their goddess, Ahuicha, sleeping in the reeds. As would be their custom with other conquered races, the Incas allowed the Uru culture to remain intact, requiring only taxes, and worship of the new god, the sun. However, they so despised the Urus for their poverty and way of life, that one emperor contemptuously directed that they be taxed on lice.

But the Urus from the remote past are still standing on the waters of Titicaca. They have seen the conquistadors come and go, and the Incas, and the Aymaras, and others before them, each like the passing of a season.

The sail lowered, and four men began to dip an oar each into the bottom sky. The lowest stars to the side and stern flung themselves about and disappeared as the boat splashed and squeaked towards the east.

Not long after a floating village slipped by to port, the wind came.

From the air, Lake Titicaca takes the outline of a puma; Titicaca is the Inca word for 'Rock of the Puma'. And the bite of the puma's jaws is with the teeth of the wind: the thin air needled through every stitch of our clothing. 'Get down, Señores,' the men warned us. 'Stay in the bottom of the boat or you'll become sick with the cold.' There seemed, at first, to be a clear space for two among the cargo and eleven huddled bodies. But one of the men had relieved himself there while rowing earlier. We decided that it was important not to get wet, and alternated between squatting in the remaining dry spot and sitting up in the cold.

The journey lasted eight hours, six of them jackboxing in and out of the iceberg wind. At two in the morning, the oars were used to pole the *San Martin* into a rock wave-shelter. Julie and I stumbled out, numb with cold, on to the rocks. We would have to find a sleeping space out of the wind.

One of the men approached us. 'Come with me, señores. I am Ernesto. You will sleep at my house.'

'You are very kind, señor. *Eres muy amable.*'

'Not far, señor. A few minutes.'

It was a two hour climb in such darkness that only Ernesto's feet saw the way clearly up the rocks. Ernesto's house sat on the other side of the island, only a little below the summit, fifteen hundred feet above the lake. Two hours short of daylight, he left us in a candle-lit hut, saying that he would bring breakfast in the morning.

The walls were of mud, studded with rocks. The wooden slat door Ernesto had shut behind him covered the only opening to the outside. The room breathed through a gap between two of the door-slats, and through the straw roof. Pieces of loose straw jutted into the room over the top of the walls, evidence of rats or mice living in the roof. A few straws lay on the earth floor, always a few inches from the foot of the inward-sloping walls. A flimsy table dominated the space, leaving a narrow walk-way between it and the sleeping platforms at both ends of the hut. Each platform was a double space, consisting of two cane mats laid side by side on a raised slab of rock.

Not long after first light, the door opened. A rat, caught in the act of peering down at us, squeaked and disappeared into the straw. Ernesto stepped over a stone rat-stop in the doorway, followed by two men, a woman and a small girl. One of the men carried a plank, the other a coil of rope. They stood inside the doorway, silently staring at the bleary faces of their guests. The little girl stood close to her mother, scanning the clothing over us, trying to decipher the outline of our bodies.

'*Buenos dias,*' Julie greeted them.

'*Buenas, buenas, buenas,*' Ernesto beamed in response. But then he fell back into silence with the others. He was about eighteen years old, the picture of his name, but with a counterbalancing shyness.

'Is it early?' I asked, knowing that it was.

'I have been awake for a long time,' Ernesto replied. All five continued to stare.

Julie propped herself on one elbow, an uncomfortable position on a rock bed. 'What's your name?' she asked the girl. But the small eyes widened, and the girl backed closer against her mother.

'She does not speak Spanish,' Ernesto explained. He pointed to the plank, which now lay on the table. 'We're going to put a shelf on the wall.' The two other men began to tie the rope between the rafters and the plank, stopping to stare again when Julie and I scraped our bones off the bedrock. It took patient questioning to determine that Ernesto and his brother Raymondo, one of those fixing the shelf, were the only Spanish speakers. The rest spoke Quechua only. The woman was Ernesto's mother, and the little girl his sister. The other man on the plank was the owner of the *San Martin*, not part of the immediate family.

'Your family haven't seen gringos before?' I ventured to Ernesto.

'Not in this house. You are the first. When you return to the mainland you must tell all the other gringos how good our house is, what good meals we have here, and how cheap the price.'

So much for our status as travellers in distress. 'It's an honour to stay in your house. But how much do you charge?'

'For the bed, thirty soles. For the meals, forty.' Twenty cents for a bed that would be bug-proof for ever. 'And we know that Americanos like Coca-Cola, so we have brought some on the *San Martin* from Puno. And some beer. They will go on the shelf.' He surveyed the finished shelf with pride. Raymondo was already packing it with as many bottles of Coca-Cola and beer as would fit.

'Ernesto, why is your family doing this?'

'Because we like people and because we want to have some money.'

The eye of Ernesto's house focusses on the mountains of Bolivia – east of Titicaca. It's winter: the white caps lilt unbrokenly from one end of the horizon to the other. The eye slides easily down the exuberant white slopes to the far shore of the lake. From there the eye draws inward, dancing the blue waters to the shores of Taquile, then rising steeply over green hedges, brown fields and grey rock to Ernesto's house.

Above the house, on the summit, are the remnants of an Inca prison. The ruins oversee the island, but with tenuous command – Taquile's strongest voice is that of peace. The island juts abruptly from the sea, but its ruggedness is lazy and hazy, a mediator between the emerald and the opal.

On one of the dusty paths, Julie greeted a teenage girl walking the oposite way. The girl halted, presented her back, and placed the front of her right foot over the front of her left. Her toes curled and uncurled in the dusty earth. Her heels were dry and cracked. She wore a long, jet-black veil, draped over an off-white woven shirt, and a long red skirt behind a black apron.

'Do you speak Spanish?' Julie asked. But the girl only tucked her bottom lip under her top teeth and bit down. She looked out the sides of her eyes keeping us just in sight. Presently, she turned her head enough to see us clearly with one eye. She shrank when Julie smiled, but kept looking.

'Have you seen other gringos on Taquile?' Julie asked. 'Just nod or shake your head if you don't want to speak.' The girl's face turned away again, reappeared, and then she walked away with lowered face. Black apron strings jiggling on the red skirt.

I met two men, both knitting as they strolled. They stopped, shy, but smiling. 'You stay at Ernesto's house,' said one in Spanish.

'Yes.'

Both men wore black baggy trousers, drawn in at the ankle. Black sleeveless waistcoats hung over their off-white shirts. Brilliant red cummerbunds snugged their waists. Each man wore a red woven hat that sat squarely at the base, but was so tall that it flopped over one ear.

'They're beautiful,' I said, pointing to their knitting. Both men were on the last stages of hats similar to the one's they wore. The two looked at each other, smiling, but said nothing.

On Taquile, long isolation had led to unique cultural development. The women tilled the soil; the men were famous for their knitting. The males did some field work, but spent much of their time strolling the island with four needles clicking, and four balls of wool unravelling in their pockets. They coaxed intricate, highly coloured patterns into their work, knitting so closely that individual stitches were difficult to see. Yet, as with these two, they supervised their own work with their fingers, seldom glancing down as they walked.

'Are there other gringos on Taquile?' I asked.

'No, you are the only ones,' they said, clicking needles, and smiling and looking out over the lake.

'Some gringos come here, but they do not stay long,' Ernesto said. He didn't know the Spanish word for abbey, but he was certain no one had talked about such a place or thing.

As always, he had walked in without knocking. It wasn't rudeness; there were few socially closed doors on Taquile, and not one physically locked door. Honesty was so built into Taquilan culture that in the unlikely event of material dishonesty, the culprit risked banishment from the island.

Ernesto had brought the evening meal. Soup and fried potatoes in pasta. 'Tell Raymondo he is a good cook,' I said. The islanders grew nothing but potatoes, which meant that Raymondo had specialized, somewhat. Each evening we ate soup and fried potatoes with pasta, or soup and fried potatoes without pasta.

Ernesto nodded. He reached for Julie's half-empty beer glass and finished it off. Drink was entirely communal. Food was communal once you had eaten as much as you wanted. If Ernesto was hungry, he would help himself to my left-over fried potatoes, and would expect us to eat his left-overs another day.

This morning, the shelf he was so proud of had collapsed, spreading a frothy sea of Coca-Cola and beer across the floor. When we told him it had collapsed on its own, the possibility that we might have lied to avoid paying for the bottles never occurred to him. The bottles he did ask money for were those we drank; and he charged us fourteen soles for bottles that cost seventeen soles in Puno.

'You would like to buy this?' Ernesto held up a hat, two-thirds complete. It contained the symbols of the Taquilan seasons; a display of such fine detail, that it must have taken at least a week to make, even for a Taquilan expert. Normally, a Taquilan would not press us to buy, but Ernesto was young, enthusiastic, and an opportunist.

'I can complete it for you before you go,' he said to Julie. 'It costs two hundred soles.'

'A dollar forty?' I exclaimed. But Ernesto misunderstood my tone.

'One hundred and fifty soles is alright,' he said, embarrassed.

That night I fell ill. Literally. I fainted over the rat-stop doorway. In the small hours, in delirium, I pounded a rock in the wall with my fist. My nose bled.

The night was filled with feverish dreams, of which one was to return to me again and again in the following weeks. In it, I walked alone on a track in wild, open country. It was a very high place. I came to a small, distinctively shaped rock that had, by an accident of nature, come to rest with a flat surface uppermost. A peculiar animal, about fifteen inches high, sat on that surface, mincing its paws. It looked like a cross between a rabbit, a squirrel and a racoon. It was partially obscured by a clump of tussock which grew alongside the rock, but spread above it.

The *San Martin* was away in Puno. But two days later, by chance, a motorboat moored near the wave-break. Julie supported me down the track, and Raymondo and Ernesto carried the packs, patient with our long, slow descent to the lake.

'You are good friends,' Julie said to them.

I was feeling more feverish by the minute then, and said nothing.

But I felt, also, the sour taste of failure. We had missed our man, and the first direct link with the abbey. Taquile had been a dead end.

'We are all friends,' Ernesto said.

16

Fever chopped the trip to Puno Hospital into jigsaw pieces: long stretches of totara weed slid by to the accompaniment of a slow throbbing sound. People ran across a great weed-coloured mattress, floating in the water, and the mattress heaved and shook under them. Two men, gringos, pushed me into a Peruvian army truck. A woman's voice said with crisp authority, 'No, I can't do anything for him. He must go to hospital, immediately.' Julie's voice reassured me that she was nearby. She sounded distant, which seemed a contradiction.

I found myself looking at a huge stomach. I adjusted my head position so as to focus better, then saw part of the stomach move by itself. With further adjustment of my head, I found the face that belonged to the bulge and the new life inside it. It was the face of a nurse. And it was regarding me with a hostility that was veiled razor-thin.

'*Buenas*,' I ventured, around her stomach. My voice was little more than a whisper, as it had been for at least two days.

'*Buenas*,' she replied in a raised monotone, stripping every shred of courtesy from the word.

A voice spoke from the other side. 'You have severe infection of the trachea and bronchial tubes. You will stay here.' The doctor scribbled on a piece of paper, turned and gave it to someone behind him. Julie. 'He will need these drugs. We don't have them here – you must go into Puno to buy them from a chemist.'

The nurse motioned a porter to wheel me away, using a movement of the head that was in the same class of politeness as giving me the fingers. Julie had just enough time to touch my hand as I rolled away.

The hospital corridors were wide and almost bare, but the porter succeeded in ramming every piece of furniture there was. He used the front end of the trolley to test the soundness of doorways. He charged double swing-doors, making them slam panic-stricken into the walls, only to rebound on to the trolley next to my head. After a last running battle with the ward doors, he halted alongside a bed.

'*Saca!*' he shouted. Get out.

'It's difficult,' I whispered.

'*Saca! Saca!*' His face darkened. I rolled my top half on to the bed, pausing to rest. He shovelled my sluggish legs off the trolley, threw the blanket after me, and departed. I lay face down for some time, hearing animated conversation from somewhere in the room. I heard the word gringo again and again.

Rough hands removed my sandals, and jerked me backwards and forwards to work the bedspread over the top of me. Two nurses left me half-sitting and half-lying, slightly askew on the pillows: they looked to me like the replay of a film taken with a tilted camera. Another nurse, a sister, trod through the doors to join the conversation. All three cast glances in my direction that made me wonder if liver trouble was an occupational hazard for nurses.

The sister strode to the end of my bed. 'Why didn't you remove your clothes before you got into bed?' she shouted. She returned to the other two without waiting for an explanation. But in half a minute she was back, wielding an even louder, sharper tongue. 'Keep your head to the centre of the pillow!'

I tried to imagine that my hearing was defective. I tried to think that she had really said, 'I suppose everything is strange for you here. But don't worry, because we're going to look after you.' But it didn't work; the clash between the face she should have worn and the face she did wear set up too much mental static.

There were four other patients in the ward. All watched me, brown faces made momentarily identical by their unabashed curiosity and their hospital surroundings. Above the floor, the room shone clinically with recently painted, light-coloured enamels. The floor might have contributed to the abundant reflected light, if it had not been covered with a layer of dirt. Dried blood stained most of the bedspread of the man opposite, and blood had been splattered across the ceiling high above him. But if it was his blood, he must have recovered, because he was showing no less interest in me than the other patients.

An air-conditioning pipe crossed the ceiling above my head. An access cover had been removed from the pipe, sending a cold airstream on to the top of my head.

The sister loomed up again at the end of the bed. 'Keep your head to the centre!'

'It's cold,' I whispered, pointing to the pipe above me and trying not to sound pathetic.

'Hah!' she sympathized, and left the ward. She was one of those rare individuals who can use their muscles to make their bottoms almost disappear. Eventually, a ward assistant, an Indian woman, pushed my bed into a different position when the nurses were all out of the ward.

'They hate gringos here?' I asked her. But she said nothing to me, then, or at any other time.

When Julie came with the drugs, I held her hand and muttered to it, 'I've got to get out of here.'

'I'm not strong enough to help you,' she said. 'And you might need special equipment. If you walk out, you could disqualify yourself from further help.' She grinned. 'You'll just have to be patient.'

'This is no time for bad jokes,' I complained, but knew that I had to stay.

My four varieties of medicine lay on a bed-table beside me. At first I waited to be told when to take them, but it soon became obvious that any action depended on the whim of the floor sweeper or the ward assistant.

On the second day I asked the doctor for the dosage frequencies, and kept my own schedule. For injections, I asked the least hostile nurse. But the second time I did that, she took the antibiotic away before filling the syringe. That injection felt much less painful than her first.

I still had my clothes on. I thought that if I didn't get a wash soon, the ward might have to be evacuated. No one objected when I left my bed and asked where I could shower or bathe. 'Downstairs,' they said. But the people downstairs told me I was on the wrong floor, that I should be looking upstairs. By the time I reached the upstairs floor again, I wanted rest more than I wanted to be easy on my own nostrils.

An old Indian man was wheeled into the ward that night, replacing a patient discharged earlier in the day. He was propped over a basin, set up with drip feed, and left in the care of his son.

All night the old man shouted a nonsense word, 'Noee, noee, noee,' on every breath, except when he spat frothy blood into the basin. There were no drugs on his bedside table.

'He needs a specialist,' his son pleaded when the night sister came on duty.

'There is no specialist,' she replied, and departed after checking the drip feed. Every two hours she returned to check on the old man. Each time, she threw a master switch which turned on every light in the room, including the bedlights. Each time, the old man faltered in his shouting, coughed up more blood, and resumed shouting. As the night ground on, the old man's back bowed further and further, his voice weakening until, by morning, it was a mumble.

After breakfast, a specialist arrived. The old man was trundled away. There was a subtle change in the way the other patients looked at me, an element I interpreted as accusation. I wanted to leap out of bed, shake each man by the shoulders and say, 'I am not a rich Americano.' I didn't say anything to anyone, but I took my wrist watch off and put it in a drawer.

For a short time on the third morning, I thought the sister might be thawing. She had watched me trying to con the doctor into releasing me. After conducting him out of the ward, she had returned to the end of my bed and said, 'Ah, gringito.' And she had been shaking her head, trying not to smile. Gringito is an affectionate form of the word 'gringo'.

Shortly, she regretted her lapse, and drew hostility back into the lines around her mouth. An hour later, she returned to tell me that three was another gringo in the hospital. She gave me the ward number. 'You go and see him,' she suggested. I didn't understand, because, by then, her eyes had reverted entirely to their usual iceberg condition.

I walked into the appropriate ward, finding the patient entirely on his own. His face lit up with pleasure and surprise. His eyes were bright yellow. 'Good day to you. Don't come near me, I'm in isolation; I've got infectious hepatitis.'

We talked, from a distance. He was Bruce McDonald, a Scot, and he had no relatives or friends in South America. His Spanish was fluent which helped him considerably, but compensated little for the antigringo atmosphere in the hospital. He didn't know why the feeling was so marked. He had run short of local currency. By the time we'd completed a remote control money exchange, I was tired again, and shuffled back to bed.

That night, my dreams doubled up. First the Crucifixion dream; then the peculiar little animal, waiting for me on the flat rock.

On the fourth morning, I made my bed according to the hospital method, then lay on it with my sandals on, to wait for the doctor. The sister, the nurses and the patients all knew instantly what I was doing. The sister said, 'Hmmmf, gringito.' But her tone did nothing to fill out the potential warmth of the word. There had been a mocking look about her ever since I talked to the isolated Scot.

I made a determined effort to extract a conversation from one of the patients. I thought it worth trying, because there had been one common spark between me and the other patients when the soup was served the day before. It had tasted so unbelievably foul, I raised my eyes to look at how the other patients were treating it. I found all of them watching me expectantly. 'It's called "Lake Titicaca",' the man on my right said, and there had been brief smiles around the room. In appearance, and probably in taste, the soup resembled the portion of lake by the Puno foreshore, where small boys defecated in the green scum.

Today, only the man on my right would be drawn into conversation, and then reluctantly. He kept his dignity in front of the others by speaking with a harsh clipped tone, a smirk, and a wandering gaze. He was a Puno policeman, I found. To extend the brief conversation I asked him about the abbey. But no, he didn't know anything about it. He asked how I knew of the abbey in the first place. But, during my answer, he remembered the flapping ears of the other patients, and smirked to the room, 'So the gringo looks for a Peruvian abbey.'

When the doctor came, he peered briefly at my throat, then started to walk away. 'Doctor,' I called hastily, 'I'm well now. I've been out of bed all morning.'

'No. You stay.' He disappeared.

Well, it would have been better to leave with an offical discharge; but I wasn't staying another night. Julie was due to come in an hour; I'd leave with her.

After half an hour, the policeman invited me to play poker. When the hands went against him, he changed the rules, explaining that Peruvian poker was different. I cheerfully agreed to the new rules: we were playing for matches, and I was counting only the minutes until Julie arrived. The play went against him again, which led to further amendment of the rules. 'Yes,' I said pushing the matches in his direction. 'Fine. *Por supuesto*.'

After three-quarters of an hour, the sister came to the ward. 'Hey gringo,' she called loudly from the doors. All patients looked at her. Two nurses stood behind her. 'Gringo, you can go.'

Whereupon nurses and patients all laughed at the gringo who'd been taken for a ride. From all the happy faces it seemed that patients, nurses and the doctor had become party to the conspiracy during my last excursion down the corridor.

'A joke, eh?' I said uselessly. The patients laughed louder, and the nurses sneered their way down the corridor. For a moment, I was tempted to say, 'Well, I was going anyway – when my friend arrives.' But I didn't say that. As a face-saver, it would have been little better than threatening to tell my mother.

'Hey gringo,' the policeman held out his hand. 'Adios. Good luck.' By refusing his hand I would seem to have been annoyed by the joke. So I shook it. Then a suspicion wriggled.

'What sickness do you have?' I asked.

'Typhoid,' he said.

After a few touchy seconds I remembered that I had recently been innoculated against typhoid. After that, only the knowledge of his intention and the heaviness of the atmosphere affected me. The faces of the other patients were stony and cynically amused.

'Thank you for wishing me well,' I said to the policeman. 'You're the second to shake my hand today. The first was the gringo with hepatitis.' His reaction was gratifying at the time. But when I left the hospital I knew that the nurses, the patients and myself had all lost the game.

142

17

Once in Tarabamba, we went straight to the government tourist office. Our success at Puno's ministry of tourism may have been temporary, but it had been the most promising so far.

We were half-way through our third explanation, when a thin, wiry young man leapt to our sides. 'Señores, did you say "abbey"?' He could only have made a more dramatic entrance with a large red 'S' on his chest. 'Are you speaking of the Brotherhood of the Seven Rays?'

'Yes!'

'You are looking for it, yes?'

'Yes!'

'*Muy bien!*' He threw his hands in the air, completing his entrance. 'Señores, I am Cesar Sucarr. I don't know where the abbey is, but I am going to help you find out. I have been waiting for you. A big party of Americanos tried to find it last year. And ever since, I have thought much about it, waiting for the next people to come to find it. What country are you from?'

'New Zealand,' Julie said, blinking. 'Did the Americanos succeed?'

'New Zealand? You have come a long way to find your abbey, yes? No, the Americanos found nothing. One moment.' He turned to the office employee we had been speaking to, a man twice his age. 'Call Señor Cevallos. Tell him I'm too busy today.' He beamed at us. 'I have thought so much about this abbey, but until now, that is all I have done. So your presence here is like adrenalin in the backside. And I can help you because everybody knows me, and I know everybody.'

'This is Julie Scott. I'm Michael Brown.'

His eyes flashed with humour. His handshake with me was brief, as if he had little time for formalities. He lingered with Julie's hand, though not because of the demands of protocol.

'Now,' he said, giving his head a little shake. 'You have a hotel? No? Then I will arrange one for you. How much do you want to pay?' We told him, and could detect no change in his enthusiasm. '*Claro*. But, for now, I have something I must do: so you will meet me here in two hours.' It was a command. Two of the nearby office staff glanced at each other but were careful with their expressions.

In fact I met Cesar, elsewhere, in less than half an hour. Rather than wait for him at the office, I set off to explore Tarabamba, and found him striding purposefully up a side street. Behind him, puffing, trotted a worried looking man. 'Miguel,' Cesar called, without slowing, 'come with us.' I fell in beside him. 'We are going to the police. My friend here . . .' he introduced his friend with a single wave of a hand. 'My friend's guitar has been stolen. But we know who did it. I'm going to put him inside for ten years.'

'*You're* going to put him inside?'

'Yes. I have the pink paper.' My incomprehension must have been obvious. 'It's to make the police arrest whoever I say. That one who stole my friend's guitar – it's known that he takes drugs. It will go hard for him.'

'You are that powerful? How?'

He smiled – a wide, generous smile, with a hint that if he hadn't decided to like me, his response to my question might have been different. He showed his palms, and his smile, to the sky, expressing appreciation of good fortune that was only his due. 'My father is head of a United Nations department.'

A drunken Indian woman tried to intercept Cesar, calling out to him in slurred Quechua. But he raised his hand cheerfully towards her saying, '*Salud mamai,*' and she stepped away out of his path.

At the police *cuartel*, Cesar went straight through to the courtyard. There, at least thirty officers were gathered around the Tarabamba police chief. Local teachers were to hold a demonstration march today; the police chief's orders would be related to that.

Cesar strode through to the police chief as if his men were no more than chaff on the ground. He cut the chief off in mid-sentence, introduced his friend, and explained the situation. The policeman asked two questions, and spent most of the time nodding. Obviously, Cesar didn't need to carry his pink paper on him.

Cesar left his friend with the police, and walked out of the circle through the path that had stayed open for him. He grasped me by the arm. 'Miguel. Already I have arranged a room for you in the Hotel Iquitos. Come, we will find your Señorita and I will take you. Then we will find out where to look for the Abbey of the Brotherhood of the Seven Rays.' He rolled out the abbey's name with a flourish. 'La Abadia de la Hermanded de los Siete Rayos.'

Room seventeen of Iquitos was sunny and clean. In the midst of our expressions of delight, Cesar dived at one of the beds and punched the mattress. His twenty-two-year-old face turned impish. 'Now I will tell you why I chose this room. Last night it was my room. Usually I stay in Hotel Granada, but yesterday I watched football, I found a girl, and last night I bounced my own balls, eh?' He chuckled, delighted with himself; and, reassured that Julie wasn't offended, he thumped the mattress again. 'It was this bed.'

Julie luxuriated in the warm sunlight streaming in the window. We had spent many cold nights recently, including my nights in Puno Hospital.

'Plenty of sun in the morning,' she observed.

'Yes, but it comes too early in the morning,' Cesar said, with sweet rememberings in his voice.

'It was generous of you to get us the room,' Julie said. 'How did you do it?' Even as she asked, I could see she knew that a question like that, to a man such as Cesar, was inadvisable.

'The owner is a friend of mine. I suggested to him that room seventeen was available, and he agreed.' Cesar's eye fell on an ashtray still half-full from the night before. 'Now, I'll show you something very Peruvian.'

He took a piece of printed paper from his pocket, glanced at it, then rolled it into a cone. He tipped all the cigarette ash into the cone which he took to the open window. He studied the pavement below, waiting for the right moment, then emptied the cone into the air, and closed the window. 'Very Peruvian,' he said. 'Now, we look for the abbey.'

For the first three days we found nothing. Even Cesar Sucarr, who knew everybody, and whom everybody knew, could find no one who knew anything. And it wasn't for lack of effort. He never used a car; he covered scores of miles of Tarabamba on foot at a tireless clip. He, and we, asked officials, old men in the market, a writer, restaurant owners, the mayor, and others. Occasionally, he turned up at the tourist office where he had a job, if and when he wanted to work at it.

In that time we learned more about him than we had about almost all Peruvians. Everyone respected him. Some feared him. Many loved him. All avoided conflict with him. The important thing for people to avoid, at almost any cost, was allowing Cesar to decide that he disliked them. He was an embryo dictator, secure in the warm support of the majority, and the support of the rest.

'That Cesar, *el es loco*,' said an admiring friend. 'One time, in Lima, he had a terrible accident on his imported motorbike. He was doing a hundred miles an hour when he crashed. There was so much bone coming out of his leg, the doctor said he would never walk properly again, and you have seen how Cesar walks – the *chicas*, they faint with pleasure to see him walk, now. He had plaster from his hip to his toes, and the doctor said he must stay in his bedroom. But, he wouldn't stay there because he wanted to ride his other motorbike. So his family locked him in his upstairs bedroom with his motorbike. But they made a mistake. Cesar demanded that his wife be allowed to visit him at night – he was married already – and they permitted it. In just a few days, of course, he regained his strength. Then he ordered the maid to unlock his door, and bribed a friend to help him carry the motorbike downstairs. He stuck his plastered leg out sideways, and rode through the streets of Lima to the beach where his friends were having a party.'

On the third evening in Tarabamba, Julie and I treated ourselves to dinner in a tourist restaurant. For the first half of the meal we were alone, enjoying the extravagance of trout from the lake. Then Cesar bundled the restaurant doors aside and made straight for our table. We hadn't told him where we were going to eat.

'*Buenas tardes*,' he said, sitting down. 'The karate teacher has left Tarabamba. So still we know nothing.' He clicked his fingers impatiently for the waiter, who was arriving but still six feet away. 'Three Pisco sours.' He drummed on the table with his fingers. 'Don't worry, we'll find out. Someone knows.'

'You were interested in the abbey before we came,' I said. 'Why didn't you start looking before now?'

Cesar was momentarily short of words; a rare event. 'Because even if I had found out where the abbey is, I wasn't ready, in myself, to go.' Julie and I looked at each other in surprise, then back with renewed interest to the young playboy. 'Those Americanos who failed to find it . . . when they returned, they said there was no abbey. They said the book you talk about is about an abbey of the mind only. And, at first, I thought they were right.'

'Why did you change your mind?'

Once again Cesar hesitated. 'I am not sure. Perhaps . . . perhaps it's because it would be terrible, horrible, if there is *not* such an abbey. Now, I want to know, to be certain one way or the other. You tell me about the way the stones of Sacsahuaman have been cut; and about a man who says he has stayed in the abbey; that makes me feel good. And I have thought something about the group of Americanos: that they travelled with no eyes and ears for the things around them. So they learned nothing. No one would want to tell them where to go. That's why they didn't find it. *Comprenden?*'

He sat back in his chair, surprised at himself. 'This is good. I like talking philosophy with you. And, I am an eyes man. I can see from your eyes that you are serious people. You think. You use the head.' He jabbed a finger at his temple.

Julie said to him, 'So are you ready to travel to the abbey now?'

Before he could answer, the Pisco sours arrived. '*Salud!*' Cesar proposed, and swigged healthily, with a stylishly hooked index finger. Immediately, he blaaghed in disgust. 'Ai! Ai!' he shouted at the waiter. '*Que horrible!* Get me the ingredients. And a shaker and ice. I will do it myself.'

'There is no ice, Señor Sucarr.'

'Aach.' Cesar waved the waiter out of his sight. He turned to us. 'I will take you to a party where I'll show you how Pisco sour should be mixed. When I was seven years old, my father had a bar in his house. When he had important guests, I was the barman. I was the youngest barman in the world who could mix perfect Pisco sour when drunk.'

We could see he hadn't forgotten Julie's question. 'It's Colonel Pomar's birthday,' he continued: 'He is a friend of mine.' He began to stand up, motioning us to stay seated. 'But first, I need to find a girl as beautiful as Julie so I won't feel lonely. Wait here.'

He steamed to the other end of the restaurant where a young couple were seated. In two minutes, Cesar returned with the girl, leaving the man sitting on his own – too far away for me to read his expression.

'This is Cecilia. Miguel. Julie.' Cesar said peremptorily. Cecilia was subdued but smiled to both of us. She began to sit down, but rose immediately when Cesar beckoned us to the door.

'The bill?' I asked.

'It's arranged. Let's go.' He looked steadily at me; and, without pause, followed up with an answer to Julie's question. 'One day I will look for the abbey. But I am not ready yet. I'll help you find someone who knows where it is, but I don't want to listen when he tells you. When you come back from the abbey you must tell me what you learned, but not how you got there.'

Cecilia went through the restaurant doors ahead of Cesar, so she didn't look back at her first partner, who was still sitting in the same position. Once out of the restaurant, she smiled more, but didn't come near to laughing.

Cesar flung Colonel Pomar's front door open and coasted inside, giving the impression that the door had actually been open all the time. Cecilia, Julie and I swirled in his wake for the first two or three steps, then ground to a halt.

The Colonel was well-off by Peruvian standards. His house, although not large, was of modern concrete block construction. The living area was open plan, and for the party, a partition between two lounges had been drawn aside. To our left, in the smaller room, was a fully uniformed military brass band, playing a patriotic march. To our right, in the larger room, were thirty to forty party-goers. Three-quarters of them were army officers in full uniform, with pistols on their hips. Some of them danced with a hand on their holsters to prevent being bruised by the movement of the pistols. There were three or four men in civilian clothes, and half a dozen women.

Greeting everyone in general and no one in particular, Cesar marched through to what looked like the kitchen area. He had, after all, come to show us how Pisco sour should be made. Cecilia followed him to the kitchen.

The band played on. Some officers eyed us, and one or two nodded. One of the men in civilian clothes swayed in my direction. He wore a bright red shirt, but was too drunk for us to tell, from his manner, if the colour was symbolic. 'Escucha,' he confided in my ear. 'Peru es el culo de mundo.' Peru is the arsehole of the world.

147

The man glanced about him, abashed by his own bravery. But only Julie and I heard him. He came back to my ear, and spoke with exaggerated lip movements. 'And do you know what came out of the hole? Tarabamba.' Thoroughly pleased with himself, he swayed back to the centre of the floor.

It was ten minutes before we became sufficiently unobtrusive for the party to become smooth again. In that time we discovered two things. First, that it was a mistake to assume that the toilet of a colonel would be any cleaner, or work any better, than other toilets. Second, that we were gatecrashers: the Colonel staggered towards us, bringing as much dignity with him as he could carry. He spent a frowning moment studying us.

'We're with Cesar Sucarr,' I said nervously.

'Welcome to my house,' he said thickly. 'It's good to have visitors from other countries. I'm very happy that you can share my birthday.' He paused. 'And Señor Sucarr, also, is welcome in my house at any time. Viva Peru!'

'Congratulations for your birthday,' Julie said quickly. 'How old are you?'

'I'm a hundred and seven,' the man chuckled. 'Viva Peru!' With raised glass he returned to the corner with the greatest concentration of uniformed and armed officers. Extraordinary, I thought, that he had chosen the very age my father chose when he used to tease me. Perhaps the Colonel had children. I looked at his wife, seated near a bowl of carnations she'd arranged. Every now and then she'd adjust a flower, surveying the total effect with pleasure.

'He is fifty,' said a voice at our side. And that opinion attracted more voices. Five drinkers began to debate the Colonel's age, placing him between forty-five and fifty-one.

The red-shirted man with the medical opinion about the nature of Tarabamba and Peru, came to our sides. 'The Colonel is a *militar*,' he said nastily. 'I don't like *militares*. Or the police.' His voice was loud. 'Viva Peru,' he said mockingly in a sing-song voice.

'What's your job?' I asked him. It seemed a safe diversion?

'I'm a farmer, I don't like *militares*.'

'What are you doing here, then?'

But he shrugged; the gesture that covered every situation – the communication cosmetic.

Cesar walked out of the kitchen threshing a drinks shaker with such energy that his feet were obliged to join in the rhythm. 'Here it is,' he crowed. 'There is no more ice, so it's not perfect. But it will do. Try it.' He handed me the whole shaker. 'What do you think?' he asked eagerly as an unmanageable amount poured from the shaker into my mouth.

'Fantastic,' I said, when the floor stopped drumming against my feet. I gave it back to him. If he never became a political leader he could at least make an economic killing by marketing his concoction.

Julie, noticing my glazed eyes, accepted a dance invitation before Cesar got to her with the shaker. She danced with a man in civilian clothes, trying to get rhythm from the tuneless dirge presently dripping out of the brass instruments. Her partner showed early signs of wanting to communicate on a purely physical level.

'What's your job?' she asked.

'I'm in the secret police,' he answered.

Julia pushed slightly to give her room to focus on him. He didn't seem at all perturbed to have given away one of the State's secrets. 'I've never met a secret policeman,' she said gravely.

'There are many of us.'

'What does a secret policeman do?'

'We are needed in Peru for people who don't respect the uniform,' he said matter-of-factly. 'Viva Peru,' he added, attempting to slide his right hand on to Julie's bottom.

Just before midnight, a uniformed officer proposed a toast to the Colonel. 'Salud,' the company shouted under their glasses. One officer, whose uniform had slipped and changed colour throughout the evening, began to sing Peru's national anthem. 'Somos libres. Seamos lo siempre . . .' But his performance was so drunken it was s social disaster. Unaware, he rolled his way throbbingly through line after line, right to the end. None of the company dared stop the man. With faces frozen into careful blankness, thirty individuals directed their gazes either on to another individual's back, or on to wall surfaces higher than six feet. The Colonel could perhaps have ended the show, but he needed all his concentration just to remain standing.

Cesar threw up in the corner soon after. But when we asked if it was time to go, he insisted that the party had just started. So we left him with Cecilia, who wiped his face with a wet cloth. No one had danced with Cecilia except Cesar.

Just after farewelling our host, and before we reached the door, the red-shirted man plucked a bloom from the Colonel's wife's bowl of carnations. He halted us by the door and loudly presented the carnation to Julie. The prickling sensation in our backs didn't cease until we had lost sight of the house.

The first direct information about the abbey came late the next morning.

Julie stayed in the hotel room that morning, washing her hair. Cesar took me to a courtyard near the centre of Tarabamba to meet his mother. But, after introductions and polite exchanges, I saw Cesar looking back at the street, some fifty yards away. A dark figure waved at us, framed by the arched entrance to the courtyard.

'One moment,' Cesar said. 'There is someone waving to me.' He strode off towards the street. I hovered uncertainly, then nodded to his mother and followed him.

Even from the distance, the newcomer looked well-dressed. Closer up, I saw that he was impeccably outfitted in a dark suit: dapper from his shiny black shoes to his trilby hat. In Savile Row he would once have been inconspicuous; in Tarabamba, he looked as if he had stepped out of an imported and dated fashion magazine.

Cesar had an intent look on his face. The newcomer was speaking soberly, making no gestures except when he nodded in my direction. Cesar's face became excited. He started to move towards me, but saw how close I was and stayed still. 'Miguel. This man knows where you have to go!'

My temples prickled and I took a deep breath. Saying nothing, I tried to weigh the man up before he spoke. His outfit seemed ludicrous; although, when I thought about it, his appearance was possibly more realistic than that of the image I had unconsciously built up. For some reason, I had been expecting the final directions to come from an old man in a long flowing robe sporting a white straggly beard.

But the man wasted no time in studying me. 'Ask at Yungacocha,' he said, And he began to walk away.

'Wait, who are you? Who do I ask for?'

He shook his head firmly. 'Ask at Yungacocha.' And he left, placing his shiny shoes carefully so as not to get them dusty.

'Did you know he was coming?' I interrogated Cesar. 'Do you know him?'

Cesar stared after the figure dwindling in the direction of the main shopping street. 'I didn't know he was coming. I have never met him, but I have seen him before. I know what he does. He's a bank manager from Malacancha.'

'A bank manager!' I grabbed Cesar by the shoulders. 'You are joking with me. You arranged this. You arranged it with him.'

Cesar pushed out his jaw, tucked his elbows into both sides of his stomach and protested with palms up. 'Miguel, Miguel, I swear to you I did not arrange it. I have never met him, I only know who he is. He must be visiting here on business and heard about all our questions around town. There is no other way. If it's a joke, it's his joke.'

The dapper bank manager turned a distant corner.

Part Three

1

Julie shook her head. Wet hair clung, water-bound to the movement. Her hair was never blonde when wet. Drying under the thin winter sun, it glistened darkly as her head shook slowly, side to side. The gesture was by her, but not of her: it seemed to belong to the loneliness sucking up from the depths of the courtyard well where we sat, side by side.

'I'm not going with you, Michael,' she said.

The conversation was inevitable and predictable. We knew the lines as if we had rehearsed them. 'You've made up your mind,' I said heavily. To lose this wonderful companion now, so close to the abbey, when we had been through so much together . . .

'Michael. You know why. This is what we discussed back home. The area around Yungacocha is going to make the Inca Trail look like a Sunday stroll. If I couldn't go any further, you would be bringing me back to here. And that could stop you altogether.'

'Can you give up the abbey just like that?' I pressed. 'Won't you have any more questions?'

'I still have questions,' she answered. 'But they sit easy with me. They'll get answers eventually, wherever I go.' I rose and walked a brittle circle on the concrete apron adjacent to the wall. 'And what about you?' Julie continued. 'I know how much you have to solve the dreams. But you know you've already got answers without the abbey. Why not do it slowly? Is the fast answer worth the risk?'

'Yes.' If I returned to New Zealand still dreaming the Crucifixion I would go under again, and this time I wouldn't get up. That must never happen, I thought. Images of the mental hospital chattered in my head like shrill voices in a narrow corridor. No choice. No peace, until I had found the solution.

'Yes,' I repeated. Julie pushed her hand out and curled a little finger in mine.

But if I went, I risked never seeing her face again. When Cesar had finally discovered the whereabouts of Yungacocha, he had been alarmed. 'It's very high, very cold. There's nothing to breathe on the altiplano. And there are animals; wild animals and human animals. *Ten cuidad*. And, Miguel, you must look after Julie.' Well, perhaps

153

Cesar would now relax a little. But neither Julie nor I could relax, knowing that I might not return. And yet, if I turned back at this stage, my days with Julie were numbered anyway. My problem, unsolved, would drive her away. Besides, there was another dream pestering me now. The peculiar animal on the flat rock was visiting me every night. No choice. No choice. My whole life was being directed from the pillow.

'Yes,' I said for the third time. 'I go. I've got to go.' And Julie said nothing in response to all my repetition. She gazed down into the well, and it occurred to me that she didn't blink much these days.

Julie and I spent most of that afternoon in bed, trying to discover how to lie in maximum physical contact. Sometimes, though, we just lay with our foreheads together, hands clasped. I could feel Julie trying to pour strength into the aching space between the centre of her eyebrows and the centre of mine. Once, she held my temples in both hands which, for some reason, made me close my eyes tightly. 'Michael, Michael, Michael, take care of yourself,' she whispered fiercely.

We arranged that she would wait six weeks for me, in Pension Rosales, La Paz, the capital of Bolivia. Before that time, I would return to civilization, either to join her in La Paz, or to send a message that I would be staying on at the abbey. If she hadn't heard from me in that time, then she must assume that I was ill, injured, or dead. We didn't discuss what she should do after the six weeks was up. In the meantime we had one more day together.

Next morning, Julie went to buy a bus ticket to Bolivia. I set off for the army headquarters to find a topographical map of the area around Yungacocha.

'Where are your headquarters?' I asked three soldiers sitting in the Plaza de Armas. I gave them a town map so that they could point out where I should go. They held the map in four different ways, trying to make sense of it, and finally gave it back to me. 'No hay,' they said. No headquarters.

Eventually, at headquarters, I was ushered into the frowning presence of Colonel Pomar. It was an awkward meeting. He pointedly made no reference to the party of two nights ago, and held his head as if he had a bad headache.

He listened. He said that yes, the army had all the topographical maps, that I should wait while he found the correct one. After ten minutes he returned without a map, saying that the area I wanted had not been surveyed yet. His tone and expression suggested that his headache would probably depart when I did. I persisted becasue there were no more army headquarters on my route north of Tarabamba. But the effort was wasted. And, for all I knew, the area might indeed be so remote that it had never been mapped.

I thanked him and angled my feet for the door.

'How is Cesar?' the Colonel crisped.

'He's well. He enjoyed the party. And so did I.'

'*Muy bien*. He is always welcome at my house. And so are his friends.'

The waiting duty officer escorted me back to the main gates.

An hour later, I bought an alpaca poncho and a wide rimmed sombrero at the market. The thinner the air became on this trip, the more ideal a garment the poncho would be. At high altitudes I could easily go through a thirty degree temperature change in the time it took to step from the sun into the shade. The poncho would be warm in the cold and cool in the sun. The sombrero would keep the sun off my head. During the hour after that, I enjoyed my outfit so thoroughly that the apprehension of the coming trip took a brief holiday.

Back in Puno, I'd had my nose cauterized. It had been a painful procedure, but a routine one for the doctor because the high altitude made the complaint a common one. Now, I still had the bandages across my nose and face. The bandages, my black beard, the sombrero and poncho all combined to somewhat dramatic effect. It struck me that it might be considered strange to dream of Jesus Christ, and yet to relish looking like a Mexican bandit.

The normally stolid Indians in the market place did double-takes wherever I went. Little boys followed me, trying to determine where I was keeping the ammunition belt. A few adults, who didn't notice my presence until almost face to face with me, dropped jaws and shifted into reverse. After that I scowled and allowed my knife to show occasionally. The ripples improved. Killer Gonzales had come to town.

'Hey, Mexicano, go home,' shouted someone from the back of a passing car. Youths yelled unintelligible things from bus windows. Little girls held up their mothers by clasping them around the legs and peering at me from behind, as it were.

Not everyone got the image right. A shopkeeper announced confidently to his clientele that I was a racing-car driver from Britain. One man thought I was a missionary and told his friends as much. I knew that Christianity had something to answer for in Peru, but this much? In any event, it was insulting of him to describe Killer Gonzales as a missionary. I considered staking him out for the ants.

Those pleasant waftings came to an end when I walked back to the market place to buy bread. Near the area where I'd bought the poncho, a dozen Indian women surrounded and seized me. All of them yelling – at me.

But there was no opportunity for self-congratulations, because it was immediately obvious that none of the women desired my body. The only thing they wanted to commit with me was murder. For what reason, I couldn't work out; they were all yelling in Quechua.

'*En español!*' I shouted. But I didn't shout loudly enough. It was becoming difficult to maintain the Mexican bandit image with a dozen disrespectful women clutching at me and my poncho.

'*Gerroff!*' I roared in English, making flinging motions in a last-ditch attempt to salvage dignity. Nearly all the women let go, which pleased me until I discovered that the only one still hanging on was four feet six inches in height and seventy years of age. She was clinging like a limpet to one corner of my poncho. I considered lifting that corner to bring her face up to my level, but decided that a fall of one and a half feet might be fatal at her age. After long soul-searching, Killer Gonzales had discovered a depth to which even he would not sink. He would not kill little old ladies.

I crouched down to her level. 'What's happening? What do you want?'

The noise stopped, only to start again as four of the women clacked simultaneously into Spanish. Something about my poncho and money. Faces watched from all directions in a radius of hundreds of yards. A policeman regarded us with detached interest from near the coca stall.

'I have paid for it,' I shouted indignantly. It was a trick to get money off me. My image was sagging more with every minute. I should not be protesting my innocence: I should be laughing and striding away into the sunset. 'I will call the policeman. He will decide,' I shouted, congratulating myself for my cunning. That would sent the cheats packing.

'Yes! The policeman!' the women chorused. And half of them pushed me all the way. The rest of them pulled. I wondered if I had come upon the original meaning of the phrase 'man-handled'.

The policeman was Solomon reincarnate in police uniform. He was in his element and he knew it. With a gravity that would have graced the ordination of a bishop, he listened to each side of the argument. Then he presented that point of view to the opposition, rolling out synoptic truths with sonorous flourishes.

I had been charged the wrong amount for the poncho. I'd paid sixteen hundred soles; which was the full asking price. At the time, I had been surprised that such a good poncho was so cheap. The women explained, through the expressive arm of the law, that the girl who'd sold it to me was mentally subnormal, that she had only been minding the stall, and should not have sold me anything. To illustrate their point, they pushed the girl to the front for me to see for myself, even though I'd obviously seen her before. The girl was distressed and seemed not to understand what was happening. The women wanted another six hundred soles. I would never have paid twenty-two hundred soles originally, but I was now attached to my poncho. It liked me and I liked it. Bargaining started, but the women took loud offence at my every offer, and made no attempt to lower their price.

'Señor,' the policeman fingered the poncho – my poncho. 'This is very good quality. It is perhaps the best one from the stall. It *is* worth twenty-two hundred soles. In Lima it would sell for four thousand soles.' He looked at me and deliberately flicked his eyes at the still upset girl beside me. He really was a Solomon.

'Twenty-one hundred and fifty,' I said, with a small nod for his benefit. The women agreed. The policeman spat into the dust, satisfied. In Peru, everyone spits, even Solomon.

I felt shamed by my bargaining which, under normal circumstances, would have been expected. I touched the girl on her shoulder. 'Don't let it worry you,' I said as gently as I could. But the girl spoke only Quechua and didn't understand.

A few of the women did understand. Two of them looked at me with contempt; this one is not a man, they thought. Two other women were more reserved, one of them translating for the girl. But the girl remained unhappy, not looking at me.

When I left, I felt exactly like a man who dreams by night that he is Jesus Christ and likes to be Killer Gonzales by day.

2

'Want to take any bets on the bus being late?' Julie commented on the way to the station. I didn't. The thought of a prolonged departure made me feel like the wrong end of a left-over bonbon.

The bus was late. Julie and I waited at a café table. We said almost nothing, and, for me, it was the silence of limbo. Only now, when she was leaving, did I realize that much of my sense of place, of belonging, had depended on her. She was quietly miserable, and, in a way, that was comforting; I ached to lie with her again, to feel the physical contact that had once bridged the gap. Last night I had nestled my head in her breasts like a child, and the desire to do that again, now, rose and fell in me like a long ocean wave. I said nothing. And I knew she would say nothing to encourage me to step on the bus with her.

There was some relief in knowing that Dave and Jackie were in La Paz, and would be for the next week. At least for that time, she would be with people she knew. Although unhappy now, she looked forward to La Paz; she had said there was plenty to occupy her there for six weeks.

'Please don't start for another few days,' she said. 'Not until you're fit again.' I had not yet completely recovered from the Puno hospital.

'I'll mark time in Tocache for a couple of days, I'll need that time to prepare, anyway.'

When the bus turned up an hour late, I climbed on to the roof, ignored the protests of the baggage man, and chained Julie's pack to the rack.

'There are no thieves in this company,' the man barked, taking personal offence on behalf of the company.

'I believe you,' I said, 'but I always do this.'

Because of that exchange, my last contact with Julie was coloured with humour. The image of her face, pale but still smiling as the bus pulled away, stayed with me, superimposed over much that happened in the next twelve days.

Some minutes after the bus left, two gringos turned up: a young man and woman. 'Are we too early for the bus to La Paz?' the woman said out of the shadow of her floppy straw hat.

158

'You're too late. It left five minutes ago.'

'Oh Jesus,' she groaned. 'We were told twelve-thirty.' Her friend sighed and dropped his pack to the ground with a punishing thump. She spoke to me again, her voice distorted with anger. 'You know, when I came to Peru, I thought, "Gee, isn't it a shame – all those poor people in bare feet." Well, now I don't give a damn. I hope their fucking feet fall off.' She was close to tears. 'Say, did you miss the bus too?'

'I don't know yet,' I said, looking down the road.

3

Standing still in the fogged, frozen town of Tocache was like standing in a tomb of iced butter. No sounds reached me; but, at five o'clock in the morning, there were few sounds for the fog to swallow. I began to walk. My cheeks tautened against the raw globules, but the rest of me murmured in delayed appreciation of the effort. At first, I wound around the tiny circumference of the Plaza. Then, needing variety, I clover-leafed the surrounding blocks.

Half an hour later, the Plaza was still empty. I had been told that the trucks would start leaving from there at five in the morning. Public transport petered out at Tocache; the only way further north was on the back of one of the collective farm trucks. I kept walking.

At a quarter to six, three Indian women wheeled a coffee cart into the plaza. Wisps of steam crept past the urn lids, melting apologetically into the enveloping murk. I was the first customer. I wrapped stiff fingers around the hot tin mug and warmed my face in the sweet steam. The fog had been oppressive, but the hot syrup expanded me, giving me place and space in the plaza.

'When do the trucks leave from here?' I asked.

'Soon. Very soon,' they answered, eyeing me with interest. There would have been few gringos through Tocache; fewer still dressed like me and heading north.

'You don't have a pack!' one stated.

'No.' Cesar's comments about the party of Americans had led to my leaving the pack behind. With few of the trappings of wealth, I would hopefully be less repulsive to the people with information, and less attractive to the bandits. Except for one article I wore all the clothing I'd need: sombrero, poncho, wind-jacket, sweater, shirt, T-shirt, money-belt, Peruvian jeans, and my boots. In hot times, the jacket and jumper would loop through the straps of my shoulder bag. In the bag: water-bottle, compass, basic first-aid, nylon cord, matches, a woollen hat, and a plastic square for the rain. On my jeans belt: my knife (hidden by the poncho), and a bag of coca leaves. In one hand I carried a bottle of Pisco to give the driver of whichever truck carried me north.

At six o'clock, a large truck pulled up opposite the coffee cart. It

160

was empty except for two men in the cab who peered at me coming through the fog.

'Are you going to Aucane?' I asked through the driver's window.

The two men questioned each other silently. The driver answered me, looking straight ahead through the windscreen. '*Si.*'

'Can you take me as far as the turn-off to Huanchota?'

'It costs three hundred soles.' It was a fast surly answer, and he still wouldn't face me.

'How long does it take?'

'Two hours, no more.' Impossible. If his time-sense was that relaxed, he should be five times older than he looked.

'When do you leave?'

'In quarter of an hour.'

We left Tocache four hours later. In that time, the driver collected two and a half thousand bottles of beer, and forty-five Indian passengers to sit on them. I cursed myself for not anticipating that a collective farm truck wouldn't travel such distances empty.

For the first twenty minutes, the attention of every Indian was locked firmly on the gringo riding in their truck. After an hour, as long as I kept still, the number of watchers went as low as half a dozen. If I moved, even slightly, the appropriate limb was scrutinized from twenty different angles. Conversation was scarce, conducted in close-to-the-ear mutters, often with eyes still fixed on me. An hour out of Tocache, two boys – the only youngsters on board – began to play at throttling each other, grinning and laughing to the adults around them. But, the more they played to their audience, the more they lost it. The adults were too absorbed in watching for the gringo's reaction to the violent game.

'Strong men,' I said. I spoke dryly, trying to avoid both eagerness and condescension. But the effort was wasted. Faint speculative smiles on two of the women's faces vanished with my words.

After midday, the half-dozen men and women packed around me began a tough session of unmusical chairs. None of them pushed or pulled; but as soon as I moved a foot closer to my backside, or swayed a knee inwards, the space I left behind was invaded. Remaining motionless on a crate of beer was difficult because the bottles tended to dent my sense of comfort. But I couldn't allow them to force me into standing up. The air had been chilled from the beginning, and was becoming more so by the half hour. My space was no better than anyone else's. And it was considerably less comfortable; every Indian sat on at least three blankets, some of them on half a dozen.

I decided that this group of Indians must have come into contact with some other gringo who'd displeased them, and that they'd assumed all gringos to be the same. At least their hostility was passive, I thought. But I became uneasy, anyway. I remembered the warnings about the area we were heading for. '*Se fuerte, Miguel.*'

161

Cesar had said. 'Be strong. You must not appear to be weak.' By one o'clock, the stolid dislike was obvious. The unmusical chairs drifted through the line that divides passive from aggressive. If I didn't find a way to cope with the atmosphere, my unease would soon become obvious. Weakness.

For ten minutes I concentrated on other places and times, putting a far-away look on my face. Then, seeming to notice the atmosphere for the first time, I acknowledged it with an expression I hoped was amused, quizzical, and unperturbed.

'Where do you live?' I asked the man next to me. I used the plural of 'you' and meant others to hear. He turned his eyes to look at another, opposite him. Each arranged a contemptuous wrinkle in the corner of his mouth. The one furthest from me hawked and spat over the side, adding his contribution to the ecology of Peru's expectoral pastures. Then there was silence, except for the freezing, dust-laden wind, and the rattling of beer bottles.

The truck stopped at Yoma for a meal break. It emptied of Indians like a puddle emptied by a dropped rock. They flowed out over the cab, the sides, and the end. I had little desire to be pushed at the wrong moment, so stayed put until they had gone. I had to avoid situations that could force me into a fight. I stood up, watching them pour into a cafeteria. At least half a dozen men carried themselves in a way which suggested the presence of a weapon.

I found a toilet at the rear of the café. After five seconds of blessed privacy I heard a whisper, so hoarse that it was twice as audible as normal conversation. 'He's in the toilet!' Then came the sound of running feet. Once my knife came out there was no time to pull up my pants. I kept the knife low, nearly falling backwards as two figures, one after the other, raced past the door, jumping for a look through the wide gap between the door and the frame. Another two shapes stopped and tried to peer through cracks in the door.

I sheathed the knife and continued what I'd come for. It was so cold that part of my backside went numb. I came out slapping fist into palm against the cold. But when I saw the size of the audience outside the toilet, I changed the movement to clapping. Applause. But only a few children smiled; the ones not old enough to know about gringos.

In the café, salt was brought to the table with each ordered meal. But not with mine. '*Sal,*' I said quickly, before the woman could easily ignore me. Around the moment she bashed the salt on my table, there was one of those silences that happen occasionally in a room full of conversation. When I tooked around, I found that the silence wasn't a fluke after all. I wished that the woman had bashed the shaker down hard enough to smash it.

Back on the truck, I found that the bottle of Pisco had been taken. I had expected as much; better so than to have carried the bottle with me. I no longer felt generous towards the driver, anyway. In fact, I didn't feel generous to any adult inside a radius of a hundred miles. I could only speculate on the chances of the malice becoming physical as the truck moved further into the interior. While I wasn't sure, I was nervous. The more nervous I became, the less generous I felt. Killer Gonzales, come back, I thought; I'm going to need you. I regretted throwing away my nose bandages.

I allowed my knife to show as I sat down.

But, within ten minutes of leaving Yoma, it became clear that no one was going to play unmusical chairs. As if by signal, everyone unfolded the blankets they'd been sitting on and covered themselves layer by layer. Single Indians became small woollen pyramids. Groups of two or three became woven mounds swaying lumpily with the movement of the truck. Two-thirds of the eyes and faces disappeared altogether. But that was little comfort to me: the rest of the eyes became doubly oppressive, glinting darkly from narrow spaces in the blankets.

Even with all my clothing on, I shook with cold. At least twenty blankets lay around the truck unused. I was freezing in the midst of plenty. In most countries with Spanish influence, offered charity is usually considered an invasion of privacy, and for that reason it is seldom offered. Twenty men will cheerfully watch someone push his car along the road. But if that person asks for help, the men might well push it five miles for him. Charity had to be asked for with the head held high. But whether or not those rules applied to these Indians and me, I was reluctant to find out. Considering the last few hours, I could well be ignored or refused a request for blankets. If so, I would then have to take one: I was too outnumbered, too far from help, to risk appearing cowed by a refusal. And I considered that I was already close to giving that impression, having passively accepted the spitting, earlier.

Soon, I would have to do something. The cold was unnerving. The truck had been climbing steadily since Yoma. And now it began the steepest climb of all: grinding up a cliff-like mountainside on one of Peru's most insolent roads. Looking down the snow-spotted slope behind us gave the impression that we were riding an out-of-control spaghetti machine.

Suddenly, I was colder than I have ever been. Colder than I had ever imagined I could be. I resolved to try for blankets, but realized before opening my mouth that the sun was close to setting. Why was it taking so long to get to the turn-off?

'How far to the Huanchota turn-off?' I asked the nearest pair of eyes.

Silence.

'How far to the turn-off?' I repeated with a hint of anger. No one had spoken a word to me in eight hours.

'Back that way, thirty kilometres.' A blanketed arm rose in the direction of the low hills spreading out from the foot of the mountain below. I fought down a surge of panic. I couldn't walk thirty kilometres tonight. I had shaken my energy into the thinning air. Nor could I sleep on the mountain road; in this cold it would be my last sleep. I would have to stay on the truck until Aucane, twelve hours ride through the night. In which case I was going to get hold of four blankets, one way or another.

I took deep breaths; the important thing was not to squeak. 'A joke, yes? *Muy bien*. Now, how far to the turn-off?'

Four of the blankets unwound to show faces as well as eyes. Four mouths smiled with parted lips, then the blankets wound back and the eyes went on staring.

In the next few seconds, the truck came to the top of the climb. The turn-off to Huanchota was immediately obvious. And as the truck pulled up at the intersection I stood, slowly, and gazed about me. There were a few moments of silence as the driver waited for me to get off. But I didn't. I wasn't even aware of being lucky that they had stopped for me at all. I just turned on the beer bottles, taking in the raw details of the scene around me.

In every direction but the one we had come from was a vast, undulating, frozen wilderness. A plateau of snow and ice swept away to a mountain range so distant that it seemed to rise from beyond the earth's curvature. And yet, there was no haze to the distance, no out-of-focus relief to the eye. The black patches of bare ground served only as context-fixers, forcing reluctant comprehension. This was the high altiplano. Hearing of its dangers had in no way prepared me for its numbing impact on the mind.

'*Despacio*,' called a voice. The driver's head peered over the top at the cab end.

Behind him, on the corner of the turn-off, was a large mud building, the only evidence of life on the plateau. Even so, I would have chosen to remain on the truck if there had finally been real smiles on the faces of a few passengers. Real smiles would have indicated that they'd anticipated the effect of this place on a newcomer, and set me up for a leg-pull. A few smiling faces were showing now, just as devoid of humour as earlier.

I climbed down to the road.

As the truck pulled away I listened carefully for a burst of laughter. I would have understood that. Or even a scatter of jeering. There was nothing. The light was starting to fade as the truck grew smaller in the distance. But, by some trick of the optical nature of this high altiplano, the moving black dot stayed clearly resolved for as long as I watched it.

Dulled by fatigue and cold, I slowly realized that I should start moving. I'd become so cold now that I'd stopped shaking. I tried to start it again, but it wouldn't work. I turned to the mud building, where a man, a woman, and a boy stood in the doorway, watching. They didn't move a muscle as I came towards them. Fatigue dragged at my flesh and bones; my ribs felt no more substantial than long tooth-picks.

'*Buenas tardes*,' I greeted them. Please let them be friendly.

'. . . *Tardes*,' the man replied after a pause.

'Please can I sleep here tonight? I'm too tired to continue.'

'No.'

'I can't go on. I need a roof and a floor to sleep on.'

'No. There is a hotel in Huanchota.'

I turned in the direction Huanchota must lie, but saw nothing It was now too dark. Nor had I seen evidence of a town when the light was better, although it could easily be in a shallow basin.

'How far?' I asked.

'Half an hour, no more,' he urged. 'There is a hotel there.' Half an hour. It was possible. The map had shown Huanchota to be close, but the scale had been too small for accuracy. It was frightening enough just standing in this place, without launching off across it for an uncertain distance. My upper body felt sick with the cold now. If I didn't move soon, or find warmth, I would be in trouble. My chest felt paper-thin.

'What's the altitude here?'

He shrugged. 'Five thousand metres. A little less.'

Sixteen thousand feet! 'You're joking! There have been too many jokes today! I can't breathe! I'm not accustomed to the altitude! I must stay here!'

The woman and the boy took half a pace backwards. The man tensed; obvious, even in the dark. 'No.'

'Then let me buy food to eat on the way to Huanchota.' My voice shook, close to hysteria. I couldn't stand still any longer.

'No. There is a hotel in Huanchota.' For a moment I tried to see their faces, to understand why they were doing this. I considered marching inside and finding food, warmth, and a resting place for myself. But that way, I'd have to stay awake all night.

I stumbled out into the dark. A hundred yards along the turn-off my body shook again in violent, welcome spasms. I stuffed coca leaves into my mouth; and I shovelled unwrapped catalyst after them, so that it burned on the inside of my cheeks. For many hundreds of yards I walked wildly, flinging elbows, jerking knees, clacking at the foul mixture in my mouth and tossing the burning catalyst from one cheek to the other. As soon as I reduced the bulk of the leaves, I stuffed in more, going through mouthful after mouthful.

Then, I warmed, the shaking stopped, I no longer felt hungry and thirsty. I slowed down; my chest still hurt, but I felt right with the slower pace.

After five minutes I stopped altogether to take stock of the surroundings. Most of the stars were obscured, but I could see the outline of the road against the snow. I could make out individual clumps of tussock and rock a few feet either side of the road. Outside that was only the vague ghostscape, non-blackness of frozen plateau. The coca had given everything back to me except my courage. I stopped chewing because the sound deafened me. But still I couldn't listen for animals or men, because my heart went whoomp, whooomp, whooomp, making the clarity of my vision fluctuate in sympathetic rhythm.

One hour later, the howling started. I nearly fainted. It was coming from one animal, somewhere out in the darkness. It would be a domestic dog, I told myself; chained to a post by a hut. I pictured the dog, and the hut and the post, and felt better. There couldn't be any wild dogs or wolves this close to town, I said severely. And the town must be just around the corner. I kept walking. It seemed to me that my ears had grown, cupped and poised with their own intelligence.

Two minutes later, my ears took a sudden fix on changes in both direction and loudness of the howling. My picture of a dog, hut, and post, vanished; the animal was only a few hundred yards out and coming in on a tight clockwise spiral.

I sucked a gasp out of my throat as, for a moment, terror blinded me, roaring black across the eyes. Then I was calm. I drew my knife, taking a karate stance with one arm across my throat. Lower. Sensei's voice came to me. 'Bend the knee, Fleming. Beeeend the knee.' Knife low. Heighten senses. I didn't scan with the eyes. It seemed better to fix them on the apparent direction of the howls and rely on peripheral sensitivity to movement if I was wrong. Then I told myself that a wild dog, or wolf, really interested in supper wouldn't be so dumb as to howl at it . . . in which case, the animal had to be domestic. So I picked up a medium sized rock, switching with the knife to put the rock in my throwing hand.

Daddy! He's going to bite me.

It's alright. He just likes barking.

Lift me up, daddy. Lift me up. You go 'way dog! Me don't like you.

I saw it at the moment it stopped howling – a dark blob slipping over the dim white snow. At the same time, it flattened the spiral into a near circle. I couldn't see if it was a wolf, but its way of moving raised all the hairs on the back of my head and neck. The animal sized up the situation for only one third of the circle, then loped straight in, fast and low to the ground. Its only sound was a gravelled 'hhhhh' from the back of its throat.

I began to throw the rock when the animal was about seven human paces away. At the same time a sound rose up, unbidden, from deep inside me. The rock left my hand at a range of five human paces, launched with an animal snarl rasping from my chest and throat. The rock hit the dog at four paces, and my snarl ended.

I never saw the rock, not even when I had picked it up. The thump it made on the dog was so solid as to suggest a direct blow to the face or back of the neck. The dog yelped, and for a brief instant, its front half splayed in the snow. Then it ran snarling into the dark.

I held my knife towards the direction it had taken. In a few seconds the knife began to shake. My head shook with it, and my teeth ground together. I kept the same stance, rotating in a slow circle, trying to make my ears grow even bigger. Nothing. The results of the throw astounded me. I had the strong conviction that the accuracy was connected with my animal snarl.

I walked sideways along the road for a while, wiping coca-leaf saliva off my chin and cheek. In one way, the animal had done me a service; it had made me forget my fatigue. I stepped out strongly then, exhilarated with the absurdity of the situation. I had come ten thousand miles to walk on a sixteen-thousand-foot frozen Peruvian plateau on a moonless night and throw a stone at a dog. And all because of a dream. *Two* dreams now, I reminded myself, remembering the tussock of the flat rock dream. It would be interesting to look at the tussock I was passing now, when I could see it clearly.

The exhilaration passed as I began to think about the reception I could expect at Huanchota. I wondered if the family at the turn-off had any communication system with Huanchota. If they had, then I was in an ideal place right now for bandits. I knew so little. I unsnapped the clip of my knife, and walked with a thumb in my belt.

Two hours from the turn-off, I found a house. I came to within ten feet of it before I noticed it. There was another on the other side, and at least one more past the first one. No lights. I drew the knife, holding it under the front of the poncho, and trod softly between the houses. There was half an inch of snow underfoot here, deadening the sound of my feet. The houses continued, lining a curved street.

Fifty yards along I found myself close to a swathe of candlelight, pouring across the street. I couldn't understand how I could not have seen it a long way back. Men's voices curled out from the open doorway, upwards from a sunken room. I could see a box and a chair on a floor, four to five feet below street level. Steps led downwards from the snow around the door.

In the darkness, I lifted my sombrero and replaced it after removing the woollen hat underneath. The hat went into a pocket: I made a few adjustments to clothing, then brought the knife back out under the front of the poncho. I need you, Killer Gonzales, I thought, but just a little; let's not overdo it.

I stepped into the lighted doorway. It was a shop. Cluttered. Three men had been conversing; one behind the counter and two in front. None of them was near the door. All three were perfectly still, one with his hand in the middle of a gesture. Their conversation hung in the air surprisingly long after they stopped talking.

The one behind the counter began to move his arm towards something out of my sight. But the movement was easy to detect because it was the only one in the room.

'*Buenas*,' I said, looking at him. The arm stopped moving.

'*Buenas*.'

'Where is Huanchota?' Damn. Badly put.

'That way.' He jerked his head in the direction I'd been travelling.

'How far?'

'Fifty metres.' Fifty metres! And he wasn't smiling. All three had kept the same carefully blank face since they saw me. Under the circumstances I couldn't blame them. I would have to defuse the atmosphere. But I must not smile too soon. I looked pointedly at the arm still hovering near something I couldn't see. It rose slowly to the top of the counter. I sheathed my knife, letting them glimpse the blade.

'Don't be afraid,' I said. 'A man has to be careful.' That was a nice touch, I thought considering that my knees, properly harnessed, could have driven a paint mixer. 'Where can I stay for the night?'

'You can't.'

'Why not?'

'There are no hotels or lodging places.'

'Then will you permit me to stay at your place?'

'No.'

'So. You want me to die?' Good boy; almost no plaintiveness.

'It's not permitted,' the man replied.

I stepped a pace closer, looking him in the eye. He wasn't joking. Nor had he flinched at my movement. I spoke to him, to them, very softly: 'Señores, my body isn't adjusted to this altitude or this cold. If I stay outside tonight, I die. Tell me any place with a roof. I can pay whoever owns the roof, if they wish.'

'No. It's not permitted.'

I climbed the steps with one eye on the men and one on the street. Brotherly love and hospitality were as thin on the ground in this part of Peru as oxygen was in the air.

Fatigue had almost swamped me during the talking. It reduced my tracks through the snow to parallel scrapes. I wondered why I could see the marks, then saw that the moon had finally chosen to rise. It was a three-quarter moon, with a halo which I thought inappropriate for such bad timing. I stood in the snow for a while, not thinking about my problem; remembering the time long ago when I had looked into the mirror of a mental hospital trying to create a halo.

Cold began to catch up with the fatigue. I looked at the houses on either side. I could hear no noises from them, nor see lights. Back down the street two figures stood in the doorway of the shop from which I'd come. I began to move, thinking that on the next encounter I was going to insist and take my chances on retribution.

At the next slice of candlelight I found another shop, also sunk below street level. The similarity of surroundings was in keeping with the similarity of conversation. It was different in words, but identical in content, up to the point where they told me it wasn't permitted.

'*Who* doesn't permit it?' I shouted.

'The government, señor. The police.' He shrugged, his wife shrugged, and their two children shrugged. Daddy shrug, mummy shrug, and two little shruggers.

'Where are the police? Are they here? In this town?'

'Three doors that way.'

I counted three doors back, by carefully touching them in case I lost count. The third door spoke to me before I touched it. I stumbled two steps backwards, fumbling for my knife as it said, '*Que quieres*?'

'Where are the police, señor?'

'Here. It's me. Let me see your documents.'

I could see nothing of him. Not even an outline. 'Let me see your identification,' I said.

'Hah!' He was amused. He stepped out into the moonlight and swept his hand over his head. 'Look. Look at my haircut.' His tone was neutral; not liking or disliking.

Inside the one-room station, I held on to the end of an unmade bed while he examined my passport by candlelight. Someone had called him out of bed. There were two other beds in the room, occupied, each with a uniform draped over the end. They slept early here.

'Your passport has expired.' He raised his eyebrows, challenging for an explanation.

'No. Look. Here, it's been extended.' He nodded. He had already seen it. A test. A test.

'You're from New Zealand,' he said. His tone was still neutral.

'You're not from this town,' I guessed.

'No,' he said. 'It's obvious, yes?'

'Yes; because you're different, you're friendly,' I gambled. I pointed to the sleeping men. 'Even those two are more friendly than anyone I have met today.'

I won. Within ten minutes we were back at the last shop. My policeman suggested to the shopkeeper that it was permitted to give the gringo a place to sleep. He also suggested to the shopkeeper what a good idea it would be to make sure that the gringo was made comfortable and warm for the night.

In quarter of an hour I had a room to myself across the street. When they left me alone, I saw that the room contained a wooden table, two alpaca skins, and six blankets. Plus a lighted candle. I used some of my nylon cord to secure the door and both sets of shutters. I lay down on the table with the skins under me and the blankets on top. My head rested on my boots and my knife waited underneath the boot nearest my right hand.

The blankets and the skins gave me enough warmth at first. But, as the night grew colder, I rose uncomfortably towards the surface of sleep, living again and again through the attack of the dog and the snarl I had sounded. In that state of sleep my senses were awake to the slightest sound in the real world outside my bedroom. In the early hours, the careful crunch of the first footstep in the snow and shale outside spoke into my ear like a confidential whisper.

Between the second step and the third, I was on the floor with my knife. Before the fourth, I was against the wall on the hinge side of the door. Another two steps, there was a silence. Then someone began to push on the door. It squeaked, and the movement stopped. It started again; the door moving squeak by squeak until it came up against the constraints of the nylon cord. There was a quiet but determined shove, a creak in the doorjamb, and another, shorter, pause. Then, furious boots and fists crashed at the door, and heavy footsteps ran away into the snow.

I stayed by the wall, touching the back of the knife to my forehead. Upwards from my chilled feet, and inwards from the icy blade, came the certainty that I could have and would have killed another man. From now on, that certainty would go with me, parallel with my need to find the abbey. I found a gap in the shutter near my table-bed, and looked for the three-quarter moon. It still wore its halo. Yet I was certain the moon could not countenance a face to face meeting between Gonzales and Jesus. So I didn't attempt to arrange it. The two feelings would have to be kept apart; they would be reconciled in time – at the abbey.

I tightened the cord on the door, went to bed, and somehow slept well, dreaming only of the peculiar animal on the flat rock in the tussock.

4

Three children chattered conspiratorially outside my room. They sounded to be to one side of the door, on the far side of the street. I woke and dressed in an atmosphere of penetrating hush, then opened the door.

Three youngsters sidled a few steps further down the street, gaping in comic book fashion. I reflected that framing myself in doorways was getting to be a bad habit, so I smiled at them, finding that hunger and thirst made the exercise difficult. One boy shrieked and ran, trying to lead the others into a game of 'let's run away from the gringo'. But his companions didn't co-operate, so he came back. They flattened against the wall as I walked past them towards one of the town's two taps.

Water gushed continuously from the tap, preventing the pipe from bursting in the cold. The shock of the raw water on my face, and in my mouth and stomach, made me light-headed. Momentarily, the double row of attentive heads and shoulders protruding from the houses seemed like a mirage.

From the tap I continued to the end of the street, intending to examine a few clumps of tussock. But, once there, with a clear westward view across the altiplano, I forgot my immediate purpose. As it had done last night, the altiplano awed and frightened me. But this morning, it produced its trump card. Under the direct sunlight, the white wilderness was spectacularly, piercingly beautiful. It was both punishing and rewarding to let the eye roam at will. My brain numbed then tautened with final comprehension of details invisible the night before.

The altiplano wasn't, after all, completely flat, but a series of shallow basins. The nearest was a few hundred feet deep, at least ten miles to the centre, and another ten miles up the other side, trimming only slightly at the top for the next descent. The lips of the furthest basins, steepened by distance, rolled to the teeth of the altiplano, the far peaks. The slope behind Huanchota rose more steeply than most. The summit formed a too-close horizon, representing either the end of the altiplano, or the lip of yet another basin. Either way I would find out today, because beyond it lay

Yungacocha and directions to the abbey.

Hunger forced me back to my original purpose. And it took no more than a glance: the tussock was of the same type as the tussock in my dream. I became certain that a flat rock with a peculiar animal waited for me somewhere on this altiplano. I decided, then, that the whole venture only had value while I still had choice of action and free will. As I looked at the tussock, I told myself in conscious words, 'I choose to keep going. If I don't find my solution I might as well lay my body out in the snow because my spirit will already be dead.' With the vague feeling that my brain had just run itself into a neat circle, I turned back to town.

I went back to my room through a long gauntlet of eyes. Occasionally there was a wooden creak or a shuffle as someone shifted position to see me from a more comfortable position. Most sound came from my boots in the soft snow. Many of the faces reminded me of the attempted break-in last night. I concentrated on maintaining an aura of confidence, certain that it was a better defensive weapon than the knife. If something happened to take away what little confidence I did have, then I would be left with just the knife. And desperation.

The blankets and skins had been taken from the room and breakfast waited for me in the courtyard behind the shop. I ate large quantities of eggs and bread, both saturated in oil and fried black. Cold. The coffee was well oiled also, but it was strong and sweet. The three chickens running round my legs were more communicative then my hosts. And the shop-keeper looked alarmed when I offered to pay for the breakfast, I decided that his generosity was connected with another suggestion from my policeman.

'*Gracias por su hospitalidad*,' I said to the shop-keeper.

'It was nothing,' he responded automatically.

'*Gracias por su hospitalidad*,' I said to my policeman.

'It was nothing,' he replied automatically. He introduced himself as Juan. 'Now you want to go to Yungacocha, yes?'

'Yes. How far is it?' His two companions were dressing and listening at the same time.

'Twenty-five kilometres.'

'That close? *Muy bien*. When is there a truck?'

'There's no truck. There's only one truck a month to Yungacocha. But you can go with Eduardo and Mario. They're going after breakfast.' He introduced me. Eduardo and Mario were young, darkly handsome, and good humoured, but reserved in my presence. Like Juan, they had been posted here from a major centre. Because of their junior status, they were liable to 'Siberia' postings; hence Yungacocha, where they would stay for one year. They said they'd be happy to take me to Yungacocha in their friend's truck.

'Let's walk on ahead,' Eduardo told me after breakfast. 'Mario will catch us up in a minute.' Eduardo wore a small haversack, which puzzled me. But ten minutes later, Mario caught us up on foot, also wearing a haversack.

'What's wrong?' I asked.

'Nothing's wrong,' he said, feigning surprise.

'Where's the truck?'

'It's broken down. It's not working.'

'So what are we doing? Are we walking to Yungacocha?'

'It's only four hours.'

Pleasure at the subterfuge radiated from both of them, poorly disguised by an attempt at inscrutability. They waited for my decision with a patience that indicated they knew what they were asking of an unacclimatized gringo. Much less clear, was their motive. Why had they manoeuvred me into walking with them? Peruvian police didn't enjoy reputations for angelic honesty – they might be no more than uniformed bandits. On the other hand, they might just want the relatively unusual company of a gringo while they walked. That was much more likely, I told myself. If so, fine. If I must walk across the altiplano, who was I to turn down the offer of an armed police escort?

Obviously pleased with my decision, they set off at better than four miles an hour. I tired quickly, then picked up as my coca leaves went to work. When my pace evened out, I took care to keep at least three paces behind them. They, in their turn, didn't trust me and walked three paces apart from each other in order to keep an eye on me. It was a stable, mobile, geometric arrangement.

'Michael.' Eduardo used my English name. 'Are you alone in Peru?'

'No. I have eight friends waiting for me in Tarabamba.'

'Why do you wear the knife?' As if he didn't know.

'To cut things.'

'What things?'

'Bandits.'

Both laughed knowingly. Eduardo moved his hand fast and a knife appeared in it. With the blade between his middle and index fingers, he flicked the knife expertly from blade grip to handle grip, backwards and forwards with impressive showmanship.

'You see? I also have a knife for self-protection.'

'It's beautiful. But you already have a pistol. Why do you need a knife?'

'Sometimes to kill small animals.' Eduardo caused his knife to disappear.

'Up here?'

'Yes. Lizards, rabbits, birds . . . There's plenty of animal life here.'

'In this cold? What about the big animals?'

'Pumas. Wild dogs.'

'Wolves?'

173

'No. No wolves.' They showed no surprise at my interest.

'What do the pumas eat? The other animals are too small.'

'They eat llamas and alpacas from the farms – and people. But don't worry, Michael, the pumas won't eat *you*.' They laughed knowingly again, and I opted not to chase the reason. I stayed careful.

In one hour, we reached the end of the Huanchota basin and rested. Another gentle slope angled down in front of us; another basin. Yungacocha, then, would be on the altiplano.

The new stretch of altiplano was a more compact version of the vista behind us. The mountains were closer on this side, no higher than normal, but dominating the fierce landscape. At first sight, the new white lands were devoid of any colour or movement that hinted at life. There was a shocking beauty in the apparent absence of life and death. The illusion emphasized the constancy of impermanence and change.

As if to underline what it had taught me, the altiplano produced a small black dot in the middle distance, moving from right to left. At first it appeared to move across the snow, but that was an effect of the road in that place, curving behind swollen ground on the edge of a lake. The dot changed direction, curved towards us, appeared on the road and grew larger. It was feeding on the road – a rolling snowball on negative film.

It resolved into an Indian on a bicycle. He halted beside us, as incongruous as if he had been pushing a baby buggy. I expected Eduardo or Mario to ask for an explanation for the bicycle.

'*Documentos*,' Eduardo said.

The Indian produced his papers. He sat astride his machine, not at all surprised to be asked for documents in the middle of the altiplano. Nor did he look surprised at the company the police were keeping. His bicycle was old, but showed no signs of rust. I picked up a handful of snow from the roadside, and it poured through my fingers, dry as dust.

As the Indian pedalled off towards Huanchota, I saw a grey-green lizard, a foot long, watching us from between two stones.

'What's that called in Spanish?' I asked.

'*Es un lagarto*.' Mario drew his knife. 'Shall I kill it?'

'No. I only want to know the name.'

'Ah! You like animals?' Mario looked tolerantly surprised.

'Yes.'

The lizard blinked, bringing his lower eyelids to meet the upper eyelids in the middle of the eye. Its expression was that of granite wisdom. Arcane knowledge.

'Is it poisonous?'

'No.' Eduardo replied. 'But if you see one a metre long, very ugly, that one has a poisonous bite, but it's good to eat.' He grinned. 'Like

174

a woman.' He carefully watched me as he walked, curious for my reaction.

The good humour and the jokes increased, building bridges between the corners of the moving human triangle. The tight configuration loosened as the distrust lessened. I offered them some of my coca, Eduardo accepted the leaves but refused the catalyst, explaining that he liked the leaves just for the taste. Experimentally, I made a defamatory remark about the desirability of owning such tastebuds as his. He laughed with pleasure. Eduardo was the talkative one; inquisitive and eager for comparison between two cultures. Mario was just as interested, but inclined to let Eduardo do the questioning. Both kept an interested eye on the sweat on my face, and the shake in my legs. But they didn't slacken the pace.

'How much is the beer at Yungacocha?' I asked.

'There *is* no beer at Yungacocha. No alcohol.' They both looked sorrowful.

'The shops don't sell it? You're joking.'

'There *are* no shops. Yungacocha is a private alpaca station. *Una estancia*. Many people and very few supply trucks.' Eduardo's face grew longer with the self-inflicted reminder of how dry the next year was going to be.

'So what do you drink?'

Eduardo glanced swiftly at Mario, then assumed an innocent expression. 'Oh, Cuzceña or Arequipeña.' Very popular brands of beer.

'But you said there was no beer,' I protested, leaping right into the trap and thumping the trigger.

They roared with laughter, breaking their stride to slap their thighs. Then they explained in high glee: 'Cuzceña' and 'Arequipeña' also translated as 'the woman from Cuzco' and 'the woman from Arequipa'. I matched their laughter, and they were delighted that a gringo could appreciate such jokes. With expressions of religious reverence, they lifted imaginary buttocks to their chins and sipped delicately at the frothy liquid therein.

'Michael.' Mario pronounced my name as Meekaaell. 'You have a woman in Tarabamba where your friends are?'

I decided to tell at least one truth. 'I have a girl-friend in La Paz.'

They stopped dead in their tracks. 'She is a gringa? She's waiting for you?' Words tumbled out in a stream of frustrated wonder and envy. 'What's she like? She's very beautiful, yes? She has fair hair? *Es una rubia*? Why is she not here? There aren't any eligible women on the altiplano. We don't get women until we get back to Tarabamba. Are you going to marry her? You must bring her to Yungacocha and introduce her to us. Does she speak Spanish like you?'

'She understands it better than me.'

'Aaahh.' Appreciative nods. We walked in silence for a few

minutes while they contemplated the vision inflated from my words and their questions.

Soon, they increased the pace, striking out on a cross-country short cut. In the warmest two hours of the day we were sometimes in snow, sometimes on spongy ground. But the respite from the cold would only last another few minutes. A bank of clouds had begun to march on the sun. I would welcome the return to cold; too much of my energy had been run off as sweat. With the increased speed, I had to shorten my talking, concentrate on keeping up.

Eduardo and Mario had energy to spare. Mario began to sing, in a clear and rich baritone. It was a song of passion. Perhaps inappropriately to our recent discussion, it was the non-sexual passion of brotherhood and friendship.

> *Tu eres mi hermano del alma realmente un amigo,*
> *En todo camino y jornada estás siempre conmigo,*
> *Aunque eres un hombre aun tienes alma de niño,*
> *Aquel que me da su amistad su respeto y cariño.*
> *Recuerdo que juntos pasamos muy duros momentos*
> *Y tu no cambiaste por fuertes que fueron los vientos.*
> *Tu corazon una casa de puertas abiertas.*

'You are my soulbrother, really a friend. Through all my ways and journeys you are always with me.' Mario's voice sounded strange, for all its quality, thinned by the sound-greedy altiplano. Someone must have had a record player or shortwave radio at Huanchota. 'Amigo' was the current popular song of South America.

Sometimes Eduardo joined in the singing, but he preferred to ply me with questions. When Mario had finished 'Amigo' Eduardo said, 'Eh, Michael, you sing?'

'A little.'

'You will sing now.'

'No. My voice is extremely ugly.' If I started singing now, I would shortly be doing it face down into a snowdrift.

But they weren't fooled. They pushed the pace even harder. It became a blatant endurance test for the gringo who hadn't yet learned how to make his lungs work efficiently. Between Mario's songs and the occasional duet, they encouraged me to talk.

'Tell us about the abbey.'

'Juan told you.'

'But there's no abbey on the altiplano. We would know.'

'Perhaps you're right. But someone at Yungacocha knows. Who would that be?'

Mario shook his head. Eduardo flung his fingers outwards negatively. 'We were there for a month last year. There is no one.'

A way of getting a rest occurred to me. I stopped near a small exposed rock. 'Momento! Tell me what this animal is called.' With the rock I drew a snow-picture of the peculiar animal on the flat rock in my dream. I gave a rough outline of the raccoon's tail, the rabbit's body, and the mincing paws of the squirrel.

'You have *seen* this?' Eduardo asked. '*Es una vizcacha*. They're very rare. It's forbidden to kill them now.'

'I haven't seen it except in a dream. They live on the altiplano?'

'*Si*. But they are hard to find.'

A vizcacha. So there really was such an animal.

Eduardo frowned as he brought his stride back into rhythm. Then he turned and spoke, aggressive with embarrassment: 'This is an adventure for you, yes?'

'Yes.' I only wanted them to stop talking.

'You see many things. Learn many things, yes?'

'Yes.'

'So, it's not important if you don't find the abbey?'

But I had no energy to give him my best answer. I just said, 'I'll find it.'

They nodded to each other, and increased the pace still more. They took another cross-country short cut, then split up at the foot of a low, saddle-shaped hill. Mario went straight over the saddle; Eduardo told me to follow him and headed round the foot of the hill. Our path was longer than Mario's but designed to bring me within three hundred metres of Yungacocha before I saw it.

I let out a groan of relief. Eduardo nodded, pleased. 'A good surprise, yes?' I blew a kiss to the cluster of drab grey buildings now within crawling distance. 'You will sleep in the police station tonight,' Eduardo said.

5

Of the seven men at the table, six wore boots, mufflers, woollen hats, and greatcoats with upturned collars. They breathed through gloved, cupped hands, sending gushes of white steam over the litter of coffee mugs and empty plates. I was the odd man out, with bare fingers protruding from under the extra poncho I'd borrowed from Eduardo. I warmed the fingers on a slow mug of coffee, occasionally pressing them against my ears, which froze inconspicuously under my woollen hat.

Nothing could be seen through the window except the snow, falling thickly and vertically in the early evening light. It was confusing to the senses that so much movement through the still air could be so utterly silent. It was as if the snow had mastered the air, freezing it into an immobile and passive medium.

The temperature inside the bare wooden room subdued conversation, even though the meal was over. The luckier men had bed-mates at night, but, normally, meals and clothing were the only sources of warmth. There was no electricity and no fuel.

And for that reason, the meals, at least for these men, were generous. At almost every sitting the plates came with potato soup, followed by more potatoes, rice, alpaca meat, and sweet coffee. Once, the alpaca was replaced by altiplano lake-trout; and, twice, the coffee came with water crackers. And these men could afford such meals. The room was the dining-room of the headquarters of Yungacocha, and the six men represented the upper echelon of the station.

To my left were Mario and Eduardo, quieter than I'd seen them so far in my two days at Yungacocha. Eduardo rested his chin on his fists at an angle off-setting the lines of the snow he stared at. Mario lounged in his chair. He played with the faint smile on his mouth, occasionally allowing it to pull his head into a series of tiny nods. He had met a girl yesterday afternoon, not long after arriving in Yungacocha, and had announced today that his heart had been pierced by an arrow.

To Mario's left, at the end of the table, glowered Sergeant Federico Paumani Alvarez. When Federico sat his six-foot-six-inch body down to the table he still seemed to be standing. He also dominated the table with the tree trunk that passed as his chest and stomach. His hands, six inches in front of his eyebrows, constantly wrestled each other. They were capable of crushing a man's skull. The eyes that looked past the combatant hands promised that such action was indeed a possibility for anyone unfortunate enough to cross him. At first sight, he looked to have as much use for social graces as Genghis Khan when questioning the captives. But I had seen good evidence of his sense of social poise: he had not asked to inspect my documents until this morning. And he had asked with a distinct air of embarrassment, knowing that I had arrived as a friend of Eduardo and Mario.

To my right, at the other end of the table, sat the owner of Yungacocha. He was an Indian, with the weathered face of those of his race passing from middle age into old age. He spoke only when necessary, with that rare form of authoritarianism that reflects two-way respect. His foreman, also Indian, sat to his right; a younger man, usually more vocal than his boss, but, for now, accepting the subdued atmosphere brought by the cold and snow.

To their right again, almost opposite me, was a third Indian, a man of at least seventy years, who had been introduced simply as Benito. Throughout my four meals in that room, Benito had not spoken one word. He had not even moved his head enough to jiggle the chullo flaps over his ears. Apart from eating, his only physical movement was with his index finger and thumb, occasionally turning a fork upside down, two or three times in succession. And yet Benito now attracted more of my attention than any of the others. He puzzled me, because, for all his surface inactivity, his deeply set eyes followed everything and missed nothing.

I had noticed particularly, that, when the abbey was discussed, Benito always kept his eyes on me. To some extent, it was natural. Every man at the table knew I had spent the whole day questioning the station workers. But his face seemed too impassive for the amount of time he watched me. The subject of the abbey was a dying one now, of course; the other five men had told me from the beginning that no one at Yungacocha knew of such an abbey. The only reason the subject had still been alive at the midday meal was the tolerant amusement my failing efforts provided. Perhaps my status as guest depended on how long they were amused. So far, this meal, the abbey hadn't been discussed at all.

'Eh, Miguel. Still no success?' Federico, not hanging on my predictable answer, threw the last of his coffee into the cavern between his teeth, and sniffed loudly to prevent a drip starting in his nose.

'Not yet.' I was aware that Benito had his eyes fixed on me again.

'Perhaps you'll find it,' Federico grunted, heaving to his feet. 'But I think it would be faster to build an abbey, yes?' He shook his head in amused resignation. Eduardo and Mario began to leave with him. So I left the table too, because it would have been inappropriate not to leave with the men who were paying for my meals.

Benito watched me as I went out the door.

I followed the three policemen back towards the barracks. The snow fell more thinly now, allowing a complete view of the bumpy white expanse that was the village of Yungacocha. There were some thirty loosely scattered dwellings, housing about a hundred people. Except for headquarters, each building seemed to have shrunk, lonely under the oppressive white blanket. For the policemen, this treeless, warmthless place was a more convincing Siberia than Siberia.

'What does Benito do?' I asked Federico. But he didn't answer; he had stopped to look at two pigeon-like birds huddling on the edge of the church roof. He pulled a sling-shot from his pocket, uncovered a pebble with his boot, and fitted it into the sling without taking his eyes off the birds. He set his jaw and fired, the stone exploding the snow in the two-inch space between the birds. The birds flew away, dissatisfied with the dubious sanctuary provided by the church.

Federico grunted. 'They're good to eat,' he said, stuffing the sling-shot back into his greatcoat. 'Benito? He's an old man. He looks after the alpacas sometimes.'

'Why does he eat at headquarters?'

'Who knows? He has always been there.'

Next to the station headquarters, the police barracks was the most luxurious residence in Yungacocha. It boasted three plaster-lined rooms, three iron-frame beds, and a two-way radio. In the entrance room were thick files of official police communiqués, framed quotations guiding the actions of good policemen, and a table and chair – both too weak to sit on. The room to the left of the entrance was empty except for more files, a bench, the kerosene cooker, and two pots. The room to the right was the most decorated room in the village. Pistols, rifles, machine-guns, batons and ammunition belts hung over the three beds and next to the tiny shrine in the corner. In the shrine, a statuette of Jesus smiles forgivingly at the armoury about him.

Last night I had slept in the bed closest to the shrine. Eduardo and Mario had top-and-tailed, leaving me to try for warmth under five alpaca blankets and four ponchos. Tossing and turning under that weight had been difficult, and my muscles had begged to be spared the effort.

Federico had reeled into the bedroom late last night, proving with each step that Eduardo and Mario might not suffer too badly from dryness in the coming year. Federico had capacity left to be concerned for my state of health. 'Hey, gringo. Are you well?' he had roared wetly into my eardrum. And, getting a positive response, he had thrown up in his chamber-pot and gone to sleep under one

180

blanket. He only survived the night because Eduardo threw more blankets over him.

Now, the light outside was beginning to fade.

I collected a pot from next to the cooker, and went out through the snow towards the village tap. Close to headquarters I saw Benito shuffling away from the dining-room, his old legs sending small dry puffs of snow into the air with each step. His feet didn't quite rise clear of the four-inch layer.

I left the tap and went to his side.

'Señor.' I had never spoken to him directly before. 'Señor. Can I speak to you?'

He stopped with back bent to the sinking snowflakes. He didn't look surprised, but screwed up his eyes as if the snow was striking his face in flurries.

'*Que quieres*?'

'Not here. In your home, if that's alright.'

He didn't say 'Yes' or 'No', but began walking again, in the same direction as before. He led me to the east side of the village, towards the alpaca corral. All the alpacas were inside for the night, with a wall of stone between them and the pumas. As I passed the gate they were bedding down, with the snow on the ground for their bottom sheet and the snow on their shaggy backs for the top sheet.

Benito stooped into a hut close to the corral, leaving the door open behind him. He prepared to light a candle, using the outside light to see what he was doing. I waited outside the door, uncertain, but he gestured impatiently, motioning me on to a wooden chair. He closed the door, placed the candle on a low-level shelf, and sat back on his bed – the only other piece of furniture in the one-room hut.

'*Que quieres*?' he repeated, leaning his back against the wall.

'You're the man who knows about the abbey. I've come to ask how to get there.'

He gazed at the tip of the candle flame. 'Yes. I know about the abbey.' He nodded absently, bringing a hand up to pick at a scrap of food between his teeth. His teeth were good, showing none of the punishment inflicted by the coca leaf. 'You have read a book, yes?'

He looked at me directly, then; his eyes hidden pools in the side-long candlelight. 'Señor, there is no such abbey. The abbey is not made of earth or stone. It has no physical existence.'

He sat up from the wall and spoke to the disbelief on my face. 'There have been others like you. Always they are directed to me. But you must understand, the abbey is esoteric. *Completamente esoterica*.'

I studied his face, his body posture, for every possible clue.

He continued, rubbing his elbow at an itchy spot on the outside of his thigh, 'You look for the abbey because you think it will provide you with truth for the soul and peace for the mind, yes? But that is the exact nature of the abbey. It's of the mind only. Your search is a search of the mind.'

I was unable to speak.

'This search has been difficult for you already, yes? You have learned many things? *Por supuesto*. That is your abbey.' He leaned back against the wall, as if fed up with the subject.

There was a long silence. I wished I was warmer so that I could think clearly. It seemed to me that Benito was saying too much. He was trying to feed me the only verbal argument that could make me give up.

'No!' I said, too loudly. Then, more quietly, 'No. I understand what you're doing. This is a screen, to send away those who are half-hearted about finding the abbey. I need to find the abbey. I must find it. Let me tell you why.'

I told him about my dreams of the Crucifixion and the walking on water, and the preaching on the hill. And I was afraid of his reaction to that, so I explained the second dream. 'And in the last few weeks I have dreamed about a strange animal that sits on a flat rock in tussock waiting for me. It's the tussock of the altiplano. I have been told that the animal is a vizcacha, and I'm certain that I'll meet it close to the abbey, I have walked that far in my dream, and I'll walk that far in reality when you tell me where to point my feet.'

He pursed his lips, looking first at me, and then at the floor. He gave a slow and melodramatic shrug, rounded out with a sigh.

I waited.

'You must ask at Pasceña,' he said.

'Who do I ask?'

He spread his hands in a don't-know gesture. 'Ask everyone. Be patient. Perhaps there is someone there who knows if the abbey exists.'

'But you just said . . .' My voice was half-pleading, half-angry.

'Ask at Pasceña.'

I realized that this refusal to commit himself must also be part of the screening process. With the thought, my control returned. 'Thank you. But it's a long way to Pasceña. Are there trucks?'

'Very few. There will not be another one for many weeks.'

'Then if the weather clears tonight, I'll walk there tomorrow. It's possible to walk the distance in one day?'

'Yes. But the way is long and very difficult. You must take great care.'

But I dismissed his warnings as yet another screening device. 'Then I'll need to take food with me for the journey. Is it possible for me to take some meat and potatoes? Who should I ask?'

'I'll talk to the station owner,' he said. 'If the weather's good, and you still want to go, talk with me after breakfast.'

*   *   *

The three policemen asked no questions about where I'd been. I waited some time, pretending to pore over my road map, then told them that I intended to try my luck in Pasceña. Eduardo and Federico drew me two separate maps. Both contained different detail in some sections, but didn't, at that stage, seem to contradict each other. Both maps were from hearsay only; none of the three knew of anyone in Yungacocha who had been to Pasceña.

They were adamant that I couldn't lose my way. They had heard that the road was clear all the way to where the tracks stopped, and the mountain track from then on was also clear. They were certain.

'Does the road branch off anywhere? Or the track?'

'No. No forks. It will be easy. Six hours, no more.'

'How high is Pasceña?'

'It's not high. It's very low. Pasceña is half-way down from the altiplano to the jungle. Breathing will be very easy in Pasceña, even for *you. Bastante oxigeno para los gringos.*'

There was no need for top-and-tailing that night. At eight o'clock, Mario bounded out the door with the spring of a stag in the season, and a voice suitable for the male lead in *Don Juan.* As he disappeared into the night, he punctuated his aria lines with kisses to the snow, the sky, and the darkness.

And while he was discovering a few of the advantages of love in Siberia, I slept badly. There was not one second of my dreams that I didn't recognize and know as a dream; but they gripped me as never before, mostly with fear.

6

Morning. Wednesday morning. The sun rose into a clear sky. In its first hour, it found a challenger in the altiplano; an adversary which parried the aching light with chilling mastery. The body of the brilliant challenger swept continuously, unbrokenly, in almost every direction. The very perfection of its composure wrought mischief on the eye and the brain. It distorted the shape of the white world, bringing the nearer mountains so ridiculously close that the illusion proclaimed its own deceptive nature. The brain and the eye danced on the snow, but not in step.

It's been eight days now, Julie. I hope you're safe; dear God I hope you're safe. I want to see your smile again: the one you left me is so pale. Don't be afraid. I'm alright. I'm alright. I love you.

After breakfast I waited in the courtyard outside the dining-room, assuming that Benito would wish our conversation to be private. But he came out in the company of the station owner, and spoke to me immediately: 'You're going.'

'Yes.'

'You want food.' Benito's voice was distant and harsh.

Disconcerted, I tried to determine the relationship between him and the station owner. But I could only tell that Benito didn't speak like a man who is in the presence of his boss.

'Yes,' I said. 'If that's alright with you.' I used the singular form of 'you', but looked at them both, uncertain of the situation.

'Come with me,' the owner said. Leaving Benito standing in the sun, he took me to a storehouse, in the corner of the courtyard. There he counted out ten water crackers, placing them loose in my hands.

'Twenty soles,' he demanded.

'One moment,' I said, and walked back to Benito. 'I think there's been a misunderstanding.'

'No misunderstanding,' said Benito.

'Twenty soles,' repeated the owner who had followed me.

'But I can't walk a whole day at this altitude without something more substantial than water biscuits.'

'Perhaps.' Benito shrugged with studied indifference in his old, bowed shoulders. 'That's your choice.' The station owner extended his hand for the money. Fourteen cents. This was a play, an act. I debated asking if I had offended them in some way, but turned, instead, to look at the altiplano through the courtyard entrance. I had a slab of chocolate and a quarter-pack of wine biscuits left over from two days ago; a miserable supplement for water crackers.

I faced Benito again, hurt by his indifference, and disturbed by the change in him. 'Water biscuits aren't enough.'

His expression said, 'I don't give a damn.'

'Then let me buy more crackers.' I pleaded

'There are no more,' said Benito.

'Twenty soles,' said the owner of Yungacocha.

I paid him, and he promptly walked away. I looked into Benito's eyes for many seconds, but could find no hint of encouragement except that he had allowed me to look.

I left him without a word or a nod, placing the crackers in my shoulder bag as I went.

Mario led me out into the altiplano. He pranced and postured across the snow, contemptuous of the toll exacted by a winter's night of spring fever. But he didn't neglect his body. Other love victims might eat little, sigh much, and claim not to live by bread-crumbs alone. Mario, on the other hand, had just eaten with gusto the fastest, biggest breakfast in Yungacocha. The energy must have gone straight to his leg muscles. Anyone coming across his tracks in the snow later today would probably turn pale and cross themselves.

Mario stopped at two parallel depressions in the snow: wheel tracks. There, he began to say goodbye.

'When does this track join the road?' I asked.

'This is it. This is the road. But don't worry, it's clear right to the end.' He shook my hand, screwing his face against the glare, becoming unexpectedly sober. 'Suerte amigo. Walk strongly. The altiplano isn't kind at night.'

I pushed myself, not trusting the cheerful estimate of five hours given me by the policemen last night. The snow didn't slow me: surprisingly, the depth off the road was only six inches, and the depth over the wheel tracks down to three or four.

I used the woollen hat as snow goggles, the loose weave stretching enough for me to see where I was placing my feet. The system worked well until an hour out of Yungacocha. Then, my solitude in the vast white space fluttered my breathing. At first, it was comforting to have my eyes behind the woollen hat. I realized that I was only using the age-old ploy of the child who hides under a blanket, reasoning that if the head is hidden, the monster can't see him. That was fair enough, I thought. The monster is normally in the child's head, so it follows that a blanket over the head will play havoc with the monster's vision.

But that piece of reasoning led me inevitably to the thought that

185

pumas, wild dogs and bandits couldn't all be figments. The woollen hat began to feel oppressive. Every hundred yards, I snatched it off, only to replace it, afraid of snowblindness. It was a complicated manoeuvre; I had to double-shuffle the sombrero and the woollen hat, occasionally juggling them with coca leaves and catalyst. I built up a shrill suspension of claustrophobia and agoraphobia; monsters in their own right, charging and receding from me on the otherwise soundless plateau.

The coca made the experience tolerable until I found paw prints crossing the road. Even at first sight, the prints were too big for a dog. As a journalist, I had once been sent to investigate large paw prints on a beach north of Christchurch. I had examined them alone on a foggy beach, then walked nervously through the sand dunes to phone the story through from the nearest store. Before I made the call, a customer at the shop had laughed and insisted that the prints must be from his dog, a Great Dane, that he'd been exercising on the beach. When I took him back to see the paw prints he turned white and said, 'No sir, that's sure as hell not my dog', and beat me off the beach. It turned out to be a tiger, escaped from a circus.

These snow-prints were smaller, but still too big for a dog. They were blurred by perhaps half an hour's melting, but it was still obvious that there were no claw marks. Which meant a cat. Puma.

I put my woollen hat into the shoulder bag, and spent some time hunting with my eyes for a tawny shape against the snow. Nothing. I kept going. The hat stayed in the bag; and, regardless of snow blindness, my hands refused to even put it on my head, let alone cover my eyes. I wondered why I didn't turn back. While continuing to scan the shallow ridges and dips around me, I indulged in a fantasy. I pictured myself riding a skinny nag through the snow, tilting at windmills. Don Quixote had all the virtues, I thought: honesty, courage, wit, chivalry . . . He was also completely crazy.

After three hours, I came to the fork in the road. I had just been congratulating myself that bare ground was starting to appear under the hot sun. So, I was in the mood to believe that this little problem could be solved quickly. I swung my head back and forth between the two possible routes looking for the one that was obviously wrong. My head began to feel like a mechanical toy, so I dragged out the two hand-drawn maps. A quick study showed that the differences between the maps corresponded to the differences I could see from where I was standing. Both roads went in almost opposite directions, into terrain too different for them both to have the same destination.

I had an hour and a half to spare. If I didn't have an answer in that time, I'd have just enough light left to return to Yungacocha. Rather than make a random choice, I sat with eyes closed at the fork, trying to open my mind to some suggestion of the correct path. After five minutes, it seemed to me that one of the roads arranged on my mindscreen glowed slightly.

I followed that road, eating a third of my biscuits on the way. I felt worse and worse about the choice as I went along. The road began to climb into low hills. It shouldn't climb, I told myself. After thirty-five minutes, I turned a corner to find a condor standing on the road, some distance away.

'How do you do,' I whispered. But, not unreasonably, it didn't answer. Nor did it fly away.

Carrion eater. I turned back immediately, shivering, angry at myself for allowing superstition to influence my actions. On the way back to the fork, I ate another third of my biscuits, and almost all of the chocolate. At the fork, without making a conscious decision, I took the other route, instead of returning to Yungacocha.

After one hour, the road reached the first of the mountains, turned left to avoid them, but began to climb, forced upwards by the now tilting altiplano.

'It's not supposed to climb,' I informed the clouds in a reasonable, matter-of-fact tone. Clouds! I hadn't noticed them. At the rate they had formed, I could expect bad weather in an hour, and no visibility after dark. I was committed. There was no way to return to Yungacocha before dark.

Far ahead, a long way off the road, I saw two human figures. Not knowing what their reaction to me would be, I went through an elaborate approach, using rocks and a low hillock as a screen. Regardless of who they would turn out to be, I was drawn to them out of loneliness, only taking care that they should not prepare for my arrival.

But it was a wasted effort. They showed no surprise when I stepped out from behind the hillock. I assumed they must have seen me when I first saw them. They hardly glanced at me. They were poking sticks around under the bank of a small stream.

'Buenas,' I said, out of range of the sticks.

No answer.

I moved around them to higher ground. They kept poking the sticks under the bank, but shifted slightly to keep me just visible.

'What are you doing? Catching trout?'

No answer. But I noticed then that three small trout lay on a spread of exposed moss in the tussock close by. One was still twitching.

'Are they for eating?' I persisted, and that ridiculous question got a response.

'Si.' Silver flicked out from the bottom end of the bank, sending one man swiftly to the closest shallows, where he scooped up his flopping prize.

'Which way to Pasceña?'

The frantic fish rose between two hands, which pointed in the direction I had been travelling.

'How long?'

'Two hours. No more.'

I stayed with the fisherman for about half an hour, poking my arm under banks for them, and picking fish out of the shallows. They gave me a place in the fishing, accepting my efforts without comment. After a while I remembered that I was supposed to be going to Pasceña.

'*Adios.*'

No response.

I only went five yards. Then I came back, overcome by the fact that some of the fish I'd taken out of the water were still twitching. I killed them quickly with the knife. The two men looked strangely at each other, but still said nothing as I went away.

It didn't occur to me to ask where their hut was. It didn't occur to me to bring away a fish to eat on the road. Nor did it seem strange to me that I had accepted their estimate of two hours at face value, or that I had then forgotten Pasceña for half an hour.

When the snow started, I told myself there was no need for the plastic square. I decided that it was too cold for the snow to melt on me. I enjoyed the sight of the white layer thickening on my right shoulder. Every now and then I took the sombrero off to admire the snow on top of it. Each time, I laughed and put it back on my head carefully, so that none of the snow spilled off.

I felt a dreamy lightness, and I told myself that the feeling was appropriate because I had matches in my shoulder bag just like the little snow-girl in the fairy story. The altiplano kept tilting upwards, which I thought incorrect, because if the billiard table isn't kept level, the ball tries to run downhill. A peculiar sensation touched my stomach at times, to which I couldn't put a cause. But I decided that it couldn't be fear.

At two o'clock, I came to the end of the altiplano.

Without realizing it, I had allowed myself to climb to the top of a pass, which must have been a good fifteen hundred feet above the level of Yungacocha. That meant that I was now at seventeen and a half thousand feet. The snow was falling more thickly. I had four hours of daylight left, and I was only now about to begin the descent.

Seventeen and a half thousand feet. While I walked, I imagined that I was a huddled frozen body on the peak El Plomo. When the first modern climbers reached the summit of El Plomo, they found that the Incas had beaten them to it by five hundred years. In fact, a boy of eight or nine years old had beaten them to it, and he was still there, preserved by the cold. To that boy had come the honour of being sacrificed to the sun. The modern climbers found him with a pouch of coca, which had numbed him against some of the pain of his death by freezing, and a little bag with all his fingernail parings and baby teeth.

I saw all my teeth falling out, and my fingernails crumbling away at the ends. I opened my eyes to watch it all hitting the ground and realized that, although I was still on two feet, I was huddled on one spot. With a cry of terror, I stumbled across towards the highest point of the pass, dragging at the coca bag. If I couldn't reach Pascena, I could at least survive a night out if I found a low enough altitude.

I only went a few steps from that spot. Then I stopped again, my mouth full of leaves, Beside the track was the flat rock. I whimpered at it. My legs rocked, surging to move. It was *the* rock; it had the right shape, and the tussock beside it was in exactly the right position. But where was the vizcacha? Where was it?

I became petulant. 'Where are you?' I cried, twisting back and forth. 'Where are you?'

Nothing came. I began the steep descent. At first my head throbbed with the thudding from my boots, but I soon thought of myself as a billiard ball rolling down the bedspread that slopes from the end of an unmade bed to the floor. I thought that up on the sheet of the bed, a little animal must be hopping on to a flat rock to keep a late appointment. He did it continuously; not up and down, just up.

Thousands of feet below the pass, the snow turned to cold rain, melting the snow on the poncho. My sombrero turned soggy, and limp, which I thought to be a great pity. So I cried about it for a while.

At some unknown time, I saw a man on the track ahead of me. But he disappeared while I was turning a loop in the track. I remembered being told that someone would appear on my path at the right time. 'You're not supposed to disappear again!' I yelled to the empty spot. But I laughed bitterly, because there was no doubt about my path at all; it was perfectly clear at this point. It occurred to me that I had voluntarily chosen to walk on the crooked and narrow. So I laughed for the river which roared down the valley below me, much straighter, and much wider, than my path.

Sometime after dark, the billiard ball stopped rolling to urinate, having suffered from hydrostatic pressure for hours. 'Basic law of hydrostatics,' I said to the rain apologetically. 'I don't want to steal your thunder, you understand.' I giggled, and threw the front of the sopping poncho over my shoulder in order to commence pressure reduction. The movement made me stagger and caused a commotion a few feet away. I had stopped near a pen of llamas. I giggled at them, bowing as I hauled the poncho back into position.

I didn't think to look for a farmhouse. I giggled my way down the track I could hardly see.

I was standing on a grassy mound, led there by the track.

A little girl wandered across the far side of the mound with a pitcher and a lighted candle. The tin reflector on the candle showed me a wall with a door. She was walking towards the door.

'Where's Pascena?' I said. And I collapsed on to the sodden grass,

189

with the girl's terrified candle-lit expression fixed in my mind.

Then I was surrounded by a ring of bodies and bright faces. I took them to be bandits. '*Ladrónes!*' I shouted, and thrashed around, trying to draw my knife.

The last thing I noticed was that a man was holding my upper body in his arms. He was blowing gently on to my mouth saying a word in English . 'Brother, brother.' He rocked me like a baby, breathing air into me and saying in Spanish. 'Be still brother. There are no thieves here.'

'My knife. My knife.'

'Be still, brother, you don't need your knife. There are no thieves.'

'Is this the abbey?' I whispered to him.

'No brother. This isn't the abbey. You're in Pasceña with friends. *Se tranquilo.*'

7

In La Paz, hundreds of miles away, Julie's head began to buzz. All
morning she had sat in her room, chilled with apprehension. No
pictures in her head, just the certainty that something was going
badly wrong. She took headache tablets, and they might as well have
been sugar pills.

Round and round in her head went the argument: what could she
possibly do? It would take days to get to Yungacocha. When she got
there what then? There was no guarantee that she would find the
abbey contact. Even if she did, and supposing she found out where I
had gone from there, would her presence help? It could hinder. If it
wasn't too late already.

But no, she thought. If it was too late, she'd know.

She forced herself out on to the night streets, and walked. She
wandered into the Plaza San Francisco, following people-currents
until one took her up the steps of the Cathedral. For a few seconds she
was uplifted by the sound of hundreds of singing voices echoing in the
marble spaces. Then she realized that they were singing to the tune
she knew as 'John Brown's body lies a moulderin' in the grave'.

She returned to her hotel where the manageress was keen to con-
sole and advise.

'You must lean on your faith,' the woman said. 'But you are right,
it is possible to know such things of a loved one far away. When my
mother was dying a month ago, I was in the United States. I knew
exactly what the telegram would say before it was sent, and I got
there just after she died.'

Julie laid her map of Peru out on the counter of the travel agency.
'What's the fastest way I can get to Yungacocha from here?' she said.

8

At first, I thought I was in a deep, warm bath. But my feet hurt, detracting from the perfect luxury; so I tried, unsuccessfully to lift them out of the water. The failure woke me. Rude memory arrived simultaneously with realization that I was in bed. Beyond the end of the bed was a white tin box, painted with a large red cross. The unexpected, familiar sight caught in my throat.

'He's awake,' a voice said.

The room was large, containing two sets of bunks, my single bed in the corner, and plenty of open floor. Three uniformed men stood between the door and the bunks, forming an arc focused on me. Police.

'Are you well, señor?' I knew the sound came from the oldest man, but didn't catch his lips moving. The three were like statues, well suited to the bare lifelessness of the room.

'Yes . . . well . . . thirsty.'

With my awakening the statues came to life. In less than twenty minutes I was propped against the bedrail, sipping hot coca tea. The senior policeman held me by the shoulders, warning me sternly not to gulp the liquid. No liquid had ever tasted as vital or satisfying, though the cracks in my throat seemed large enough to prevent any tea from reaching my stomach.

Through the steam, I saw my knife, poncho, and sombrero, lying on one of the bunks. I felt a pang of separation from them, which the older policeman must have detected, because he scooped up the pile and placed it on the end of my bed. He looked about forty years old, but moved with almost adolescent vigour. The sombrero was little more than a sodden rag. The same policeman grinned sympathetically at me and picked up the limp circle of cloth for my inspection. Then he helped me off with my belt and sheath, rejoined them to my knife, and looped them over the bedrail behind me.

'No more bandits?' he inquired with wry solicitude.

'No.' I responded, pained at the memory.

'And pumas,' he continued.

'Pumas?' I didn't remember that one.

'Last night you heard a cow, and you thought it was a puma. You

192

wanted to get out of bed to fight it, but there was only me here, so you tried to fight me.' He bared his teeth in huge enjoyment.

'*Madre de Dios*,' I muttered, raising a hand to cover my face. The three men laughed, the younger two shifting their bodies into a more relaxed stance. 'Are you the one who called me "brother"?' I asked the oldest.

'Yes, it was me. I saved your life. You were nearly dead, but I revived you. I am Cristóbel.'

'Then I'm alive because of you. How can I thank you?'

'By getting well, brother.' He placed his hand firmly on my shoulder. 'How do you feel now?'

'Much better. Like a new man. I'm Michael.'

He introduced his younger colleagues, Simón and Tomás. Both were in their first years as policemen. Both had been too shy to speak, standing further back than Cristóbel, watching the conversation behind bushy, stylish moustaches and bushy black eyebrows.

Shortly, Cristóbel nodded to Simón who left the room. While he was away, Cristóbel and Tomás stood about with hands in pockets. They kept a conversation going, but avoided the questions an unexpected stranger might anticipate. I leaned outwards to look under my bed. But, once again, Cristóbel understood, and dragged my boots out for me, then replaced them. I pulled my feet out from under, removing the socks to find out what was so painful. Five toenails were a purple-black colour. I would lose them, but at least there was nothing seriously wrong with my feet. My toes gave Cristóbel more food for inconsequential conversation.

The light through the window was that of late morning. Simón returned with a thin-faced, slightly built man in his late forties. He wore a grubby poncho and sombrero, but carried an air of authority that he didn't try to amplify or diminish. He also carried hot coffee and fried batter, which he delivered into my hands during his introduction. Then he stood back, even further than Simón and Tomás, passively observing. His name was Fernando.

'You're alone,' Cristóbel commented.

'Yes.'

'Where's your pack? Up the valley?'

'In Tarabamba.'

'*Verdad*? You've walked from the end of the road, yes?'

'From Yungacocha.'

'From Yungacocha?' Cristóbel glanced back at Fernando, his expression seeming to request confirmation. Fernando confirmed nothing. His expression didn't change. Cristóbel quickly returned to the matter almost at hand.

'You have come to look for the abbey,' he stated.

'Yes.'

'There is no abbey.'

I already expected it, so I was studying Fernando's face as

193

Cristóbel spoke. But I learned nothing. He hadn't altered his expression since entering the room.

'I'm not the first to come looking for it?'

'No.' Cristóbel continued. 'Since 1974, fourteen gringos have come to Pasceña looking for the abbey. You are the fourteenth.'

'To how many did you give directions to the abbey?' I asked. But the effort was wasted, because all attention was taken away from me by the appearance of a breathless teenage boy at the door.

'The truck! It has crashed off the road near the pass!'

The authority in the room leapt off Fernando's shoulders and on to Cristóbel's. With the style of a universal policeman, he extracted from the boy that the town's supplies were scattered down the mountainside, and that the driver was unhurt. In that order. He told me to rest well, then departed taking Simón, Tomás and the boy with him.

'How often do the trucks come?' I asked Fernando, who was about to leave also. The trucks came seldom. So, whatever answer he gave, it would be double-edged: one for the dependent town of Pasceña, and the other, of blunted iron, for me.

'Sometimes not for three months.' He watched my expression for a moment. 'Can you walk?'

'Yes.'

'Then you can look at Pasceña this afternoon, and have dinner with my family this evening.'

Pasceña is a mud spot on a violent green sea. It hangs between the crest of a ridge and the river, between the altiplano and the jungle. About thirty huts season the tiny shelf, which, although the best village site, threatens to slide its grey cluster into the river. All around Pasceña, even on the steepest slopes, is the low, green vegetation that eases the valley into the jungle. Condors hover over the valley, often directly over the village, as if hoping for a body, even there. Their magnificent wings are so perfectly in control of the upward sighing air, they seem to have been painted on to the sky.

For the first two hours, a group of children followed me around the village. An adult eventually sent the children to where they could only watch me from a distance. And, by mid-afternoon, there were times when I moved around unobserved.

It was in one of those times that I came across a boy playing soccer in the plaza, on the town's only piece of concrete. His manner of concentration on the plastic ball indicated that he had been waiting for me. He was about twelve, with unusual reluctance to stare.

I sat on the steps a few feet away and waited, looking out and down the valley at the jungle. When the ball came in my direction, I picked it up and threw it back. Ostentatiously, he trapped the ball with his feet, in silent rebuke of my use of hands. I kept my eyes on him, but feigned a look of temporary distraction by the view. He was very good; a twelve-year-old expert. In my school days he would have been star of our senior team, just on the basis of his ball-handling.

He allowed it to slip again. I leapt up, trapped it with my feet and returned it from the inside of my left foot: an imitation of his own style. I returned to my seat and my view. He stood silent for half a minute, rolling the ball in a tiny circle by describing that shape on the top surface with his big toe. Then he used the same foot to roll and flick the ball into his hands. He seated himself, also on the steps, but a careful eight feet away. There, he also watched the view, spinning the ball on a vertical axis provided by his two index fingers.

'You play football?'

'Used to,' I said. And both of us continued to find interesting things in the distant jungle.

He spat on the ball, drew the spittle into a circle with his toe, then drummed the ball between fingers and concrete so that the wet patch described a circle relative to his hand.

'Who taught you to handle the ball?'

'No one.' He shrugged with modest pleasure. 'Where are you from?'

'Nueva Zelandia.'

'Ah! Holanda!'

'No. Nueva Zelandia. *Es diferente.*' Ever since Peru had played themselves into World Cup contention by drawing with Holland, I had had the same reaction.

'Oh. They have schools in . . . in your country?'

'Yes. And in Pasceña?'

'No. The teacher went away. There was a strike.'

'What did you learn when he was here?'

'Singing and writing. About the President and Peru . . . and Lima.'

'Which way is Lima from here?'

He used one hand to direct the current path of his ball (down the left leg and up the right) and pointed up the valley with the other hand.

'That way.'

'And Yungacocha?'

He pointed in the same direction.

'And the abbey?'

He shrugged, and concentrated on the ball. 'I don't know.' He stood up, and began a push-bounce-shuffle technique off the bottom step.

'You're following the World Cup?'

'*Sí*. Peru has the best team in the world.'

'But how can you follow it without a radio?'

'There are radios in Pasceña. And Cristóbel has a watch. What time is it?' He clamped the ball and came closer to inspect my watch.

'Half-past three. You have a radio for hearing music?'

195

'No. They are for speaking.' He threw the ball backwards over his head, but with a forward spin. It bounced slightly forward, and, without turning, he heel-tapped it back over his head and into his right hand.

'The ball is part of you. You are a master,' I admired.

'*Sí.*' He confirmed the fact with dignified, serious pride.

Like every other building in Pasceña, Fernando's house was made of mud and thatch. Unlike most of the others, his house contained three rooms sufficiently large to form most of a small courtyard. A rock wall completed the enclosure.

One of the rooms served as bedroom, dining-room, and storage room. A wooden bench bisected it wall to wall, with one end disappearing under a factory-made table, which leaned tiredly against the wall. On one side of the bench was an iron-frame bed, used only for storage. On the other side was a double-size sleeping bed: bamboo frame supported by rocks. I could see no evidence of a radio.

Fernando instructed me to sit on the bench, and peered at my bare feet. 'Very sore,' he commented.

'*Más o menos*. I think two nails are infected.'

He brought a medicine box from the factory bed, producing from it cotton wool and a bottle. The liquid inside was some form of antiseptic and drying agent, a brilliant red colour. Fernando watched with polite humour as my feet turned into something resembling suet dumplings decorated with glacé cherries.

'Very pretty,' I said ruefully. And he smiled openly for the first time. He indicated that I should drop the used cotton wool on the floor, then he climbed over the bench to return the medicine box. His right shoe fell off, and that led to my giving him enough of my braided nylon for both of his shoes. He walked out into the courtyard and back, delighted with the new laces. But after that one display of pleasure, he didn't look at his shoes again.

In the long, silent wait for the meal, he remained standing because the bench was too close to me, and the sleeping bed too far. He was perfectly comfortable standing that way, passing the time with strain, in a manner that seemed like the way the village of Pasceña passed its own markless time.

I gazed through the open doorway to the courtyard where the late afternoon rain had turned into a steady, cold drizzle. An old woman shuffled into the yard carrying firewood, the miserable rain splotching squarely on to her bent back. She arranged some of the sticks under a sheet of corrugated iron suspended on poles against the courtyard wall. Then she journeyed to a room near ours, returning with a container and a flaming stick. She poured a thick, clear liquid on to the sticks, set light to them, then returned the liquid to what must have been the kitchen. Thereafter, she sat under the shelter, befriending the fire and coughing in the smoke the corrugated iron threw down on to her head.

'My wife's mother,' Fernando said.

A baby girl crawled out into the rain from the kitchen. Progress was difficult for the child, because her one garment caught between her knees and the uneven rock slabs. At first, this obstacle only made the child more determined; so much so that her knees became redundant, and she waved an impressively soiled bottom at the rain as she went. But the combination of an inexperienced body and cold mud and rock became too difficult. She sat back on her bottom, sniffled twice, then began to howl with her face turned up to the rain.

A small boy, about four years old, also appeared from the kitchen. His objective was to catch sight of me; and he achieved that at a safe distance by walking straight out into the rain near the baby and turning to stare through my doorway. The little girl beat forlornly at the rain with her arms, shifting her voice into top gear. The rain pushed a forelock of the boy's hair down over his forehead.

'My son,' Fernando said. 'And my daughter.'

Daddy, I want to play outside.

It's raining.

I like playing in the rain.

No. You're in your good clothes.

You are a naughty, naughty daddy!

A young woman in pigtails appeared from the kitchen, and retrieved the adventurous crawler without a word to the child or a glance in our direction.

'My wife,' Fernando said. The pride in his voice had been equally generous for all his family.

I kept my attention inside, then, on a magazine picture above the desk. It was a centrefold picture; an artist's impression of one of the Spanish methods of discouraging Inca unrest. Four conquistadors were using their horses to pull an Inca Indian apart. A long line of chained prisoners watched the event, waiting for their turn. The artist had focussed their eyes on the present victim, at the moment the ropes tautened sufficiently to just lift him off the ground. Their expressions were focussed much further away, to some point in the distance where their deaths marched inexorably towards them.

Fernando's wife entered with the first course, her pigtails swinging over the plates. She walked across the room, placed the food on the desk, and retreated – all without taking her eyes off Fernando's shoe-laces. When she had gone, Fernando squatted on the door stoop to eat. First course was soup with chunks of potato and pig-meat sausage. Main course was the same, but without the soup. Thick, sweet black coffee followed, coaxing the heart to illusory peace.

'Thank you,' I said to the woman, when she came to remove the mugs. But she lowered her head still further, and moved quickly out into the rain between our room and the kitchen.

'She doesn't speak Spanish,' Fernando said. He spent some minutes in silent observation of the old magazine pages that lined part of one wall. Then he said, 'Why do you want to find this abbey?'

The responses I had previously given to this question suddenly seemed inadequate; so I didn't answer immediately. There was no hurry. While I waited for a better answer to occur to me, I felt my stomach twist with the conviction that I was very close now: only one more physical effort and I would be there.

The baby began another foray into the rain. As I watched it, my gut tightened hard. I wanted to put my body through the last effort the way a starving man wants food.

'I need to find it the way a starving man needs food,' I said to Fernando. He nodded and continued to scan the magazine pages on the wall.

Later, he lit a candle and placed it on the floor. He scraped a smooth area into the dusty clay, then drew a careful sketch with a twig.

'You must return up the valley, the way you came, as far as the pass. But once you get to here, you go this way, then this . . . These lines are ridges, very low. You come to another pass here, with a small hill shaped like this . . .' He drew an outline. 'Once here, you must be careful to walk to the left of a rock shaped like this . . .' He drew another outline. 'And after that, you will find a path.' He glanced at me, then waved his hand at all the sketches. 'Perhaps this will take you where you want to go.'

Perhaps!

'But I will end up only a few hours away from Yungacocha,' I said. But, as I spoke, my frustration changed to understanding. Fernando raised his eyebrows, in humorous acknowledgement of the beauty of the arrangement.

Then he turned serious. 'I must warn you. At this altitude, climbing back up the valley is not the same as coming down. There is a strain on the heart. You must be careful, particularly because you have no equipment – you have to do it in one day.'

Scare tactics, I thought. 'I'm young, my heart is strong,' I said.

'Perhaps. But you must still take care. Even a young heart needs to work in sympathy with the lungs. Leave early in the day, travel slowly.'

'I will. I'll leave the day after tomorrow. Saturday morning.'

'No! That's a mistake. Stay for a week, two weeks, until your body recovers. Then go.'

But Fernando's baby was, once more, howling in the rain. And last night, during the Crucifixion dream, my hands had hurt for the first time. And the vizcacha! Yes, I thought, this time, I'll see the vizcacha. Everything directed me back up to the pass. 'I must go the day after tomorrow,' I said. 'I'll take care, as you say. But I must go. I'll leave at four-thirty in the morning and move slowly.'

After a long pause, Fernando said, 'Very well. It is for you to decide. You will need breakfast before you go, yes?'

'Yes.'

'You will come here that morning. We always begin cooking before that time.'

'Four-thiry?'

'Yes.'

'Could I buy food from you, to take with me? And perhaps coca leaves and sugar?'

He frowned. 'It is possible. I will see. But food is scarce, especially now that the truck has crashed. And meat is expensive, even here. And you may change your mind about leaving so soon.'

9

Not a single word was exchanged between the three people in the cab.
Julie would have liked to identify the cause of a dry 'sshhkk, sshhkk'
sound from the load, but her companions had made it clear that
conversation wasn't part of the deal. Nor was friendliness in any
detectable form. For all that the couple looked to Julie's side of centre,
they might as well have been wearing blinkers.

But Julie decided that she had to count herself lucky. Her companions would obviously have put her on the back if the load had been
any smaller. But considering the way other truckers had treated her
back in the Plaza, these two could well be the most agreeable company north of Tocache.

After three hours of silence, she made calculations in her head.
Then she spoke directly to the driver, startled by the sound of her
own voice. 'Señor, I want to get to Yungacocha tonight. You can take
me that far?'

'No.'

'Of course I will pay you more money, for the extra petrol.'

'Petrol is expensive now.'

'Yes. You are right. I'll give you four hundred soles more.'

'That much petrol costs two thousand soles.'

Yes. Yes, she thought. But I must not seem too rich, or too desperate. She shrugged her shoulders, and found something interesting
outside her window. 'I'll stay in Huanchota.'

'For fifteen hundred soles, I can take you.'

'Impossible. Eight hundred soles. No more.'

10

I ate all my Friday meals with Fernando. He made no direct pleas for me to delay departure. But, in spite of my obviously improving health, his manner still indicated that I should change my mind about leaving the next morning.

The rest of Friday, I spent alternating between barefoot walks through the village, and resting on the bed in the barracks. During one of the latter times, late in the afternoon, Simón and Tomás overcame their shyness. They seated themselves on the lower two bunks opposite my bed, obviously intending to talk. I realized that no one had asked to see my documents.

'Miguel. You go in the morning,' Simón said, knowing the fact already.

'Yes.'

'You're disappointed that there's no abbey?'

I thought quickly. 'No, I'm not disappointed. I learned many things on the way to Pasceña. I'm happy.'

But their minds hastened to other things. 'You have a girl in New Zealand?'

'Yes. But she's in La Paz.'

Both men leaned forward, lower arms resting across their knees. 'This is true? Why are you not together?'

'Because she didn't want to come here.'

'She permits you come here alone? It doesn't worry her?'

'Yes, she's worried. But she doesn't let or not let.'

Both men looked astounded. Tomás said, 'They do this in your country?'

'Some of them.'

'It's different in Peru,' Tomás said with finality. Then he added: 'And you don't know what she's doing in La Paz. That doesn't worry you?'

'No,' I said, wondering if I was showing red stripes as I came out of the tube.

There was a short silence. My turn. 'The gringos that come to Pasceña – are they all looking for the abbey?' And this question had a remarkable effect on the two men. They shot to their feet and gesticulated around the room, both talking at once.

'Stop!' I said. 'What are you saying?'

'There was an Americano who came here with *six* women. All Americanas! The Americano was tall, very tall; perhaps two hundred and twenty centimetres. They stayed here, in this room. And the women were dancing *naked*!' Simón stopped to watch my reaction. Tomás sat down on his bunk and got up again.

'What were they doing here?' I asked, but Simón had started talking again.

'Betty slept here, Audrey slept here, Angelique slept here . . .' He stabbed variously at the bunks and areas of the floor.

'Angelique?' I questioned. Surely they weren't making the whole thing up.

'. . . And the Americano slept here on the floor between Lizzy and Barba.'

'Barbara,' I suggested. 'What were they doing here?'

'They talked to everyone. They wrote in their books and made drawings of Pasceña. The Americano spoke Quechua. And he played a guitar while the women danced naked!'

'Perhaps he was from a university. They weren't looking for the abbey?'

'No.' Tomás leaned against one of the top bunks, captured by a new line of thought. Then he swung on me. 'The bachelors in New Zealand live in separate houses, yes? And they have parties, yes?'

'Many of them. Have you been reading . . .?'

'And single women come to those parties, yes?' His voice poised for a crescendo.

'Ah. Yes, but . . .'

'*Desnudos?*'

I winced. 'Sometimes. And then not until they get to the party.' I added that I hadn't been to any such parties.

'Oh.' Tomás's enthusiasm folded. 'Why not?'

'No one invited me. I would have been too embarrassed when I was younger.'

Simón beat an authoritative finger at me. 'When you return to New Zealand you must tell all the single girls that there are two extremely handsome men, very lonely, very eligible, waiting for them in Pasceña.'

'I'll tell all of them,' I promised.

Cristóbel stomped in. He sat heavily on a bunk, tired from an errand up the valley. He'd spent much of the last day supervising sorties to recover the town's supplies from the head of the valley. 'Hola,' he said. 'What are you talking about?'

'He says he's embarrassed at nude parties,' Tomás grinned, jerking his head at me.

But Cristóbel had other things in mind. He smirked once, so as not to be rude to Tomás then frowned at me. 'You still go tomorrow morning.'

'Yes.'

'It's too soon.' He stood up, in spite of his fatigue. 'Tomorrow, you'll get to the top of the pass, your heart will feel bad, you will fall over and die. Eh brother! It's better to wait until you're strong again.'

'I *am* strong again. And I *have* to go tomorrow.'

He must have anticipated my answer, because he pulled a sachet of colourless liquid from his pocket and said, 'Then take this. Put it in your water-bottle when you are near to the top. It's adrenalin. It'll make your heart keep going.'

I took the sachet, looking at him, 'Thank you, brother, I already owe you my life.'

'Perhaps you will change your mind in the morning,' he said flatly. 'But if you don't . . .' He paused. 'This is a good thing you're doing. *Tienes cojones*. But it's also stupid. *Loco*.'

'Yes.'

'Good luck, my friend. I hope we meet again. And if I see your body again, I want you to be in it. Understand?'

I went to bed early that night. And not long afterwards, Tomás also settled down for the night. Ten minutes after pinching the candle, he shouted out, '*Documentos! Documentos!*' And a minute or two after that, he sat up and spoke to me through the dark.

'Miguel, are you awake?'

'Yes.'

'Was I talking in my sleep? Did I shout something?'

'You shouted "*Documentos*".'

'Oh.' There was a short silence. Then, 'This is very bad to talk during sleep?'

I said something I hoped was reassuring. He grunted and rolled over and was soon asleep. Then I slept dreamlessly for the first time in many weeks.

11

The owner of Yungacocha frowned at the wall, tapping his index finger on the desk. Then the movement halted as he came to a decision. 'Wait here,' he said harshly, and strode through the door.

Julie wanted to retreat within herself for a rest. Ever since that brief glimpse of the pre-darkness altiplano, she had been talking sweetly to her panic-stricken lungs, convincing them that La Paz had given them adequate acclimatization. And this office was little comfort; the walls were bare and the candlelight reflected relentlessly off every surface. The windows were black with the night.

She closed her aching eyes, but still felt the lap and flick of the flame. So she walked in circles, touching a boot to her pack on every circuit.

After half an hour, the door opened. The station owner entered, followed by old man.

'*Que quieres?*' the old man demanded, wasting no time on preliminaries.

'I'm sorry to interrupt your sleep.'

'You're looking for the gringo. Why?'

'He's sick and in danger. Can you tell me where he is?'

The old man sat in the chair opposite the desk. He was so frail in the frozen chamber, he seemed little more substantial than the breath that flashed and vanished in front of his face. 'He's not here.'

Julie thought he seemed hardly aware of why she was here. She knew how important these moments were and kept her voice even. 'He asked you where the abbey is. Is that where he's gone?'

'The abbey doesn't exist. It's esoteric. A challenge from the spirit. *Completamente esoterica.*'

'I'm not looking for the abbey.'

The old man stared at her. 'Why not?'

'Because . . .' Julie paused, and her heart hammered. 'Because I have already seen much of your abbey in another place. And I know I'll see more of it in other places as I grow older.'

The old man watched the floor in front of his knees and snorted. 'Mmmmf.' He spoke to the other man in Quechua, both showing traces of amusement.

'Wait here,' the old man said. And Julie was left alone again.

When they returned, they looked at her in a way which seemed different from before.

'Tomorrow morning, you will come here,' said the old man. 'Late in the morning. We don't know yet if tomorrow is the right day. But, if it is, you will have to walk across the altiplano for a few hours. A boy will go with you, because the way from here is hidden and complicated.'

'Thank you,' Julie whispered. 'Thank you, Señores.'

12

At four-thirty in the morning, Fernando's house was black as coal, and silent. I beat at the courtyard door a long five minutes before candlelight sprang at it from the other side. Fernando's wife pulled the door aside and paddled back across the yard, without word or motion to follow. I followed.

In the kitchen she oiled fire-sticks in a clay hearth. As she reached for the candle, Fernando strolled in, yawning and tucking shirt to trousers. '*Hola*,' he greeted me. Then he strolled straight back outside. '*Momento*,' he said on the way, '*poco de piss*.'

The fire-sticks came to life, throwing slow red light on to the woman's face, and coiling smoke up to the closed ceiling. The first crackles from the wood mingled with a splashing sound from outside.

Fernando returned.

'There's nothing prepared,' I said, without accusation.

He shrugged; a thin motion in the firelight, as if made with razor-blade shoulders. 'It was impossible. The supplies have . . .'

'Alright,' I said resignedly. 'I understand why. But it won't work. I'm leaving now, anyway. Do you understand? I have to do it today. I can't wait any longer.'

Fernando pushed tangled hair away from his eyes. 'You won't even get to the pass without food.'

'I have half a packet of biscuits,' I said, and started to leave.

'Wait. Have breakfast with us first. It will only taken ten minutes to prepare.'

I stayed. The sight of last night's potato and pig-meat-sausage soup lifted the gloom that had been settling on me. I picked out two chunks of sausage, and started to open my shoulder bag. But Fernando halted my arm. 'No, there's no need.' He lifted three plastic bags from beside the hearth, and held them out for inspection. Cooked llama meat, two bread rounds, and a few ounces of coca leaves, with a paper twist of sugar to sweeten and cool the catalyst.

In the first hours I moved fast, taking advantage of the relatively low altitudes to gain time. Before dawn slipped over the pass, my muscles had warmed to a much lower level of pain than I had expected. Even my toes kept low profile, held away from the front of the boots by the constant upward climb. Before sunrise, I consciously gathered will-power from every part of my body, and focussed it on the effort to be made before sunset.

Pasceña stretched further up the valley than I had thought. Three nights earlier, I had walked past many farm houses, not realizing how close I was to safety. Now, after dawn, the houses were turning people out into the fields. Groups of llamas swung their stately heads as I went by, astonished by my passing.

Not long after sunrise, as the climb steepened towards the head of the valley, the altitude ambushed me with the leaded weights I had worn three days earlier. I stopped worrying about pumas and wild dogs. The much more dangerous enemies would be my body and my conscious mind. At first, I watched out for the crashed truck, but soon gave up that effort also as wasted.

By nine o'clock I was half-way up the head of the valley, about two thousand feet below the pass.

Until then, I had made the pass the day's major intermediary target, reasoning that everything beyond the pass was either flat or downhill. But, as I tired, I began to look for closer targets. I thought myself from resting place to resting place. Each became a prize to be won and consumed.

Each change from rest to movement demanded intense mental concentration. Once moving, I would pick a spot three to four hundred yards away, and use its promise to lever me up the slope. Once there, the view of the valley would be a degree more impressive than the time before, a shade more worthy of prolonged admiration.

The ingrained habit of the five minute rest always overcame that creeping logic; it pulled me to my feet, oblivious to argument. But I had no habit that controlled how often I 'took-five'. The distance between resting places became shorter.

Eventually I had to admit that my method was coming to pieces. Increasingly, I caught my body in the act of having stopped between resting places, without permission. As well, my body wouldn't tell me how long it had been standing idle, or why it hadn't put the wasted time to better use by sitting or lying down. Instead, it gazed vacantly at the bright shale at its feet, basking its head and shoulders in the unusually warm sun.

I began to rhythm-step, forcing my feet to hook up with the count. *One*, two, three, four. *One*, two, three . . . On each rest, I hung my head between my knees, less and less tempted by the sight of condors hovering below me. The vizcacha is waiting for you, I told myself. He'll applaud you with those little paws, because when you get to the pass, the worst is over. Okay, up you get. *One*, two, three . . .

Five hundred feet to climb. Seventeen thousand feet above sea level. Clouds reached out for the sun much earlier than usual, and fog settled inside my head.

I'd once been ordered to run five miles with boots, rifles, and pack. At the end of the run, we were supposed to clamber over a six-and-a-half foot wall, with the equipment. For the whole five miles I had fretted about that wall, trying to conjure up the power that positive thinking was supposed to sell me. When the wall loomed up, I had to trample on a sniping suspicion that my equipment and I were about to become an untidy heap at the bottom. But I whistled over the wall. So did most of the platoon. Not that the sergeant laid on any champagne; he just demanded to know if we'd learned anything.

Now, with the pass rearing just a few hundred feet above, I tried the same approach. But it got out of hand. I made it to the top and over as Tarzan, Mr Universe, Roger Bannister, James Bond, and, finally, Superman. I got a bit carried away with myself on that last one. When I came to, I was taking another unscheduled rest stop. Flat on my back.

Alright! On your feet, Brown! Knock off the rocks 'n cocks, the socks are *on*. Any man still in bed on the count of three cleans the bog all day. Christ, Brown! If you can't swing it faster than that, I'll cut if off and clean my rifle barrel with it. *What's funny, Brown*? Did I tell you to laugh? From now on, Brown, if you even want to breathe in, you'll wait till I give you permission. Understand? Shuffle your trotters you disgusting little ham. Christ, man! You think sore feet is bad! When I'm through with you, your feet will be like Christmas Pudding in July.

By the time the slope eased for the last two hundred feet, an enormous hollow had developed inside me. Every rest stop, I ate bread or biscuits, chewed more coca, and drank adrenalin water, willing it all to fill the hole. I knew that food wouldn't do it, but food was all I had. I stopped eating when I was in danger of vomiting.

When the top of the pass shuffled on to the horizon, I used the siren sight to beckon me. I filled the hollow in me with the fantasmagorical anticipation of how it would feel to stand on top. Every step of the way my brain automatically projected the slope into vertical distance remaining, because that was the only dimension that mattered. Fifty feet. Forty. The vizcacha would be almost in sight now. Unthinkable that he might not be waiting. After all, this was the last big effort. In forty vertical feet it would all be over. Twenty feet. Stop. Go. Ten feet.

With half a dozen steps remaining, I looked for, and found, the flat rock, a few dozen yards away on the other side. I had difficulty focussing. But the vizcacha was undoubtedly sitting on top; a fuzzy, vertically-elongated blob.

At the highest point, I halted, swaying and giddy. I could have stopped the movement, but was unwilling to apply the effort needed. I swallowed more adrenalin water, keeping sights fixed on my patient friend on the rock.

Walking towards him on the slight downgrade felt like my first time away from the handrail on ice skates. But, I had made it. Obviously nothing had gone wrong with my heart. The remaining twenty or so kilometres would be a Saturday afternoon stroll by comparison.

I halted scuffily, squarely facing the vizcacha six feet away. His winter coat was much more sleek and beautiful than I expected. He minced his front paws at me, expressing polite, dignified interest.

'*Buenos dias*,' I said, also unwilling to take hasty liberties with our relationship. Apart from a hesitation in his dainty paw movement, he didn't discourage me in anyway. I noticed that the flat rock had grown an ice-needle down one side.

'I did it,' I boasted. 'How about that, then?'

This demand for recognition produced an astonishing reaction. He stopped the tuck-and-cuddle movement of his paws, and began batting the air, chittering loudly. This is what the little pugilist chittered to me: 'Here. This is for you.' And immediately afterwards, a tiny duplicate of the ice-needle on the rock entered my chest, left of centre.

'Oh,' I said carefully. 'Oh. That wasn't fair.' But the vizcacha hopped leisurely away to another rock, where he boxed the air again and chittered in emotional support of the correctness of his action. After that explanation he fielded his paws, returning them to the polite mincing of before. Knitting needles wouldn't have looked out of place in those paws. I pictured him sitting with the women who knitted while watching the guillotine at work.

'Why did you do that?' I called across the cold ground to him. 'It's not supposed to be like this.' But he spurned the pathetic appeal by hopping away through the patches of snow.

For ten minutes I sat on the road, talking myself into calm. The argument went like this: obviously I could not be my normal, rational self at this altitude, especially considering the strain of arriving. Therefore any decisions I made were suspect, probably based on worthless, emotional pseudo-logic. In that case I should look for a less emotional, more rational cause for the ice-needle in my chest. If I could find such a cause, I could stop worrying.

Then I had it. Of course! It was heart-burn from all that fast eating on the way up. The diagnosis was heartburn. The remedy was time, and the prognosis excellent.

I set off across country, following Fernando's directions. I wallowed in righteous indignation at Fernando and Cristóbel for their unnecessary scare-tactics. Since when did a man of twenty-nine years have to worry about heart trouble?

I was so absorbed in willing the chest pain to fade, that I didn't see the herd of pure white alpacas until I was twenty feet from the nearest bunch. Pure white! They so entranced me that I attempted to count them. They moved around so much, I ended up with only a 'guestimate.' Six hundred. Pure white, and no sign of a herdsman.

Then I realized that not one alpaca had shown any reaction to my presence.

'Hullo there,' I called out. But not even the nearest animal, only fifteen feet away now, gave a twitch of notice. How perfectly white they were. A horrible commercial came to mind, but my temples went cold, so it wasn't funny.

I walked again, wanting to leave the herd behind. But I couldn't help seeing that one animal in that vast herd wasn't white. It was a youngster, perhaps the only youngster there, coloured the usual autumn browns. It was running frantically through the herd, bleating, looking for something. In the same moment I realized that, apart from the youngster, I had not heard the faintest whisper of sound from the entire herd; not even from those cropping the grass close by.

In the next half-hour, I rhythm-stepped, just to rid my mind of the chest pain and the alpaca herd. I tried to hypnotize myself into a non-thinking, non-feeling state. Even the count, I tried to turn into a vectorless, numberless pulse.

The ice-needle began to expand. It pushed nothing aside, it simply enveloped everything in its path, around it and through it. At the same time, another pain, vice-like, seeded in the centre of my chest. When that pain, too, could no longer be ignored, I classified it under the category of 'interesting' on the grounds that I couldn't think of any single organ under the centre of my chest.

I pulled out the water-bottle to finish off the rest of the adrenalin water, spilling some down my chin and poncho as I walked.

Daddy. Me have spilt *all* the milk. Heh, heh; aren't me a silly billy. Andrea! Stuart!

The afternoon snow started.

Brown! Keep in step, you horrible little man. If you haven't got any sense of rhythm I'll have you out on the parade ground beating a base drum until your ears fall off!

But I'm afraid.

Lawd help me. I asked for soldiers and they send me idiots. Get this firmly entrenched in what passes for your head, Brown. Twenty-nine-year-old hearts simply do *not* mutiny. Got it? . . . even *your* heart. Though, sometimes I seriously doubt you're made in God's image at all. For Christ's sake! Look at the way you've been mowing through Peru's national crop. That much coca would make anyone hallucinate.

But I thought it was impossible to hallucinate on coca leaves.

Don't flap your chin at me, Brown. What do you know about cocaine absorption? You know, your smart-ass attitude is giving me the fast prune. You wanted a hard time, didn't you? Well, then, intersect the dentals and enjoy it, man. Look at it this way: you have six hours of daylight left and all you have to do is lift your feet up and

210

down. Got it? The earth moves under you. A into G, soldier! That's better. That's better! By God, Brown. For a while there, you were in danger of tripping over your lower lip.

The ice spread through my left side from shoulder to stomach. I walked with a lean to the left. Snow fell on the other shoulder. I talked out loud to Julie, as if, by the precision of sound, I could get her to hear me.

'Julie? Julie. Listen to me, I'm in trouble. I feel bad. I feel real bad. Julie?'

There was, of course, no answer. So I made believe that she said something comforting to me. Which deserved a response:

'Yes. Oh, yes. It's wonderful to know you're there,' I said. I convinced myself so well, that a lump formed in my throat. 'The sergeant trick isn't working very well, Julie. The ice is taking over. I'm walking with a lean to the left. I'm the crooked little man, Julie, and it's not sea-sickness. No, it's not sea-sickness. Tell me what to do. Please! Give me strength . . . Yes. Thank you. I will. Keep telling me. Don't stop . . .'

But talking out loud was a costly business. Every quantum of energy lost as sound seemed to shake another hundred snowflakes on to my right shoulder. So I continued the monologue in my head.

Julie? The ice is pushing down to the bottom of my hips and hard up under my skull. It's all through my chest, my stomach; it's spreading towards the other side. The pain, I can't stand the pain. My legs won't walk any faster. I must keep the ice out of my legs. Rub them Julie – yes. just like that. It's so cold inside me, I can't stop. I mustn't stop, or I'll die. It's the ice of death, Julie. Warm me, darling. Warm me. Warm me. Warm me or I die. Die. Die. Die.

As the ice reached out for the right-hand side, I knew I wouldn't have to lean to the left much longer. And the crooked little man screamed out to the crooked little sky, 'Noooooo! Stop! It's too much! I don't want to die! Don't let me dieeeee!'

Then, after its absence of three years, the tunnel came back to find me. I felt its presence before I saw it. I felt it when I saw myself lying dead in the snow, some distance ahead. I didn't look about me for the tunnel, because I was trying to see the facial features of the body in the snow. Although I knew it to be my body, curiosity directed me to make visual confirmation of my identity.

But, as I walked past it, I couldn't seem to focus on the details of the upturned face. I could only see that the body was lying on its back, and that snow had built up on one side; even though there was, as yet, no wind.

As the body passed out of sight, I raised my face to greet the tunnel. Its black walls swept around me and above, below, and to the sides. All at a radius of two to three kilometres. Even though the tunnel was such an immense size, the walls converged to a point in the far distance. At that point, and growing larger than a point, was the light at the end of my tunnel. There were two differences between the tunnel now and the tunnel of three years before. Now, there was nothing between me and the light. Now, the tunnel was huge, and it sang the song of the void.

I looked above me. Snow twinkled through the roof. The walls began to close in. I walked on, towards the light, as the blackness tightened around me.

Julie. Julie.

I continued the monologue very softly in my head. Flat and even. Julie. The tunnel. It's here. It's come back for me. The light is coming, Julie. The light is death. I looked for it, and now I'm going to find it, and it's death.

Yes. I wanted you to know. I've seen my body, Julie. I'm going to die. But I don't want to die. I want to be the father to my children. They won't understand. They won't understand. Julie. The walls are here. I only need to stretch out my arms to touch the walls and I'll die. But I don't want to die, Julie. The light is so far away, yet. I must keep walking. I *must keep walking*.

Brown! Get up, you lazy, fucking bastard. *Get up*! Or I'll kick your fucking head in. Up! That's it. Now walk. Walk! Two . . . Three . . . Four. *One* . . . two . . . three . . . four.

Julie? I fell over! I musn't do that. Fell over. Fatal, that is. Long way to go to the light. Getting closer. I'm so cold. Everything is so cold. The wet head is dead Julie. The tunnel's near my elbows. Mustn't touch the wall. I'll die. Naughty boy. Musn't touch.

Brown! Brown! You did it again, you gutless son of a bitch. Roll over. Roll over! More! Pull your knee up, push with your hands. No. No, come *on*, Brown, or you'll kill us all. Up! Up! On your knees, then. That's my boy. Now crawl. Crawl man, crawl. Crawl to the count. One. *One*! That's it. Now, two! . . . three! . . . four! . . .

Julie. I'm not going to make it. Can't crawl in this poncho. Can't move. Stand up, stand up, but I can't. Can't raise head. So cold. I'm nearly dead now, Julie. I'm going to die. the tunnel. The light . . .

I fell for the third time. I knew I wouldn't get up again, so the sergeant left me alone. But I felt a strong urge to open my eyes, and after a while I did so.

Two men were watching me. Looking down at me. I waited for them to fade, or dissolve away. But they remained full, substantial. A snowflake fell on top of one man's boot and stuck there instead of falling through. I knew, somehow, that that man was a fisherman. Then I knew that the other man was an alpaca herdsman. Perhaps, perhaps, it wasn't too late. I could yet be saved.

Hope and despair came back to me, mingled together. I raised my head. 'Help,' I said clearly. And the effort closed the tunnel walls to the last half inch.

I pleaded with my eyes. Help. Help me. Help me.

They walked away. They didn't fade, or flick out of existence: they just walked away through the snow. My head fell back into the prepared hollow. Why? Why?

The snow fell on to my face and into my open eyes. I ceased asking why. I ceased wanting, or desiring, anything.

White light filled my head. It filled the air around my head, and it filled my body. It filled the earth under me, the falling snow, and the sky. It was a soft, a very soft, radiance. It stretched away to infinity in all directions. It was with me, and it was with all other matter in the universe; living and non-living.

I knew myself to be still lying in the snow, and felt newly dissatisfied. I wanted to stretch out, to expand. I wanted to become one with the light, to reach out and encompass the things of infinity. The separation between me and the light distressed me. I yearned to lift up from the ground and merge with it. I struggled to be free from the cross of my body. I was a fragment seeking unity with the whole.

I failed. And one clear thought answered the efforts of my will: not yet. Not yet.

The moment sight returned to my eyes, a series of impressions rushed in with it: I was alive. The ice had gone from my head, remaining everywhere else above my hips. My body was in terrible pain. The tunnel was still with me, further back now, at arm's length. It had stopped snowing. A wild dog was ten feet away, coming in on a cautious, but confident lope.

Terror swept upwards, snarling and bubbling out of my throat and mouth. I wanted to live. I wanted desperately to live. And the thought of my body being eaten, pulled another animal snarl on to the end of the first.

The dog fell back in surprise, matching my sounds with its own. In a fury it began the first of a series of feints and passes, inviting me to show my hand. I drew my knife; so slowly and awkwardly that I knew the weapon would be useless. But the effort exerted far less pull on the tunnel walls than I expected. Encouraged, I manoeuvred in preparation to stand.

While I was still on my hands and knees, the dog took its chance and went for my ankle. It snapped its teeth on the boot leather, which added insignificantly to my store of pain, and gave no injury.

The fresh wave of terror threw me to my feet. I tried to whirl on the animal, but the movement was so slow, he was ten feet away before the knife came between us. I kept turning as the dog circled, twisting the blade of the knife, to make sure the dog saw it flash. The tunnel walls tightened significantly with all the movement, but didn't envelope me. The dog continued to circle, but didn't lunge.

Not today, brother. Go eat something else.

There was hope. Hope. I decided on a direction and began to walk. The dog quietened, and settled in behind, trotting from side to side. I wasted a great deal of energy turning to check on it, before deciding that it was now playing patience with me. By the time I settled to looking where I was going, there was no choice anyway: the walls were, once again, courting my elbows.

I walked as an automaton.

I kept warm little more of my brain than was needed to drive my legs. My arms hung loosely at the sides. My back was erect. My face stared wide-eyed and slack-jawed down the length of the tunnel. I made no attempt to direct the eyes through the tunnel walls. I would be safe from the dog as long as I moved. I saw only the bleak altiplano at the end of the tunnel. No light. That was behind me now.

I walked through the shadow of the valley of death.

I walked so as to stabilize the equilibrium that formed between my body and the tunnel walls. And the energy that held the walls at bay was not my energy, it wasn't of my making. It expanded inside me, coming out of a point within a point. It drove the legs yet it maintained the ice, the pain, and tunnel walls in a state of constancy. I knew, at last, what it meant to tap the universal reservoir. And the energy that ran out of the tap was a gift from God.

I had to utilize the gift to the full. I couldn't waste it. I developed an energy 'watch', which was at once both an act of worship and an act of control. I sped up for a down grade, and slowed for a rise. The change in speed varied according to the slope. If the legs or the lungs fluctuated in their demands, or if some sleeping part stirred or murmured, speed was altered to compensate. Even when I resumed my mental monologue with Julie, I slowed the appropriate tiny amount.

Julie? I'm still here. I'm still alive. I think I was dead, Julie. I'm not sure. Things have changed. But I'm alive again. The light is keeping me going. I met it. It's giving me energy. Does that sound crazy?

My mind filled in Julie's answers much more successfully this time, and I encouraged the illusion, because I so much wanted comfort.

Michael! Keep going, – I got Julie to say – don't stop.

I'm not stopping. I'm not even stopping for a rest. It's hard to explain, Julie. I've got to keep going until I get there. But there's so far to go. There's so much pain . . .

Keep going, Michael!

I am, Julie. I am. This is forever. There's nothing as long as this. Talk to me. It's so good to hear your voice.

To strengthen the illusion, I placed Julie's face out along the tunnel. I made it so big, it superimposed over half of the tunnel. I chose the expression I remembered best, from the parting so long ago in Tarabamba.

Wonderful to see your smile, Julie. But you're looking a fraction pale today. Have you had a good day? I do hope it was better than mine. Mine was lousy.

Michael! Keep going. Please keep going. I'm waiting for you.

Glad about that. Really want to hold your hand. Touch your

breast. But I can see you. Lovely smile. You deserve flowers with a smile like that. But I can't send you any. No flowers here. Did you know? Very high.

Michael! Where are you? Please keep going!

Depends on your point of view. I'm going to the abbey. In the longest tunnel in the world. Private entrance, you know.

Michael! Oh God! Michael, it's you! Keep going, my love. Keep going. Can you see me? I'm coming to meet you. I can see you!

That's nice. I can see you too. Ravishing creature. What are you doing tonight? What say you and I find ourselves a candlelight dinner? Wine? Silver? But the white table-cloth is out. Very bad taste that. Don't you think so? I do. In view . . .

Keep going. Keep going, my darling. I'm coming.

A small boy appeared in front of me. He gaped at me, walking backwards. I knew better than to ask for help this time. And, sure enough, he ran away down the tunnel like a gnome down a rifle barrel. He also ran right through Julie's right upper lip, as she smiled at me, superimposed over the tunnel.

My control was deteriorating. The gift of energy would only last as long as I could put it to work. My finely tailored model for body management was turning to patchwork. The appearance of the boy confirmed that. My brain was leaking somewhere.

He appeared a second time, much further away. On his third appearance, he brought a new Julie with him. Together, they walked through the face of the other Julie.

The new one wasn't smiling like the other one. It stopped a few feet away, and said, 'Michael.' It looked ghastly, and drew back and to the side as I got closer. It was wearing a poncho, and I knew Julie didn't have a poncho.

So I ignored it. With my brain leaking that badly I was better off with something familiar. I returned my attention to the other Julie. The smiling one. But the new one was persistent. It touched my left arm, and drained energy out of it, slowing me down. 'Michael. It's me. Julie.'

I've got to keep walking.

It drew back, and I concentrated hard on the other Julie. But the new one walked by my side talking at me.

'I'm with you, Michael. I'm going to help you. There's not far to go.' And it was crying. Really unpleasant. I kept ignoring it, but it poured along beside me, out of the leak in my brain.

The other Julie kept smiling; pale, but smiling.

'Look, Michael. We're at the top of the valley. There's the shelter.'

I'm at the top of the valley, Julie. Maybe I'm going to make it. Julie.

'Can you walk a few steps further? Come over here. I want you to see . . . Look, down there. No, look down. You don't have to move

215

your head. Just lower your eyes. There, down on the valley floor. See? The abbey. Now, look, over on the track. People coming up. You're safe. It's all over darling.'

Julie? Can you hear? I've found the abbey. There're people. I'm going to make it. Can you hear me, Julie? I'm looking at the abbey.

Part Four

This world set embraces the stage of physical matter,
where we are all cast as players
to ourselves, the audience.
And if we would return radiant to the glowing hearth,
we must hear the spirit between the lines,
before the play is ended.

I'm sitting at my favourite place in the hidden valley: a grassy ledge, fifty feet up the curve that introduces the valley floor to the wall. A tributary to the main river runs below. If I sit at the front of my ledge, I see and hear the water pooling its way to the flats. If I move back a few steps, most of the sound cuts off, almost as sharply as the sight. Back a step or two further and there's no more than a faint liquid murmur.

It's early evening. As is usual at this time of day, a cloud ceiling hovers thousands of feet above the floor and thousands of feet below the altiplano, cocooning the plunging valley. But, in the soft evening light the cloud is not oppressive. It lends the valley intimacy, an evening companion to its permanent guest – tranquillity. Regardless of weather and time, tranquillity, the mother of serenity, rests in every corner.

On the far side of the valley, a little to my left, the trail drops out of the clouds. It's a dark line, twisting down through grey rock, green shrubs, and through waterfalls that trace fine silver on to the inner walls of the cocoon. The trail is a thin line. It has never felt the weight of motor vehicles or material wealth, but it knows the tread of people, who bring only themselves with them when they come. The trail is the one connection between the rest of the world and the abbey. And yet, in spite of its narrowness, no man walking the trail has ever trod exactly in the footsteps of any other man before him.

Opposite my ledge, one of the valley's contributing streams tumbles down the mountainside, soaring out at the last in prolonged free fall. But such escape from itself cannot be sustained: the stream always finds itself waiting at the bottom. Afterwards it chooses to overcome its pride on the tortuous rapids between the fall and the flats. And, finally, calm and strong it joins other tributaries at the main river, which flows in front of the abbey.

Now, the abbey dominates the landscape. Its normally sombre grey walls have taken on some of the colourful evening light. But, as even that light fades, the abbey's shape sharpens into silhouette, and draws distant human shapes in across the darkening fields.

This grassy shelf is where I best find my point within a point. Here, the brothers' teachings weigh and balance themselves. I need only relax my mind away from specific concern, and the knowledge I am ready for settles of its own accord. The teachings that mean nothing as yet, or seem worthless, either store themselves in surface memory or are forgotten. As the days pass, less and less is actively rejected as worthless.

I know, now, just how closely I allowed the pit of insanity to erode the ground behind me as I came here. But I don't need to speculate on what might have been. The pit has been left behind. I won't need a mental asylum again. I need only look forward; my mind knows its direction, my days have purpose, my nights are restful. Now that I know their meaning, the dreams could have stayed and not troubled me, but they have gone. Now, I know who I am. I know why I am here. They tell me that my physical recovery will take some time: but it turns out that I have quite a lot more time to play with than I ever imagined. So time is no longer important.

I don't have all the answers. In fact now that I know what questions to ask, I have more of them than ever. And I look forward to answering them with something of the enthusiasm of a small boy who anticipates getting into the senior grades at school – where all his big brothers and sisters have been studying for years.

Like the others before us, Julie and I have undertaken not to reveal the location of the abbey, nor to describe its interior, nor to describe the teaching methods employed. The purpose of this restriction is to encourage the seeking for first-hand experience of the nature of the abbey.

Julie was at ease here from the beginning. She nursed me in the first days, and spent her spare time immersing herself in the ways of the abbey. She has taken strongly to what she once called the 'quick' answers. But now she calls them the 'conscious' answers.

We are both looking forward to returning to our normal lives, taking those answers with us. The abbey is not, after all, an escape from the world. We came here with a purpose, but we will return to the world with a much stronger purpose. The abbey is a way, not a destination. It is a means, not an end. The spiritual knowledge it has given us is not kept only in the bottom of a mountain valley. The true spiritual anchor does not rust in the depths; it rides every wave and every tiny ripple in the living sea.

But what IS the Truth? What IS the Ancient Wisdom?
What IS it that the weaver weaves?
You didn't say!
Brother, brother, I cannot say.
A man who knows much says little,
and I have already rattled words like seeds of grain.
Beware of the man who claims to bear Truth's kernel on his tongue,
for just as the grain seed must grow to reach the sun,
so must you grow inwards and outwards to find the kernel.
For now, if but one pulse had echoed in your mind,
of the purpose that lay with you in your dawn,
then you have begun the journey and I am satisfied.

IN SEARCH OF ANCIENT MYSTERIES
by Alan and Sally Landsburg

In the middle of the Atlantic Ocean is an area known as the Bermuda Triangle which covers approximately three-hundred thousand square miles of open sea. Within this comparatively small patch of ocean more than a hundred ships and aircraft have been permanently listed as missing during the last two centuries . . . .

What really happened to these fated vehicles? Could they somehow have wandered into an ancient force-field, left by an alien technology who once tried to colonize Earth?

Alan and Sally Landsburg found themselves on the trail of this and other enigmas of history – colossal temples and monoliths built by the Incas, parts from a digital computer dating from 50 B.C. and the brilliant architecture of the ancient Egyptians – when they began their journey – In Search of Ancient Mysteries.

0 552 09588 5   85p

THE SECRET OF THE ANDES
by Brother Philip

High in the Andes mountains on the northern Peruvian side of Lake Titicaca, is the Monastery of the Brotherhood of the Seven Rays. Here, in this Shan-Gri-La lies secret knowledge which has been hidden away for thousands of years – and will remain hidden until the children of the Earth develop a spiritual perfection which will allow them to use it once again. Here, and in the many other monasteries set up throughout the world by The Masters, are stored away the Divin Truths dating back to the times when the highly advanced civilisations of Lemuria and Atlantis inhabited the Earth.

0 552 12173 8   £1.25

RETURN TO THE STARS
by Erich Von Daniken
author of the world bestseller
CHARIOTS OF THE GODS?

Not long ago the world witnessed the drama of a crippled American space-craft being nursed back to earth. Supposing it had landed on another planet at the same stage of development as the earth was 50,000 years ago, what would the astronauts have taught the inhabitants? What remnants of their efforts to return to earth would they have left behind? How would the inhabitants remember them in myths and art? The answers we would give fit exactly the vast numbers of unexplained mysteries which have been found all round the world. RETURN TO THE STARS is another fascinating examination of a part of our history which has been, until now, neglected.

0 552 09083 2   £1.95

MIRACLES OF THE GODS
by Erich Von Daniken

Today's most original investigator of the unexplained takes a penetrating look at miracles, visions and all the supernatural wonders that Churches throughout the centuries have recognised as 'holy'. What are visions? Are they supernatural phenomena, or the product of mass auto-suggestion? Can they be divine revelations, or extra terrestrial communications? Erich Von Daniken's theories are far more fascinating than any of these . . . In this latest book, the best-selling author of CHARIOTS OF THE GODS?, RETURN TO THE STARS, THE GOLD OF THE GODS and IN SEARCH OF ANCIENT GODS turns his ever-questioning mind to Christianity – and the religions that reach back far beyond Christ . . .

0 552 10371 3   £1.50

HOVEL IN THE HILLS
by Elizabeth West

This is the unsentimental, amusing, and absorbing account
of the 'simple life' as practised by Alan and Elizabeth West
in their primitive cottage in rural Wales. The Wests – she is a
typist, he an engineer – moved from Bristol to North Wales
in 1965, determined to leave the rat race for good. But the
daunting task of converting a semi-derelict farmhouse and
turning the unproductive soil into a viable self-sufficient
unit was to prove a full-time job. The author describes the
very individual and resourceful ways she and her husband
tackled the problems which faced them – from slating the
roof, curing a smoking chimney and generating their own
electricity, growing a wonderful variety of fruit, herbs and
vegetables on impossible soil. With a preface by John
Seymour, author of "The Complete Book of Self-
Sufficiency" "Hovel in the Hills" is a heartwarming and
salutary tale which will either leave you yearning for a
chance to get away from it all or convince you that the
comfortable security of the nine-to-five is not such a bad
thing.

0 552 10907 X   £1.25.

A SELECTED LIST OF FINE BOOKS
AVAILABLE FROM CORGI

ORDER FORM